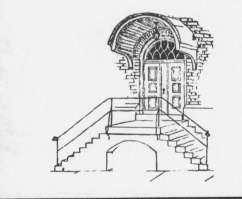

'HOUSEHOLD BUSINESS': DOMESTIC PLAYS OF
EARLY MODERN ENGLAND

THE MENTAL AND CULTURAL WORLD OF TUDOR AND STUART ENGLAND

Editors

Paul Christianson
Camille Slights
D.R. Woolf

VIVIANA COMENSOLI

'Household Business':
Domestic Plays of
Early Modern England

UNIVERSITY OF TORONTO PRESS
Toronto Buffalo London

© University of Toronto Press Incorporated 1996
Toronto Buffalo London
Printed in Canada

ISBN 0-8020-0733-3

Printed on acid-free paper

Canadian Cataloguing in Publication Data

Comensoli, Viviana
  Household business : domestic plays of early modern
  England

  (The mental and cultural world of Tudor and Stuart
  England)
  Includes bibliographical references and index.
  ISBN 0-8020-0733-3

  1. Domestic drama, English – History and criticism.
  2. English drama – Early modern and Elizabethan,
  1500–1600 – History and criticism.   3. English drama –
  17th century – History and criticism.   I. Title.
  II. Series.

  PR658.D65C65 1997   822'.309'355   C96-931485-X

University of Toronto Press acknowledges the financial assistance to its
publishing program of the Canada Council and the Ontario Arts Council.

This book has been published with the help of a grant from the Humanities
and Social Sciences Federation of Canada, using funds provided by the Social
Sciences and Humanities Research Council of Canada.

For Elaine

Contents

Epilogue   147

Acknowledgments

I am deeply grateful to the many individuals who have assisted me during the various stages of this project. Kay Stockholder and Joel Kaplan were inspiring teachers who offered valuable insights when I began thinking about the volume. Sara Munson Deats, Linda Woodbridge, C.E. (Ted) McGee, and my colleagues Joyce Lorimer and Anne Russell generously read and commented on portions of the manuscript. I also extend warm thanks to my students and research assistants, Viona Falk, Dianne Krynicki, and Beth Wolf, for their insights and hard work.

I have also benefited by the helpful comments and suggestions provided by the anonymous readers of the University of Toronto Press and the Canadian Federation for the Humanities. Suzanne Rancourt, Barb Porter, and Miriam Skey of the Press have been generous and expert editors. The assistance and expertise of the staff at the British Library, and of Amy Menary and Karen Scott at Wilfrid Laurier University Library have also been invaluable. Martin Dowding skilfully prepared the index.

A grant from the Social Sciences and Research Council of Canada funded research assistance and travel. I am very grateful to the Office of Research at Wilfrid Laurier University for course remission and a book preparation grant. Paul Tiessen, my Department Chair, has been unstinting in his consideration and support. Thanks to Joanne Buehler-Buchan and Sandra Wallace, our Department secretarial staff, for their incomparable efficiency.

A version of chapter 2, 'Fashioning Marriage Codes: Sixteenth-Century Griseldas,' originally appeared in *Renaissance and Reformation* n.s. 13 (Summer 1989). A version of the discussion of *The Witch of Edmonton* in chapter 4, '"Retrograde and Preposterous": Staging the

Witch/Wife Dyad,' originally appeared in 'Witchcraft and Domestic Tragedy in *The Witch of Edmonton*,' in *The Politics of Gender in Early Modern Europe*, ed. Jean R. Brink, Allison P. Coudert, and Maryanne C. Horowitz, vol. 12 of Sixteenth Century Essays & Studies Monograph Series (Kirksville, MO: North East Missouri State University Press, 1989). I thank the publishers for permission to reprint portions of those essays. Segments of other chapters have been presented as papers at various society meetings and conferences: the Renaissance Society of America; the Glasgow International Renaissance Conference; the Canadian Society for Renaissance Studies; the International Patristic, Medieval and Renaissance Conference; and the North East Modern Language Association.

I reserve my deepest gratitude to my family for their patience, encouragement, and good humour. My parents, Giulia and Inaco Comensoli, have as always given unqualified support. Most especially, I thank my partner, Elaine Auerbach, for listening to my ideas, reading and commenting on the manuscript, and for her understanding during the years when writing this book was a regular feature of household business.

'HOUSEHOLD BUSINESS'

LORD AVERNE: Forreigne[?]
LADY: nay domestick.
tis howshould busines all.
(Heywood, *The Captives*)

Introduction

I

The English domestic play originates on the popular stage towards the end of the sixteenth century. Its literary roots are predominantly native rather than classical, and its mainspring is the presentation of domestic conflict among English characters drawn chiefly from the non-aristocratic ranks of society: merchants, housewives, labourers, farmers, shopkeepers. The prologues and epilogues often stress that the plays are fashioning a dramatic form which differs from classical or aristocratic models. 'Look for no glorious state,' advises the Prologue of Thomas Heywood's *A Woman Killed with Kindness* (1603), 'our Muse is bent / Upon a barren subject, a bare scene' (ll. 3–4).[1] The declaration echoes Tragedy's induction in *A Warning for Fair Women* (anonymous, c. 1593–9): 'My Sceane is London, native and your owne, / ... my subject too well knowne ... ' (ll. 95–6), a claim reiterated in the Epilogue in Tragedy's reminder that the events we have witnessed are 'home-borne' (*Warning*, l. 2729).[2] In his *Apology for Actors* (1612) Heywood employs the double meaning of *domestic* in his description of 'our domesticke hystories' as a form of drama drawing on English subjects and on 'domesticke, and home-borne truth.'[3] The example which Heywood offers is the dramatization, 'in *Norfolke*' by 'the then Earle of *Sussex* players,' of an event 'which within these few yeares happened,' in which 'a woman ... had ... secretly murdered her husband' out of love for 'a yong gentleman.'[4] The best plays, writes Heywood, are those which have 'power to new mold the harts of the spectators'; because the 'English blood' best responds to 'the person of any bold English man presented' in a 'prosperous performance,' plays which treat everyday subjects and include characters drawn from 'among vs,' such as '*Rosamond*, and Mistresse *Shore*,' will 'proue' especially appealing to audiences.[5]

The domestic play's interest in 'home-borne' subjects and in the drama of the 'everyday' has influenced subsequent assessments of the genre, most of which have focused on the tragedies. In the nineteenth century, J.P. Collier identified a distinct 'species of dramatic representation ... which may be said to form a class of itself: – it may be called domestic tragedy, and pieces of this kind were founded upon comparatively recent events in our own country.'[6] Collier was referring to the interest of early domestic tragedies (also known as murder plays) in contemporary reportage: the action is usually precipitated by a murder, the basis of which is an actual and recent crime recorded in a ballad, chapbook, chronicle, or pamphlet.[7] In vogue chiefly between 1590 and 1610, the murder plays gave way to plots which no longer revolved around topical events but which retained the domestic setting. In the early twentieth century domestic tragedy was deemed distinct for its intense focus on the contemporary family. A.W. Ward, for example, observed the emphasis on 'incidents which gain ... force from the frequency of their occurrence in the familiar sphere of daily life'; the dramatists 'compass strong theatrical effects by the treatment of subjects at once interesting and homely ... and suggestive of the sympathy which attaches itself to any tale of eventful experiences in accustomed surroundings.'[8] This view was adopted by Chilton Powell, who considered the portrayal of 'family life' to be the genre's distinguishing feature, and by a group of Heywood scholars interested in the overriding importance of the household setting.[9] However, with the publication of Henry H. Adams's widely influential study, critical interest shifted to the genre's didactic structures.

Seeking to interpret the plays as they would have been understood by the original audiences who saw them performed in the public theatres, Adams located their widespread popularity in their Anglican impulses: 'Elizabethan domestic tragedies inculcated lessons of morality and religious faith in the citizens who came to the theatres by offering them examples drawn from the lives and customs of their own kind of people. The choice of the hero, the moralizing, and the religious teaching are ... consistent attributes of all these plays.'[10] The homiletic superstructure and the portrayal of characters from the common ranks of society led to Adams's important discovery of the genre's debt to the morality play, in which the protagonist represents ordinary humankind and the action is circumscribed by a pattern of temptation, sin, repentance, punishment, and divine mercy. Although also noting that issues pertaining to statecraft are subordinated to the focus on familial relationships, Adams considered this focus incidental to the genre's exploitation of the morality tradition. The genre became identified as 'the dramatic equivalent of the homiletic tract and the broadside ballad,' the writers' 'primary purpose [being] to teach the people by means of examples couched in terms of their own experiences.'[11]

The notion of a strong correlation between the expectations of an allegedly homogeneous group of urban playgoers and the domestic play's realistic and didactic structures also developed alongside sociological studies, carried out in the 1930s and 1940s, of the early modern theatres and their audiences. In *Shakespeare and the Rival Traditions* Alfred Harbage remarked that the homiletic superstructure of domestic tragedy has parallels in a group of comedies performed in the public theatres: 'The "homiletic tragedies" in which adultery leads to disaster are overwhelmed ... by what might be called, with equal justice, the "homiletic comedies" where a woman's constancy saves the day.'[12] The 'popular' dramatists, argued Harbage, appealed to a supposedly unified group of middle- and working-class spectators who attended plays largely for edification, whereas playwrights writing for the private theatres catered to the more decadent tastes of elite audiences. And in *Middle-Class Culture in Elizabethan England* Louis B. Wright characterized the plays of Dekker and Heywood in particular as mouthpieces for their largely 'middle-class' audiences, whose 'growing class consciousness' inspired the creation of the new drama.[13] As has been frequently pointed out, this perspective has allowed little room for differentiation with respect to individual response, and has combined under the broad rubric of a 'rising middle class' groups that in the sixteenth and early seventeenth centuries were socially and economically distinct.

In their surveys of contemporary social institutions and practices, the Elizabethan commentators William Harrison and Thomas Smith distinguish, in hierarchical order according to revenue and social standing, four major social groups: 'We in England,' writes Harrison, 'divide our people commonly into four sorts, as gentlemen, citizens or burgesses, yeomen, and artificers or laborers.' Among the gentlemen, the monarch is in a distinct 'estate,' followed by lords, noblemen, knights, and 'they that are simply called gentlemen.' The 'citizens and burgesses' are described as having 'next place to gentlemen,' and they include merchants, manufacturers, and other 'citizens' who 'serve the commonwealth in their cities and boroughs, or in corporate towns where they dwell.' The third group consists of 'yeomen' or 'freemen born English [who] are also for the most part farmers to gentlemen ... or at the least-wise artificers.' Yeomen, explains Harrison, 'have a certain pre-eminence and more estimation than laborers and the common sort of artificers,' and they 'commonly live wealthily, keep good houses, and ... come to great wealth ... ' At the bottom of the hierarchy Harrison lists 'the fourth and last sort of people,' the group which in England comprises 'day laborers, poor husbandmen, and some retailers (which have no free land), copyholders, and all artificers, as tailors, shoemakers, carpenters, brickmakers, masons, etc.'[14] Andrew Gurr has noted that each of these subgroups could be distinguished from the others 'in education, occupation, dress and income.'[15] Although, as Ann Jennalie Cook has suggested, the 'privileged' or middle stratum generally defined the majority of spectators in the London theatres, audiences spanned the entire social spectrum, ranging from royalty to the dispossessed (courtiers, merchants, students, petty criminals, vagrants, and the unemployed).[16] The heterogeneity of audiences helped to make the public stage an important site of convergence for diverse segments of the population, and for wide-ranging discursive and dramatic traditions.[17]

The view that domestic drama is written for the edification of spectators in the public theatres has continued to influence studies of the genre. Qualifying Henry Adams's suggestion that domestic tragedy originates in Anglican theology, Stephen Trainor has identified 'a separate strain of domestic tragedy that was essentially Calvinist in origin and relied heavily on Puritan theories of conversion and homiletics.' While the tragedies based on Anglican theology 'followed the general Anglican format of delivering a warning based largely on the fear of punishment,' those influenced by Calvinism 'sought to replicate the emotional effect of the Puritan sermon that strove to achieve a sudden and overpowering conversion arising from an apprehension of the horrible nature of sin.'[18] For G. Nageswara Rao, domestic drama more generally portrays, 'against the background of ordinary family life ... an action of deep and commanding moral interest' with which its audience – 'the country squires and town merchants' – could easily identify; Ada Lou Carson and Herbert L. Carson have stressed 'the tragic potential of the colloquial and the commonplace' together with 'a didactic intention based upon a realistic development of materials'; and Michel Grivelet has argued that the genre (including the comedies) deals in a fundamental way with family life, its overall aim being to instruct the spectator in the exaltation of married love. Andrew Clark, like Grivelet, has proposed that the genre not be restricted to type or theme – 'to limit the domestic genre solely to tragedy is to exclude a number of other plays which have many of the characteristics of the genre and are seriously concerned with domestic themes and relations'; however, his discussion of specific plays relies heavily on their debt to the 'field of domestic doctrine and conduct which they ... evince.' And in her analysis of the representation of the family in domestic tragedies and comedies, Kathleen McLuskie, while acknowledging that 'there existed a constantly changing relationship between literary convention and real social change,' denies the plays any differentiation with respect to dramatic strategy or intent: the 'focus' of the genre is 'moral rather than social.'[19]

The homiletic superstructure has also been deemed to distinguish the domestic play from citizen comedy, a genre that developed syncretically alongside of it. In his discussion of the two genres, Alexander Leggatt has suggested that while both are concerned with characters from the non-aristocratic ranks involved in 'everyday' situations, domestic drama originates in a more distinct theatrical tradition governed by a pervasive didacticism: 'the category "citizen comedy" cuts across a variety of comic modes ... [such as] the satiric, the didactic, and the simply amusing, with everything from lightweight farce to pieces that verge on domestic drama,' the latter being a genre distinguished by 'moral earnestness' and 'a seriousness of tone.'[20] Although citizen comedy and domestic drama are not as mutually exclusive as the argument from didacticism would indicate, the major distinction between them, I would suggest, is that citizen comedy, while often including *domus* scenes, takes the city rather than the household as its fulcrum, spanning a variety of settings: taverns, London houses, streets, docks, and brothels. The city is thus continually felt as a compelling force. No single activity absorbs the action's full attention, and domestic themes are subsumed within the depiction of city life and its attendant social conflicts. The genre also engages more directly than does domestic drama the broad, contemporary affairs of state (cases in point are the war between France and England, which forms a haunting background to Dekker's *The Shoemaker's Holiday*, and the political intrigue that underwrites Heywood's *Edward IV*).

These differences notwithstanding, thematic and structural correspondences clearly exist not only among domestic drama and citizen comedy, but also among these and other Renaissance dramatic genres. Moreover, to single out the influence of the morality tradition on the domestic play ignores the fact that edification is the overt aim of all English Renaissance literature. For Thomas Heywood, every play, be it

'Tragedy, History, Comedy, Morrall or Pastorall,'[21] shares the didactic structures of classical drama, 'either animat[ing] men to noble attempts, or attach[ing] [i.e., laying hold of, fastening to] the consciences of the spectators.'[22] Heywood's defence of the stage on moral grounds recalls countless similar injunctions in early modern literary texts. Compare, for example, the commonplace promise to the reader in William Baldwin's Preface to the 1599 edition of *A Mirroure for Magistrates*: 'here as in a loking-glas, you shall see (if any vice be in you) howe the like hath bene punished in other heretofore, whereby admonished, I trust it will be a good occasion to move you to the soner amendment.'[23]

The early modern theatre, however, was not a monolithic institution which passively and unequivocally bolstered dominant moral or political orthodoxies. Heywood's *Apology* belongs to an extensive body of pro- and anti-theatrical tracts that, taken together, attests to the instability of the theatre as an institution for the inculcation of moral or social codes and precepts. As Jean Howard suggests, one of the most striking features of the early modern debates about the theatre 'is how variously this institution was interpreted by contemporaries and how differently they described the "lessons" it taught, the social consequences it effected.'[24] Heywood's description of the theatre as capable of teaching subjects not only 'humanity and manners' but also 'obedience to their King'[25] is, for example, strongly disputed by the author (John Greene?) of *A Refutation of the Apology for Actors* (1615), for whom 'Stage-Players ... to please the vulgar ... set before them lyes, and teach much dissolution and deceitfulnes.'[26] Whereas for Heywood plays 'comprehend ... what in our liues and manners is to be followed, what to bee auoyded,'[27] for Greene they 'consist ... of sundry impieties, comprehending ... damnable things, wherein is taught how in our liues and manners wee may follow all kinde of vice with Art.'[28] It was not merely Puritan practice to condemn plays for promoting idleness and other forms of disorder. As early as 1532, the monk Richard Whitford in his treatise *The Pype or Tonne of the Lyfe of Perfection* advised both a monastic and lay audience that although interludes and plays may include 'many things full devout and that might edify,' such forms of entertainment are unsuitable for those striving for a life of spiritual perfection: 'For without fayle they ben spectacles of mere vanites, which the worlde callethe pastymes / and I call them waste tymes /.'[29]

Thus while playwrights may have appealed to prevailing moral codes, they often did so in order to escape censure. We can only speculate, moreover, about what moral or religious significance homiletic discourses and dramatic texts may have had for their original audiences. Within the last twenty-five years a wide body of evidence has been uncovered suggesting that in the early modern period belief was a more problematic construct than had previously been supposed. Both popular and elite cultures, writes Imogen Luxton, 'were far less ... literate' than historians had assumed, and were frequently 'confused about their beliefs.'[30] Although villagers often shared common goals, each person might interpret those goals and assumptions differently, and have conflicting aspirations and interests. In his analysis of the philosophical, political, legal, and theological discourses of the period, Perez Zagorin has demonstrated that individuals were sometimes compelled to conceal their actual beliefs. English Protestants, for example, were 'confronted with moral conflicts as a result of the enforcement of conformity by the royal state and established church,' and treatises on the subject of conscience often referred to the problem of dissimulation. During the Tudor and Stuart reigns various groups, under threat of reprisal, were forced to prevaricate about their beliefs, the 'imposition of compulsory oaths and subscriptions on Protestant dissenters as religious and political tests occasion[ing] both controversy and evasion.'[31] Zagorin's detection of pervasive dissimulation parallels the findings of Lucien Febvre on the anxiety about double truth, doubt, and unbelief felt by many Europeans in the sixteenth century, and of Victoria Kahn on the relation between the humanist rhetorician, who 'can know nothing absolutely,' and the sceptic, who 'shares with the orator a refusal of dogmatism' and the ability to speak convincingly on any side of a question.[32]

Although the writers of homilies and domestic-conduct books upheld the principle of natural law and of immutable truth, they also knew that they were responding to fragile and transitory experience. It has been widely perceived that the dissemination of homiletic treatises and household manuals was largely a response to changes in the social structure brought about by increasing urbanization and mobility, changes led in part by the tremendous expansion of London, the financial and cultural hub of the country. The growth of the urban population far surpassed the general increase in population and economic growth. London, for example, grew from a town of 50,000 individuals in 1500 to a metropolis of 575,000 in 1700 to become the largest European city; and between 1560 and 1640 rapid growth in population and large-scale land transfers contributed to an apparent disintegration in the social order.[33] The shifting social dynamics led to changes in the distribution of wealth and property and to fluctuations in the standard of living. These in turn led to the expansion of social groups such as those belonging to the gentry, the professions, and the trades, as well as to the displacement of labourers (in particular of agricultural workers forced from the land by enclosure acts) and to an increase in the numbers of drifters and vagrants.[34] Faced with unprecedented social mobility, the English authorities sought to inculcate the respect for order in the population by appealing to traditional notions of stability and hierarchy.

On one hand, the overt function of the homilies, sermons, and domestic-conduct literature was to disseminate Christian humanist values; on the other hand, these texts served the interests of the church and state, whose objective was to monitor and control public opinion. Yet these tracts and sermons were neither always promulgated nor received in the manner in which the authorities would have hoped. Elizabeth's colloquy (1585) in which she addresses her bishops on the problems underlying a reformed ministry demonstrates the difficulties incurred by the authorities in trying to promote a uniform system of belief:

You suffer many ministers to preach what they list and to minister the sacraments according to their own fancies ... to the breach of unity: yea, and some of them so curious in searching matters above their capacity as they preach they wot not what – that there is no Hell but a torment of conscience. Nay, I have heard there be six preachers in one diocese the which do preach in six sundry ways. I wish such men to be brought to conformity and unity: that they ... preach all one truth; and that such as be found not worthy to preach, be compelled to read homilies ... for there is more learning in one of those than in twenty of some of their sermons. And we require you that you do not favour such men ... hoping of their conformity ... for they will be hanged before they will be reformed.[35]

There was, moreover, mixed reaction to the publication of *Certain Sermons or Homilies* (1547) and the *Homily against Disobedience and Wilful Rebellion* (1570). These texts preached the necessity of upholding 'good ordre and obedience,' but like all forms of dogma they had their detractors even among the church elite.[36]

It is especially difficult to determine the extent of the influence of homiletic and other socializing tracts on the so-called common people. The behaviour prescribed in these discourses – patience, deference to authority, and so on – must be considered in relation to the prevailing power structures. Keith Wrightson has suggested that 'the deference accorded to superiors,' for example, 'might be little more than a form of demeanour, a recognition of the imperatives of the particular social situation,' and an eagerness to display subordination 'in return for assistance, favour or protection.'[37] Nor do homilies and conduct books always sustain consistent points of view. Although their didacticism serves politically conservative interests, they are often riddled with inconsistencies and contradictions, the authorial perspectives varying with the kinds of readers who are being addressed. A case in point is the diversity of the marriage manuals, texts which, as Heather Dubrow observes, inscribe 'conflicting theories' about a number of 'procedures appropriate for weddings (is a church ceremony necessary? is a *de futuro* contract binding?) and about the very nature of marriage itself.'[38]

The public and private theatres of early modern England reflect the heterogeneity of early modern culture, each fostering modes of representation which sometimes promote and sometimes challenge dominant political, religious, and social systems.[39] Like other dramatists with professional ties chiefly to the public theatres, writers of domestic plays speak to audiences representing diverse social and economic interests, and in their plots they portray contrary and opposing impulses. Domestic drama includes a variety of characters ranging from the 'middling sort,' to the group that Harrison labels 'the fourth ... sort of people in England' (day labourers, artificers, masons, and so on),[40] to the poor and the dispossessed. While playwrights may well have wanted to document the lives of ordinary people in order to entertain predominantly urban audiences, some of these texts encode the material aspirations of families who wield significant power and influence.[41] To describe the protagonists and their activities as 'spectacularly ordinary people going about their daily tasks'[42] disregards the fact that a number of the male characters share a privileged status gained as a result of sophisticated and exploitative economic practices made possible by the benefits guaranteed by the institutionalization of private property and the patriarchal family. Other plays are more concerned with the poor and the powerless, and with the detrimental effects of a money economy on dispossessed individuals. The genre's discontinuous and divergent emphases indicate that playwrights by no means respond uniformly to the ideologies and institutions which entrench the hierarchies of class, gender, and status.

II

During the sixteenth century the demands of new audiences contributed to the proliferation of new literary forms and the multiplication of genres. 'It was a moment,' writes Claudio Guillén, 'of dynamic contact between traditional artistic principle and practical innovation.'[43] Early modern writers and theorists readily accommodated the new forms, which for the most part were as yet uncodified. In the theatre, stage plays altered over the decades with the emergence of different genres, the processes of accommodation and invention providing, as Walter Cohen contends, both 'the basis of similarity and the potential for divergence.'[44] Yet the fashioning of new forms was not always accomplished without anxiety or self-consciousness. In their interrogation of the traditions of classical or aristocratic forms of drama, writers of domestic tragedy reveal an acute awareness of their engagement in a complex process of restructuring, in which conventional forms are at once upheld and resisted. A number of inductions and epilogues betray self-consciousness about the process of innovation. Beneath the apologetic tone typical of these structures, we detect a mixture of authorial anxiety and bravado in the claims that spectators should not expect to see orthodox tragedies:

> Gentlemen, we hope you'll pardon this naked tragedy
> Wherein no filèd points are foisted in
> To make it gracious to the ear or eye;
> For simple truth is gracious enough
> And needs no other points of glozing stuff.
> (*Arden of Feversham*, Epilogue, 14–18)[45]

> We could afford [i.e., wish] this twig a timber-tree,
> Whose strength might boldly on your favours build;
> Our russet, tissue; drone, a honey-bee;
> Our barren plot, a large and spacious field;
> Our coarse fare, banquets; our thin water, wine;
> Our Poet's dull and earthy Muse, divine;
> Our ravens, doves; our crow's black feathers, white.
>   But gentle thoughts, when they may give the foil,
>   Save them that yield, and spare where they may spoil.
> (*A Woman Killed with Kindness*, Prologue, 5–14)

Peter Holbrook points out that the theatre in early modern England was, 'as an institution, necessarily sensitive to differences of rank and to the structure of society'; texts such as *Arden*, *A Woman Killed*, and *A*

Warning for Fair Women generally reveal 'not an oppositional orientation toward tragedy but an ambiguous, shifting pattern' in which the plots 'move in and out of ... [the] high mode, which is regarded as usually taking for granted aristocratic norms.'[46] However, the degree to which these shifts replicate or displace elite models depends upon two important factors: (1) the extent of the playwright's interest in the dialectical presentation of conflict; (2) the complex interaction between playwright and audience. An emerging genre is in general terms a working model whose diachronic patterning depends upon the interrelation between a writer's choices and audience expectation. In its self-conscious break with established dramatic and homiletic traditions, domestic drama eludes homogeneity of purpose as it reconstitutes and reinscribes (sometimes confidently, sometimes ambivalently) inherited praxes.

From the writer's perspective, a play is a pattern of inherited structures and precepts interacting with the work as it evolves. The interaction between a writer's experience and pre-existing forms, and between writer and audience, implies that no one work will embody completely all prototypical features of a given genre. Jean-Marie Schaeffer, commenting on the 'genericity' of any given text, proposes that 'insofar as a text enters into social communication,' it inevitably 'situate[s] itself with respect to the structure of the accepted literary field of its epoch – to make a place there for itself'; it does this by 'capitaliz[ing] on the partially decisional character of generic nomination, which functions as a buffer between textual genericity and accepted generic paradigms.'[47] The task of the reader consists in formulating an approximate position of influence within the coordinates of the genre. One way to effect this formulation is to examine the general field of literary conventions and influences with which an emerging form enters into dialectical relation. Literary traditions necessitate competition between writers, their fellow-authors, and the authors on whose works the emerging texts are modelled. A 'new' work, therefore, becomes 'both a deviant from the norm ... and a process of communication referring to the norm.'[48] In this context, domestic drama may be approached as a related body of texts sharing a number of overlapping characteristics and impulses (formal structure, subject matter, mood), which each text exploits in a different manner and with a different degree of intensity. Although Alastair Fowler's definition of early modern genres as 'a family whose septs and individual members are related in various ways, without necessarily having any single feature shared in common by all,'[49] is a useful preliminary criterion for the classification of specific texts, the metaphor of 'family resemblance' can be applied only loosely. One of the difficulties with the metaphor is that it subordinates difference.[50]

More important, the characteristics of a genre will vary with the author and with social, political, and cultural forces, so that genre entails mediation between texts, and between text and ideology. As a system of signification that underwrites the ideas and objectives which shape political, moral, and cultural procedures, as well as the codes of everyday life, ideology cannot, as Louis Althusser argues, be equated with 'the real conditions of existence'; rather, it is 'an imaginary,' a 'representation of the real world' that governs the 'conditions of existence.'[51] 'Each epoch,' writes Tzvetan Todorov, 'has its own system of genres, which stands in some relation to the dominant ideology,' and 'like any other institution, genres bring to light the constitutive features of the society to which they belong.'[52] But within all ideological systems there exist, as P.N. Medvedev and Mikhail Bakhtin have shown, a number of 'mutually contradictory truths, not one but several diverging ideological paths.'[53] A text's response to ideology is grounded in the dual concepts, elaborated by Bakhtin, of intertextuality and polyphony, whereby an utterance always forms part of a group of other utterances, which it appropriates and regenerates. There is no such phenomenon as an isolated text or autonomous voice, only of voices resonating with others within social space.[54] In a culture's configuration of interests and objectives, the tensions between dominant and subversive discourses will sometimes reveal similarities between apparently disparate ideas and activities, and at other times profound bifurcations. The uncovering of a culture's (and a text's) diffuse, disparate, and often shifting organization offers up a network of impulses in which instances of resistance and absorption will be manifest. A historical construct expressing human consciousness, a genre can variously represent, promote, and challenge ideological systems.

III

If a stage play engages its subject matter dialectically, audiences will recognize not only their desires and ideals but also the contradictions and struggles inherent in them. A widely held critical assumption is that while providentialism is apparent in most English Renaissance plays, it is qualified by the so-called principal dramatists, who consistently inscribe polysemous meaning. Although many canonical playwrights uphold temporal, mutable constructions, the labelling of their texts as 'major' or 'great,' as has often been the practice, has tended to marginalize a body of drama that also does not always genuflect to audience expectation or to essentialist notions of truth. A persistent criticism of the domestic play has been that it is an aesthetically 'inferior' genre. This assessment originated in the early part of the twentieth century and evolved largely out of A.C. Bradley's New Critical definition of 'Great Man' tragedy, a form which he placed at the top of the hierarchy of the so-called major tragedies (*Hamlet, Othello, Lear, Macbeth*).[55] A by-product of the 'Great Man' theory of tragedy has been the critical tendency to give greater consideration to the plays of Shakespeare than to those of his contemporaries, in particular those writing for the public theatres. In 1990 Carol Thomas Neely voiced the still valid complaint that while 'current research on women's status and women writers, on the construction of sexualities and the history of homosexuality, on colonialist discourse and popular revolts has drastically transformed the early modern period,' it 'has achieved only a barely perceptible decentering of Shakespeare, who remains the catalyst to and referent of many such explorations.'[56] The New Critical preoccupation with aesthetic quality and with Shakespeare's 'superior' craft has informed recent studies contrasting the artistry of Shakespeare's *Othello* with that of other tragedies with domestic themes.[57] What this approach has ignored is that so-called minor dramatists like Heywood, Dekker, and the anonymous writers of domestic plays inscribe, sometimes more ambivalently and sometimes more radically than does Shakespeare, discursive conventions and ideological paradigms.

While domestic drama exploits the morality tradition more overtly than do other types of early modern plays, this difference in method should not be confused with difference in purpose, which often is of degree rather than kind. Whereas some plays insist on schematic conclusions, others move towards a complex displacement of homiletic structures. Although retaining the traditional focus on the tragedies and on their 'ethical pattern' of action, Madeleine Doran has argued against a strictly providentialist reading of domestic tragedy. Many of these plays take contemporary crimes for their subject matter, and would be especially appealing as thrillers. In this context, vestiges of the morality play appear 'less like the original impulse to the plays than like a conventional moral pattern such subjects would attract'; while not denying that the genre 'owe[s] a good deal to the morality,' Doran has argued for 'a shift [of] ... emphasis in viewing the relationship.' Doran's proposal, however, that plays such as *Arden of Feversham, A Woman Killed with*

Kindness, and *The Witch of Edmonton* 'suffer distortion if viewed as dramatized homilies' is never developed in her brief but provocative discussion.[58] A non-schematic treatment of the genre has also been urged by Peter Ure, who reminds us that the writers of domestic plays, like their counterparts in the private theatres, 'had to handle character and incident before an audience,' and should therefore 'be judged as dramatists and not as homilists.'[59] To Adams's paradigm of the commoner-protagonist Ure adds the relationship between husband and wife, a relationship which qualifies the doctrinal pattern of the action: 'While ... a code of marriage' underlies the tragedies, the latter 'could not have occurred without ... [the moral] order being disturbed by the aberration of one or other partner.'[60] Ure does not go so far as to argue in favour of authorial resistance to homiletic closure: the dramatist, he writes, 'accepts the morality from which the treatises proceed,' and although the marriage code is crucial to the play's dramatic power, 'it is the agreement about this code,' which the playwright 'could assume' in the spectator, 'that contribute[s] to its effect.'[61]

Rather than categorically upholding the marriage code, writers of domestic drama reveal an interest in perversity and contrariety. A play will sometimes stabilize around a specific ideology while simultaneously approaching another. My purpose is not to provide a survey of all domestic plays, nor does this study permit more than a cursory treatment of texts only affiliated with the genre. My inquiry will focus on those tragedies and comedies that interrogate generic and ideological codes. I will begin by demonstrating that domestic drama grows out of the literary and cultural traditions of the Middle Ages, in particular medieval cyclical drama. At the same time, the aesthetic points of departure between domestic and medieval drama illuminate differences that are concomitant with the later genre's interest in the ideology of private life. The domestic play brings into relief the instability of the early modern household, together with the passions, rivalries, and ambivalence attending early modern theories of order. A number of the tragedies and comedies reconstitute inherited precepts through irony, paradox, and ambiguity, creating disjunctions and clashes of values that are not easily resolved by homiletic formulas.

IV

The domestic play's interest in the contemporary family indicates that the genre emerged out of historical changes (and continuities) in social structure. While noting the limitations of the providentialist reading, however, we must be careful not to counterbalance it with a reductive historical critique. Domestic drama is more than simply a minor species of didactic theatre which schematically mirrors contemporary social practices;[62] it is a new genre in which the historical and ideological contexts scrutinized are a composite of the world portrayed on stage and the society of the playgoer.

That domestic strife can assume tragic proportions attests to the enormous importance placed on marriage and the family, whose social, political, and economic significance in the early modern period has been well documented. Since the publication of Lawrence Stone's *The Family, Sex and Marriage in England* (1977) it has become commonplace to view the early modern family as a political institution, and the householder's private duties as complementary to religious and political obligations. Although Stone's claim that a nuclear family 'organized around the principle of personal autonomy' emerged in the sixteenth century[63] has been qualified by evidence of the existence of nuclear family units as early as the eleventh century, and of 'middle-class individualism' in England in the thirteenth century,[64] early modern treatises define the family as a distinct political category. 'The patriarchal-familial conception,' writes Gordon Schochet, had, by time of the Stuarts, 'become the chief view of political origins.'[65] In *De Republica Anglorum* Thomas Smith describes 'the house and familie' as 'the first and naturall' beginning of a 'common wealth.' Smith further defines 'the house' as 'the man, the woman, their children, their servauntes bonde and free, their cattell, their hous-holde stuffe, and all other things, which are reckoned in their possession'; the commonwealth is created by the 'multitude of houses and families which make stretes and villages, and the multitude of the stretes and villages [which] make townes, and the multitude of townes the realme.'[66] With the weakening of the feudal system of mutual obligations and rights, the family assumed a crucial function in the promotion of social stability and governance. Obedience to husbands, fathers, and masters was considered the principal duty of women, children, and servants, and rebellion within the family was viewed as synonymous with rebellion against the state. In *The Good Hows-holder* (anonymous, 1607) the writer, appealing to biblical authority, compares the structure of the patriarchal household with that of the church and the body politic: 'Every Governour should be that in *the body politick of his house*, which the *heart* is in *the natural body of man*: as it communicateth life and vital spirits to the rest of the members; so must the Master of the houshold endeavour to impart the spiritual life of grace, to all that are members of his body politick.' In *Certayne Sermons Appointed by the Queen's Majesty* (1569) the reader is cautioned that 'it is not lawful for inferiours and subjects in any case to resist or stande against the superior power'; disobedience of both public and private authority leads to 'al mischiefe and bitter destruction both of the soules, bodies, goodes and commonwealths.'[67] The household, declares Robert Cleaver on the eve of the seventeenth century, should function as 'a little commonwealth' whose rulership, both 'civill and righteous,' must be exercised by the husband or 'cheefe' with the support of his wife or 'fellow-helper.'[68] The orderly household was deemed essential to the family's preservation, and domestic crime a challenge to God's will. 'Great efforts,' writes Keith Thomas, 'were made by the State and by local authorities to see that everybody was attached to a household, and the government displayed a strong prejudice against bachelors and master-less men.'[69]

By the early sixteenth century the idea of the family as the foundation of the orderly Christian state and of matrimony as among the highest of human pursuits underwrites a wide range of political and religious discourses. Cultural historians have recently demonstrated that the post-Reformation emphasis on companionate marriage was not a distinctly Puritan phenomenon, but one which had its roots in ancient Greek and patristic discourses, and whose doctrinal assumptions were shared by Christian humanists, Protestant reformers, and Anglican conformists alike. Margo Todd observes that wedlock was generally viewed by 'sixteenth-century commentators as having three primary goals: companionship, procreation and avoidance of fornication.'[70] The Puritan celebration of marriage as, in the words of Thomas Becon, 'an hye, holy, and blessed order of life' created by 'God in Paradise'[71] is preceded by Erasmus as early as 1497 in the *Encomium Matrimonii* (pub. 1518), in which he writes that it is 'an especial sweetness to have one with whom ye may communicate the secret affections of your mind, with whom ye may speak even as it were with your own self.'[72] In *The Office and Duties of an Husband* (1555?) Juan Luis Vives, following Erasmus, advises the husband to live peacefully with his wife in order to ensure 'the society and fellowship of life'; earlier, in book two of the English translation of *The Instruction of a Christen Woman* (1529), Vives had celebrated the superiority of marriage over celibacy, praising his parents' successful union.[73]

But while the definition of the early modern family as a sacred and

hierarchical institution held together by the mutual obligations of husbands, wives, and children provided the foundation of the sociopolitical
order, the family was a more dynamic and complex institution than has
traditionally been assumed. Ralph Houlbrooke points out that the
relation 'between official doctrines and actual practice, and consequently
the speed with which changes in the former affected the latter, are
overestimated.'[74] The dominant view of marriage, moreover, conflicted
with the widespread pattern of resistance to order that culminated in
the revolution of 1640. Power relations within the family did not precisely replicate those that defined the state, and there is considerable
evidence that many individuals thwarted prevailing notions of the
stable family. Margaret Ezell has shown that English women sometimes
displayed certain forms of power that contradicted the traditional patriarchal model of the family: 'Domestic patriarchalism was a personal
authority on the family level. In theory, the husband was the head of
the house. In practice, when death often removed him before his
spouse, or in a marriage where the wife possessed the stronger will of
the two, the woman often fulfilled "patriarchal" duties.' Wives thus
'wielded considerable power, whether acknowledged in theory or not,'
but it was a form of power that was exerted largely in the private
sphere, 'not through the public institutions.'[75] Allison Coudert has
documented the rebelliousness of many wives from all social classes in
Protestant England, while Sarah Hanley has argued that in sixteenth-
and early seventeenth-century France women's 'cultural purview contained the Family-State compact' by 'counterfeit[ing] culture over time
to fashion themselves and their spheres of action.'[76] In her study of early
modern definitions of petty treason, Frances Dolan has illustrated the
paradox inherent in those definitions: while 'petty treason constructs the
subordination of wives and servants to the master of the household as
the foundation of domestic and civil order ... it also acknowledges that
wives and servants did not always cooperate; their subordination was
not a given.'[77]

Many households were laden with conflict, to the extent that families
were often unable to keep subordinates from turning to vagrancy for
their livelihood. In England the increasing fragmentation of the family
during the period from 1540–1640 alarmed church and state authorities.
The 'Homilie of Whoredome and Unclennesse' declared 'the outragious
seas of adultery, whoredome, fornication and unclennesse' to be 'above
other vices' in having 'overflowed almoste the whoole worlde,' to 'the
utter destruction of the publique wealthe'; these various 'synnes' now

comprised one 'vice,' which had spread 'so abundantly, that through the customable use thereof ... [it] is growen into suche an height that in a maner emong many it is compted no sin at al.'[78] The cracks in the official image of the orderly family led to the proliferation of conduct guides proclaiming the sanctity of the family and denouncing those who would bring dishonour to it. In *An Order of Household Instruction* (1596) Josias Nichols stressed 'what good may come out of a well instructed familie, namely, that it may bee the preseruing of the countrie and Church, in the time of extreame daunger and darknesse.' The theologian William Perkins described the family as the 'first Societie' or 'the Schoole, wherein are taught and learned the principles of authorities and subiection'; and Robert Sanderson, preaching at Paul's Cross on the need for 'the suppress[ion] of Novelties and the preservation of Order and Peace,' equated 'the Political Laws in the Civil State' with 'domesticall orders in Private Families.'[79] Yet in everyday practice the model of the 'well instructed familie' proved untenable.

The sanctification of the early modern family was only partially rooted in religious idealism; it was also a political response to shifts in and challenges to the social and moral foundation of society. Between 1560 and 1640 prosecutions of disorderly conduct increased in frequency, the most common offences being those which disrupted the notion of the well-regulated family – adultery and fornication, bigamy, scolding, desertion, and violence. 'Divorce from bed and board, with the hope of ultimate reconciliation,' comments Houlbrooke, 'was granted on account of infidelity, cruelty, and inability to live together because of continual quarrels.' Numerous instances of violence against wives 'came to judges' notice as a result of presentments made during visitations and inquisitions. Those who sought decrees of separation were no doubt greatly outnumbered by those who simply abandoned or expelled their spouses.'[80] Relying on evidence gleaned from sources such as court documents, legal theory, and popular sources, Dolan has documented other types of domestic violence which were defined as crimes, including 'acts of murder (petty treason, wife murder, infanticide) and of witchcraft.'[81] Especially disturbing to the authorities were disruptions in the gender hierarchy. During this period the scold, the termagant widow, and the unmarried woman refusing marriage were growing in number and in vociferousness, and they were severely admonished. Scolds were women who 'brought their rejection of women's "quiet" and obedience out of the household and into public view,' and they were consistently prosecuted; to the church courts the scold was guilty of 'a "breach of Christian charity"' requiring penance; to manorial and urban courts her offence was public disruption, for which the punishment was the cucking-stool.[82]

The authorities' insistence upon a system of order based on female subordination indicates that women did not always conform to the roles prescribed for them. Church court records frequently cite the insubordination of women as a reason for marital strife. In Essex, for example, an unnamed husband declared in 1562 that he desired to keep his wife, but that 'she wanting government doth absent herself'; and in 1574 another husband explained that he 'turned ... away' his wife 'for that she would not be ruled.'[83] At Norwich, the surviving decrees of marital separation indicate that the successful petitioners were primarily women.[84] 'The assertions of patriarchy that we encounter in the [domestic] tracts,' argues Heather Dubrow, 'were surely at least in part reactive, responses not only to the assertions of independence that many feminist scholars have traced in late Elizabethan and Jacobean culture but also to the degree of autonomy that the authors of these tracts were themselves ascribing to women.'[85] Although the conduct books were intended to hold up the family as a spiritual institution, some authors acknowledged its precariousness. Ideally, the husband wisely governed his wife, whose duties, we are told in the 1534 translation of *Xenophons Treatise of Hovsholde*, included being 'a good companion, and a good felow to hir husband in a house.'[86] The 'Homily of the State of Matrimony,' however, lamented 'how few matrimonies there be without chidings, brawlings, tauntings, repentings, bitter cursings, and fightings.'[87] In *Bethel, or a Forme for Families* (1633) Matthew Griffith denounced the growing number of husbands who wasted their earnings 'in whoring, idleness, drunkenness, [and] gaming,' leaving the support of the household entirely to their wives; William Gouge, in his highly popular treatises, *Of Domesticall Duties* (1622–33), admitted that whenever he instructed his parishioners in 'the doctrine of female submission and inferiority' he sensed 'a certain amount of "squirming" and "murmuring" on the part of the women in the audience'; and William Whately, conceding in *A Bride-Bush Or, A Wedding Sermon* (1617) that 'Most men' who 'enter into this estate, [i.e., marriage] ... complaine thereof,' directed his tract to those individuals who 'finde' marriage 'a little Hell.'[88]

Because the confines of the private sphere ultimately depended on the way public authority was constructed and disseminated according to the influence exercised by the state, it was not coincidental that, given the privileges bestowed on the husband as the spiritual leader, most of the political tracts and marriage manuals written during the first half of the sixteenth century were addressed to men.[89] In *De Republica Anglorum* Smith clarifies the rationale for this practice in his definition of the family as a 'private' institution whose governance mirrors that of the kingdom; 'in the house and familie is the first and most naturall (but private) appearance of one of the best kindes of a common wealth, that is called *Aristocratia* where a few and the best doe governe'; and just as the king rules by divine right, so 'God hath given to the man great wit, bigger strength, and more courage to compell the woman to obey by reason.'[90] Women in early modern England, with only a few significant exceptions, were discouraged from actively participating in public life, so that very few preached or published for a living. Men's published works about women, marriage, and family life attest not only to how men publicly regarded women, but also to how women were taught to think about themselves.[91] The few household treatises aimed at women usually instructed them in their moral obligations or in specific menial tasks such as cooking and wine-making.[92]

The marriage guides, domestic economies, and household manuals belonged to a larger body of educational literature aimed at instructing the emerging classes in civility. In addition to providing guidance on how to sustain domestic hierarchy and on practical subjects such as cooking, household medicine, and the rearing of children, these tracts included advice about manners. An important adjunct to the ideal of the orderly family was the growing emphasis on civilized behaviour both outside and inside the home. By the mid-sixteenth century the literature on civility included a vast system of codes and precepts to oversee private behaviour. Books on manners offered advice to family members not only on how to conduct themselves in public but also in private conversations, that is, conversations at home rather than outside the house. A large number of conduct guides focused on the regulation of table etiquette; they also instructed readers on menu planning and service, as well as on the content and tone of diners' conversation. 'A whole normative programme,' writes Michel Jeanneret, was 'instituted; the domestication of appetites and the controlling of nature by art' were undertaken in order to create 'a more polite and cultured society.'[93]

The rules governing behaviour within the private sphere were thus crucial to the production of the ideology of domination and subordination. 'The word *private*,' observes Anne Ferry, 'as distinguished from *public*, was frequently used in contexts which define it simply to mean domestic.'[94] But private life was not conceived as an autonomous domain disengaged from public institutions; rather, it existed in dialectical relation to the public sphere, and in particular to public authority. As Gouge asserts in *Domesticall Duties*, by the early seventeenth century the relation between the public and private spheres had become axiomatic: 'who knoweth not that the preseruation of families tendeth to the good of Church and common-wealth? so as a conscionable performance of household duties, in regard of the end and fruit thereof, may be accounted a publike worke.'[95] Indeed, an important qualification needs to be made when we refer to the distinction between public and private in early modern England: the early modern state, argues Althusser, is 'the State *of* the ruling class,' and is therefore 'neither public nor private; on the contrary, it is the precondition for any distinction between public and private.'[96] The entrenchment of what Richard Hooker and his contemporaries called 'private families'[97] was the underpinning of early modern official ideology, and the *locus* of the meaning which constructed social relations.

These relations, however, rested on a fundamental contradiction: the enforcement of harmonious interpersonal relations within a system of social hierarchies. The dominant ideologies of early modern England did not problematize familial relations; 'the rhetoric of the marriage manuals in particular,' comments Dubrow, is 'grounded in ordering in the sense both of giving commands and of establishing order,' the writers 'delight[ing] in the process of hierarchical enumeration.'[98] Yet among the numerous discourses which prescribe wifely duties, one sometimes detects confusion and contradiction on the part of the authors as they attempt to fashion a homogeneous view of companionate marriage. Although Christian humanist and Protestant discourses generally uphold the value of spiritual equality in marriage, the concept of equality is denied to socially unequal partners. Gouge, for one, rationalizes the inconsistency by reclaiming the traditional view of marriage as the blending of two identities into one, namely the husband's: if 'a woman of eminent place' is married to a man of low social rank, 'It booteth nothing what either of them were before mariage ... for in giuing her selfe to be his wife, and taking him to be her husband, she aduanceth him aboue her selfe, and subiecteth her selfe unto him.'[99] Some of the writers of conduct books celebrate companionate marriage while qualifying their praise. A case in point is Edmund Tilney's inclusion, in *The Flower of Friendship* (1568), of the Lady Isabella's eloquent denunciation of marital hierarchy and sexual inequality. Isabella's denunciation of wifely obedience, together with her speeches in favour of equality in the distribution of household duties, represents an emergent discourse which is more fully articulated in the culture at large towards the end of the sixteenth century.[100] It is also an emergent narrative whose idealism is scrutinized in a number of domestic plays.

V

The tensions which prompted widespread injunctions against the precariousness of the early modern household are crystallized in domestic drama. On one hand, the family is invested with the ability to generate social order and continuity, the dramatists typically striving for the appearance of an ordered world governed by married love. Marriage is seen as the early humanists and contemporary homilists saw it, that is, as the site where one practises active, Christian virtue. The order invested in the patriarchal family is bolstered by the salubrious, civilized household. At the outset, the plots create an atmosphere suggestive of English civility and prosperity. They do so by setting scenes in spaces that in the sixteenth and seventeenth centuries became indicative of social status among the gentry and yeomanry: libraries, studies, closets (small, wood-panelled rooms), kitchens, dining rooms, bedrooms, gardens. Stage properties include a variety of household effects (stools, beds, salters, card tables, and so on) further typifying status and comfort. On the other hand, in the staging of domestic strife and violence the plays inscribe a profound disenchantment with the ideal of the well-ordered, civilized family. The *locus in quo* of transgression is the patriarchal household, and tragic suffering arises from the protagonists' inability to abide by social codes governing civility and domestic hierarchy. Whereas the homilies, marriage treatises, and household economies invariably call for the speedy punishment of erring individuals, in a number of domestic tragedies and comedies the protagonists' rebellion against the cult of domesticity is only tentatively corrected. These texts explore the vicissitudes attending the early modern family, showing them to be concomitant with the individual's ambiguous and often painful relation to prevailing constructions of agency and private life.

The domestic play's interest in marriage, civility, and the early modern household coincides with the genre's preoccupation with the category *woman*. In many domestic tragedies and comedies the protagonists are women. While some of these plays concur with a large body of extra-literary discourses seeking to define femininity, others contest those definitions. The genre's multifarious representation of 'woman' corresponds to the rhetorical and political strategies of many early modern fictional texts. Revealing subtle ironies and modulations in the adaptation of misogynist social and stage conventions, Linda Woodbridge has pointed out that authors do not unfailingly defer to commonplace injunctions with respect to female humility; while 'the ideal ... was trumpeted from city pulpits,' the literature of early modern England 'is full of women' who challenge orthodox codes of behaviour, and whose defiance is not always denigrated by the authors.[101] Catherine Belsey has similarly shown how non-canonical dramatic texts do not easily capitulate to the patriarchal institutionalization of marriage: whereas officially sanctioned discourses often depend for their 'success on the elimination of difficulties,' the fictional narrative, and drama in particular because it speaks to a broad spectrum of audiences, relies for its 'continuation on obstacles and impediments to the resolution of conflict.'[102] Critical theory and practice that takes *woman* as a central category has often disempowered women by representing them merely as victims of patriarchal law. In her study of texts by English women writers of the early seventeenth century, Barbara Kiefer Lewalski has demonstrated 'the oppositional nature' of these texts as they 'consistently though variously resist, oppose, and rewrite patriarchal norms.'[103] Conceptualizations of *woman* and *femininity* are deployed in early modern culture in such a way that they resist uncomplicated binary distinctions between male and female, dominant and submissive, oppressor and oppressed. The woman-as-victim paradigm has ignored oppositional discourses and the numerous historical instances of feminine denial and transgression attesting to gender-specific anxiety about changing social relations.[104]

Determining the intertextual and historical contexts of a 'popular' genre like the domestic play does not mean, then, that the ideologies which inform these texts are mere by-products. A multivocal genre, domestic drama forms part of the vast network of discourses comprising early modern English culture, which was marked by disparity and contradiction. Although providentialism is a governing teleological principle of the genre, certain texts gesture towards alternatives to officially sanctioned codes and norms, be they moral, linguistic, literary, or social.[105] To describe domestic drama as fundamentally didactic, or to claim that the genre merely exalts the pleasures of the so-called common people, is to obfuscate a number of these plays' resistance to traditional praxes. Identifying the protagonists' alienation as grounded in the tension between personal desire on the one hand and social, discursive, and ideological claims on the other, texts such as *A Warning for Fair Women*, *Arden of Feversham*, *A Yorkshire Tragedy*, *The Witch of Edmonton*, and the two parts of *The Honest Whore* counter homiletic structures by inscribing change and instability above order and continuity. The patterns of resistance in these and other plays are in need of critical synthesis.

1

Medieval and Tudor Contexts

Domestic drama has its roots in the literary and cultural traditions of the Middle Ages. While the development of the genre out of the morality play has been widely observed, it is also indebted to other medieval dramatic forms. The oldest analogue of the domestic murder play is 'Dux Moraud,' a fragment of a fourteenth-century English play. The subject is the story of Apollonius of Tyre and his daughter, a victim of paternal incest. After murdering her mother and daughter at the behest of Apollonius, she murders her father for later abandoning her. Journeying to a foreign land, she continues her life of sin until she is providentially rescued by the teachings of St Augustine. The theme of human redemption, together with the homiletic pattern of temptation, sin, and repentance, underlies not only the morality drama but cyclical plays as well, which reached their peak in the fifteenth century and remained influential well into the sixteenth century.[1] The English cycles and domestic drama demonstrate considerable intertextuality in their presentation of the contemporary family,[2] at the same time that their aesthetic and ideological points of departure reveal, among other things, the domestic play's more sustained ambivalence towards the myth of the orderly family. The areas of intersection are especially significant because they contribute to the growing revisionist claim that the family in Europe developed not on the heels of the Protestant Reformation but during the later Middle Ages.

The inclusion of domestic matter in the medieval cycles coincides with the growing typological importance of the family. With the exception of high aristocratic circles, the family had long existed as a social institution for the vast majority of people. The view of the early feudal kindred family as consisting of a number of related households sharing hearth, board, and fields, which gave way to smaller, more self-contained households managed by members of a nuclear family and their servants,[3] has in the past decade been qualified by historians and demographers. David Herlihy has demonstrated that beginning in the seventh century distinct domestic units known as households were 'used as standard units in censuses and surveys,' and although the units varied in structure and size, the degree of variance had greatly decreased; similarly, Barbara Hanawalt and Alan Macfarlane have shown that ordinary people did not live in extended households in medieval and early modern England.[4] From the twelfth century in both England and France the 'hearth' became associated with the patriarchal domestic unit, a connection which would become commonplace during the late Middle Ages.[5]

The movement towards individual family units was commensurate with the church's widespread reforms, which were intended to shape and guide the secular world. Creating a comprehensive theology and canon law of marriage, the church assumed within its jurisdiction the practice of judging cases pertaining to marriage. A major departure from traditional doctrine was the affirmation, based on a series of papal decrees (1159–89), that no person or institution could interfere in an eligible couple's decision to marry, in effect sanctioning marriage based on choice.[6] Evidence of affective ties between family members has been widely observed, dispelling the notion that in medieval society people did not form emotional bonds with their closest kin.[7] The promotion of affect in marriage was evidenced by, among other developments, the evolution of the legal term *maritalis affectio* (intent to marry). By the ninth century the concept of *consent* came to be defined by church authorities as meaning 'consent by the partners themselves,' and *maritalis affectio* was gradually invested with sentiment and even romance.[8] In sanctioning affective familial ties, the medieval church was anticipating what has been regarded as a distinctly Protestant phenomenon, although one cannot go so far as to suggest that the encouragement of affective relations constitutes evidence of the promotion of individualism. As Michael McKeon observes, 'the larger purpose' which '"individualist" values ... reflect and support is not the validation of the individual but the promotion of Church interests through the subversion of kinship solidarity.'[9]

The conjecture that the Middle Ages had no distinct concept of childhood is also no longer tenable. On the contrary, medieval records and literature reveal that while some parents showed a lack of interest in their children, many formed deep emotional bonds with them. Already at the end of the tenth century Bernard of Anjou had remarked that 'rearing' and 'taking care' of children 'is the natural bent of all human beings' and a duty through which they attain 'the largest part of their happiness.'[10] Child mortality was high, and while some parents reacted by distancing themselves emotionally from their offspring, many remained close and demonstrative regardless of the consequences.[11] The parent-child bond was prominent in hagiography, especially in the cult of the infant Jesus, which was the main site for the expression of both sacred and secular attitudes towards childhood, and in which parental involvement was notable for its passionate nature.[12]

I

In the drama, a number of cycles include pageants that ground the action in the everyday world, combining allegory and typology with naturalism and homiletics. Human suffering is depicted amid evocative scenes of domestic pathos, while theological themes are subsumed under a range of dramatic situations that appeal directly to contemporary values. A prevalent *topos* is the emotional interaction between parents and children. The *topos* is poignantly dramatized in the Towneley Herod the Great (Play 16, *Incipit magnus Herodes*) during the lament of a mother whose child has been slaughtered by Herod:

> 3 MULIER. Alas, my bab, myn innocent,
> My fleshly get! For sorow
> That God me derly sent,
> Of bales who may me borow?
> Thy body is all to-rent!
> I cry, both euen and morow,
> Veniance for thi blod thus spent ...   (ll. 560–6)[13]

The refrain is echoed in turn by two other bereaved mothers (ll. 495–502, 523–33). Douglas Cole has suggested that with the exception of 'traditional plaints connected with the Passion, the situations which give rise to the expression of innocent suffering all involve some kind of domestic bond'; a 'parent's lament over a lost child' represents 'one of the more important kinds of suffering in the mystery-cycles, a kind of suffering which, because of its independence from the Passion story, could easily be adapted to the developing needs of secular drama in a later age.'[14] Even liturgical plays, however, sometimes depict human sorrow within a familial context. As in lyric poetry, the trope of the *planctus Mariae* (Mary's lament uttered over the dead body of Christ) increasingly balances human and divine sorrow, bringing into relief Mary's role as mother. In Passion plays of the thirteenth century the *planctus*, whether Latin or vernacular, is not directly addressed to the spectator but to Jesus, the Jews, Death, or the women of Jerusalem, with an implicit appeal to the audience's pity. By the fourteenth century the method of presentation in the lyric *planctus* involves Mary's revelation of her inner turmoil directly to the reader, signalling an evolving interest in the personal nature of her suffering.[15]

The psychological aspects of the lyric *planctus* are especially influential on the drama's presentation of the climactic moment of Christ's Passion and death. A case in point is the pageant of The Crucifixion in the late fifteenth-century N-town manuscript. Although Mary's sorrow has no direct bearing upon the direction of the plot, the psychological moment functioning independently of her religious status, Mary's role as mother is nevertheless brought into bold relief:

MARIA. Alas, my dere chyld to deth is dressyd!
Now is my care wel more incressyd!
A, myn herte with peyn is pressyd –
For sorwe myn hert doth twynne!
...
Al joye departyth fro me.   (Play 32, ll. 226–9, 269)[16]

The Chester Passion play sharply particularizes Mary's speeches, personalizing her maternal bond with Christ:

MARYE. Alas, my love, my liffe, my leere!
Alas, nowe mourninge, woe ys mee!
Alas, sonne, my boote thou bee,
thy mother that thee bare.
...
Alas, theeves, why doe ye soe?
Slayes ye mee and lett my sonne goe.
For him suffer I would this woe
and lett him wend awaye.   (Play 16A, ll. 241–4, 261–4)[17]

Mary's insistence upon her maternity – 'Thinke one, my fruyte, I fostred thee / and gave thee sucke upon my brest' (ll. 245–6) – renders the lament an incident of special value and intensity.

The Towneley Crucifixion (Play 23, *Sequitur processus crucis*) similarly unifies the suffering that underwrites Christ's death with bereaved motherhood. Among the additions to the basic plot line, the Towneley pageant includes a two-part *planctus Mariae*, a section in which John the disciple attempts to comfort Mary at the foot of the cross (ll. 345–66), a conversation between John and Mary (ll. 383–460), and Mary's concluding lament (ll. 461–502). In comforting Mary, John remarks that Christ was her 'faryst foine' (l. 349) (i.e., 'fawn,' offspring), 'a term of endearment'[18] that parallels Mary's tender addresses to Christ – 'Swete son, say me thi thoght'; 'Alas, my lam so mylde' (ll. 375, 410). Mary's powerful apostrophe to death during her final lament sustains the focus on her personal sorrow, and includes her anguish at having forfeited not only motherhood but also her many friendships:

> A dede, what has thou done?
> With the will I moytt sone,
> Sen I had childer none bot oone,
> Best vnder son or moyn,
> Freyndys I had full foyn:
> That gars me grete and grone
> Full sore.   (ll. 472–8)

Mary's direct address to the women in the audience – 'Madyns, make youre mone, / And wepe, ye wyfes euerichon, / With me ...' (ll. 418–20) – highlights once again the importance of the social setting. Noting the widespread use of Mary's lament in medieval literature, George R. Keiser has suggested that Mary's tragic suffering 'would have had a particularly immediate appeal to women, many of whom would have experienced the loss of a child and even more of whom would have had to comfort a relative or friend upon such a loss.'[19] In the drama, the trope qualifies the action's symbolic referents, anticipating later playwrights' need to shape domestic themes within wider secular contexts.

The secularizing tendencies in the medieval cycles are more fully realized in the Chester, Brome, and Towneley pageants of Abraham and Isaac, in which naturalistic and emotionally charged vignettes evoke the affective interaction between parents and children, and in some instances between spouses. Pathos is pronounced in the Chester pageant, which integrates Abraham's and Isaac's symbolic function as 'the Father of heaven' and 'Christe ordayned ... / to honour him' (Play 4, ll. 138, 141–2) with their roles as father and child. The lyrical strains of the dialogue preceding the sacrifice reveal that Abraham's loyalty is divided between God and Isaac, heightening the intensity of the familial bond:

ABRAHAM. My blessinge, deare sonne, give I thee,
and thy mothers with harte soe free. ...
ISAACK. Father, I praye you hyde my eyne
that I see not the sworde soe kene. ...
ABRAHAM. My deare soone Isaack, speake noe moare;
thy wordes make my harte full sore.   (ll. 333–4, 337–8, 341–2)

The Brome play focuses extensively on Abraham's devotion to his son, expanding upon the enormous personal loss which the sacrifice would entail:

In my age þou [God] hast grantyd me thys,
    That thys ȝowng chyld wyth me schall won;
I love no thyng so myche, iwysse,
Excepe þin owyn selffe, der Father of blysse,
    As Ysaac her, my owyn swete son. ...
Thys fayer swet chyld, he schereys me soo,
In euery place wer that I goo,
That noo dessece her may I fell.   (ll. 11–15, 18–20)[20]

In the Towneley version Abraham can obey God's behest only by abandoning human feeling. To kill Isaac, who has never been 'vnkynde,' declares Abraham to the audience, would be 'I thynk grete syn' (Play 4, *Sequitur Abraham*, ll. 218, 221). Sharing his pain and uncertainty with the spectator, Abraham voices what appears to him to be an unjust circumstance. Although Abraham finally yields to God, he can do so only by subduing emotion and reason.[21]

The scenes of domestic pathos in the Abraham pageants reflect in part the didactic structures of medieval sermons and conduct literature. The instructional value of these powerful dramatic episodes is evidenced by the portrayal of Isaac as the model son: obedient, respectful, and eager to yield to parental authority.[22] Abraham's entreaty in the N-town pageant – 'My swete childe, com kysse now me' (Play 5, l. 24) – is met with Isaac's promise of filial loyalty:

At ȝoure byddynge ȝoure mouth I kys.
    With lowly hert I ȝow pray,
ȝoure fadyrly love lete me nevyr mysse,
    But blysse me, ȝoure chylde, both nyght and day.   (ll. 25–8)

In response to Abraham's reluctance to undertake the sacrifice, a reluctance which Abraham expresses in an unconstrained and intensely subjective manner – 'I must go walkyn, for I haue nede' (l. 47) – Isaac reasserts his loyalty and obedience (ll. 145–60), encouraging his father to 'werke Goddys wyll' (l. 150). In the Chester pageant, Isaac's solicitude extends to his mother and siblings: 'Father, greete well my brethen yonge, / and praye my mother of hir blessinge; / I come no more under her winge' (ll. 369–71). The pathos of these scenes thus not only emphasizes the intensity of affective familial ties, but also instructs the spectator in domestic conduct: to the 'fadyr evyr most comly,' declares Isaac in the N-town pageant, 'It ovyth' his 'childe evyr buxom [i.e., obedient, submissive] to be' (ll. 109–10).

In the portrayal of Isaac as the ideal son the Abraham plays anticipate a group of Tudor academic interludes, written primarily for students, which deal with the upbringing and education of children. Although the ideology of childrearing in these texts is based on Protestant belief structures, they share with their medieval counterparts the assumption that ideal domestic conduct can promote moral and spiritual health. In his comprehensive survey of Reformation religious plays concerned with 'educational or youth-related issues,' Paul Whitfield White has observed that these interludes – Nice Wanton, The Disobedient Child, The Glass of Government, Jack Juggler, Jacob and Esau, and Misogonus – inculcate views which are commonly 'found in royal injunctions, school statutes, and the homiletic writings' of Protestant reformers who view education as 'above all else a religious undertaking' for the 'primary purpose' of 'engender[ing] piety and lead[ing] the way to salvation.'[23] In the words of John Colet, who framed the statutes of St Paul's Grammar School, the chief aim of education is 'to increase knowledge and worshipping of God ... and good Christian life and manners in children.'[24] Prevalent themes in the Protestant education plays include the need for parents and guardians to correct rebellious behaviour, to teach children the value of scripture as part of their daily instruction, and to maintain rigorous standards of discipline.[25]

In the medieval pageants, the inscription of contemporary manners and values within naturalistic scenes is also notable in plays whose focus includes the roles of husband and wife. In the Northampton (or Durham) Abraham and Isaac the extra-biblical role of Sara, Abraham's wife, permits the construction of homely vignettes that would have had an immediate appeal to contemporary audiences:

SARA. A, welcom souereigne, withouten doute;
How haue ye fared whils ye haue ben oute?

And, Isaac, son, in all þis rowte?
   Hertly welcome home be ye!
HABRAHAM. Gramercy, wif, fayre most you befalle.
Com þens, wif, out of youre halle,
And let vs go walke and I wol telle you alle ...   (ll. 318–24)[26]

The private interchanges of Sara and Abraham throw into relief the
domestic setting, to the extent that Sara's incredulity over Isaac's death
momentarily displaces the eschatological emphasis on Abraham's sacrifice:

SARA. Alas, all þen had gone to wrake!
Wold ye haue slayne my son Isaac?
Nay, þan al my ioy had me forsake!
Alas, where was your mynde?   (ll. 342–5)

In the Towneley adaptation the role of Abraham is pointedly individ-
ualized, both in the way that Abraham conveys to the spectator his anguish
over Isaac's sacrifice, and in the way that he anxiously anticipates his wife's
response:

What shal I to his moder say?
For 'Where is he?' tyte will she spyr.
If I tell hir, 'Ron away,'
Hir answere bese belife – 'Nay, sir!'
And I am ferd hir for to flay;
I ne wote what I shal say till hir.   (ll. 225–30)

   Intimacy between husband and wife frames the action of the York play,
Christ before Pilate I: The Dream of Pilate's Wife. The opening scene alerts
us to Pilate's detachment from matters of state, at the same time that it
stresses the couple's mutual affection:

VXOR. Ther is no lorde in þis londe as I lere,
In faith, þat hath frendlyar feere
Than yhe, my lorde, myselffe þof I saye itt.
PILATUS. Nowe saye itt may ye saffely, for I will certefie þe same.
VXOR. Gracious lorde, gramercye, your gode worde is gayne.
PILATUS. Yhitt for to comforte my corse me muste kisse you madame.
VXOR. To fulfille youre forward my fayre lorde I am fayne.

PILATUS. Howe, howe, felawys! Nowe in faith I am fayne
Of theis lippis so loffely are lappid
In bad is full buxhome and bayne.   (Play 30, ll. 43–52)[27]

On the moral level, the scene highlights not only Pilate and Uxor's affection
but also their carnal appetite – 'Yhitt for to comforte my corse me muste
kisse you madame' (l. 48). Theatrically, Pilate's familiarity with the
spectators – 'Howe, howe, felawys! Now in faith I am fayne / Of theis
lippis' (ll. 50–1) – draws the audience into the scene, as does Percula's reply
to his embrace: 'Yha sir, it nedith not to layne, / All ladise we coveyte ...
bothe to be kyssid and clappid' (ll. 54–5).

II

The emergence of domestic themes in medieval drama is coterminous with
developments in staging, especially the construction of private space. While
the early modern domestic play will problematize more systematically the
individual's relation to private life and public authority, and will treat the
cult of domesticity amid more elaborate representational settings, the
medieval cycles' reconstitution of biblical material within contemporary
familial contexts and distinct private spaces wields a notable influence
upon the formation of the later genre.

Although, as Meg Twycross contends, medieval open-air processional
staging was a complex phenomenon, it also offered a 'simple and eco-
nomical solution to a severe logistic problem: how to bring a vast play to a
large holiday audience without losing either detail or an intimacy of
approach'; the challenge was resolved 'by playing each episode over and
over again' to small groups of spectators – 'as many as can crowd into an
ordinary shopping street around a pageant wagon.'[28] To the place-and-
scaffold staging of the pageants intended for outdoor performance on
wagons were added multiple, realistic settings. The technique of perspective, moreover, facilitated the movement of actors from mansion or
domus to domus, permitting the illusion of functional space, in particular
functional household space. In both English and continental plays of the
twelfth and thirteenth centuries, common items in the dialogue and stage
directions already included references to sedes, estals, sièges, lius (lieux), and
loca; in later plays the most prevalent technical terms were domus, mansions,
or houses.[29] Richard Southern has observed that 'scaffolds ... were sometimes
called houses' and 'were constructed by fitting pre-fabricated frames
together.'[30] The figures Mary Magdalen, Martha, and Lazarus occupied

'Martha's house (*domum Marthe*) at Bethany,' while 'another built structure was no doubt needed for the home of Simon the Pharisee, unless one *mansion* served both Martha and Simon ... '[31] The staged *seats, houses,* or *places,* whether belonging to specific characters or else signifying areas such as Heaven or Hell, were actually 'small stages,' normally with corner posts 'supporting curtained frameworks.'[32] As early as the twelfth century the search for verisimilitude was evident in the plan for the Anglo-Norman *Adam* (c.1150), which describes Paradise and Hell as two contrasting houses, the former adorned 'with curtains and silk hangings' and 'sweet scented flowers,' while in the latter the inhabitants are 'noisy' and there is 'a clattering of pots and pans so that it can be heard outside.'[33]

The fourteenth-century impresario Leone di Somi advises that settings should foster verisimilitude and be modelled after 'ancient or modern' cities through the display of 'house fronts, squares, porticoes, streets embellished with arches, columns, statues of diverse kinds ... according to the demands of the script.'[34] In England, the compilers of pageant plays demonstrate varying degrees of interest in adapting the action to specific, recognizable locations. 'The York cycle's specific self-referential or meta-dramatic allusions to "medieval time and English place,"' writes Beadle, 'are studiedly discreet and quietly assimilated to its greater purpose,' a feature which 'is characteristic, and contrasts with the freer but less clearly motivated references to the contemporary scene that form an attractive feature of the Chester cycle and the Wakefield group'; in the York plays, 'variegated detail and the changes wrought by time are effectively subsumed.'[35] The several locations required for York Play 30 (The Dream of Pilate's Wife) include a *palatium* or separate quarter to which Pilate leads Christ in order to interrogate him, the *palatium* also serving as Pilate's and Percula's private bedchambers. The scene in which Pilate is put to bed parallels the episodes in York Play 29 (Christ before Annas and Caiaphas) and Play 31 (Christ before Herod), in which Caiaphas and Herod respectively go to bed and later awake upon the arrival of the captured Jesus. Although these episodes inspired imitations, they have no known dramatic or biblical antecedents.[36] The addition of these details to the York repertoire is consistent with the cycle's restrained verisimilitude, especially with respect to location as well as cause and effect.[37] Plays 29, 30, and 31, moreover, are indicative of the growing social and economic influence of the trade guilds, which staged their respective pageants 'from a mixture of religious devotion, civic pride and showmanship.'[38] Given that The Dream of Pilate's Wife was performed by the Tapisters (weavers or figurers of tapestries) and the Couchers (upholsterers, especially of couches, bedding, and the hangings over ornamental beds), with some assistance from the Linen-weavers, it is not surprising that the episodes set in the *palatium* should depict sumptuous costumes, furnishings, and other properties. Pilate, for example, asks to be brought to bed 'rychely arrayed' (l. 128), securing his servant's promise that he, Pilate, will 'luffely be layde' (l. 131); and Satan tempts Percula while she is asleep in 'a bedde arayed' of the 'beste' materials (l. 153).

While the addition of private space to perspective settings sustained the tradition of performing close to the audience, it also made the *platea* and the *domus* more theatrically connected. Actors' entrances and exits through '"dores" or curtains,' observes Robert Weimann, were 'now more directly related to, and motivated by, the actual content of the dramatic action, such as the dramatic image of leave-taking, returning home, or visiting.'[39] In the York Dream of Pilate's Wife, Percula's bedchamber, together with her son, her lady-in-waiting, and familiar domestic surroundings, is a source of comfort after her long journey home:

> DOMINA. Now are we at home. Do helpe yf ye may,
> For I will make me redye and rayke to my reste.
> ANCILLA. Yhe are werie madame, for-wente of youre way,
> Do boune you to bedde ...
> FILIUS. Here is a bedde arayed of þe beste.
> DOMINA. Do happe me, and faste hense ye hye.
> ANCILLA. Madame, anone all dewly is dressid.
> FILIUS. With no stalkyng nor no striffe be ye stressed.
> DOMINA. Nowe be yhe in pese, both youre carpyng and crye.   (ll. 149–57)

A set of detailed stage directions calling for concrete, recognizable domestic space and properties underwrites the temptation of Uxor in N-town Play 31, Satan and Pilate's Wife; The Second Trial before Pilate:

> *Here xal þe devyl gon to Pylatys wyf, þe corteyn drawyn as she lyth in bedde; and he xal no dene make, but she xal sone after þat he is come in makyn a rewly noyse, comyng and rennyng of þe schaffald, and here shert and here kyrtyl in here hand ...*   (p. 317)

The actors, as these examples illustrate, also gain a new, more metaphorical space: the theatrically important interior.

The growing emphasis on interior space in the drama coincides with the widespread practice in medieval literature, art, and theology of treating the private room or chamber as a sign of one's inward condition. In Augustine's

Confessions the soul and heart are architectural spaces resembling the rooms of a house: 'in that great struggle within my inner abode – which I had forcibly provoked with my soul in that little room of ours, my heart ... '[40] A common *topos* in both morality and cyclical plays is the function of the bed as the encasement of the soul. In *The Castle of Perseverance* Mankind's soul is hidden under his bed until death; and in both the York and N-town plays dealing with the temptation of Pilate's wife the latter's retreat to her private room and bed alerts the audience to her imminent spiritual temptation. The allusions in both the York and N-town plays to interior spaces draws on the late medieval practice of investing palace halls with a partition dividing the large public reception area from smaller quarters reserved for private conversation and for sleeping. By the fifteenth century most of the homes of the gentry and merchants, and of some artisans and yeomen, would contain interior divisions.[41] In the York Dream of Pilate's Wife Percula's request for complete solitude so that she can be shielded from public 'striffe' (l. 156) anticipates the early modern practice of withdrawing to a private chamber in order to be alone. In the sixteenth century Montaigne, like many of his contemporaries, describes the pleasure that withdrawal to private quarters can bestow: 'Miserable, in my minde is he, who in his owne home, hath no where to be to himselfe; where hee may particularly court, and at his pleasure hide or with-draw himself.'[42] Percula's action in The Dream of Pilate's Wife is especially significant in that it anticipates the move towards the individual's physical separation from the collective.

III

Domestic matter in medieval drama is not restricted to plays that high-light human sorrow or separation. Quotidian subjects also inform plays that combine edification with comedy. In keeping with medieval and early humanist appropriations of classical formulas, the plays with comic overtones focus on characters from the common ranks of society. Notable examples are English versions of the Noah story, which trace the movement from sorrow to hope and reconciliation through Noah's patience in marriage. The Noah pageants anticipate later domestic plays in their use of comic motifs for the instruction of popular audiences in domestic conduct. Noah's faith and obedience in York Play 9 (The Flood) bring about not only his victory over despair but also his successful taming of his obstreperous wife. In their blurring of didactic schemes with farce, however, the Noah plays also inscribe a tension between doctrinal and dramatic structures. The Towneley and Chester versions give greater emphasis to Uxor's domestic intransigence, and Noah's attempts to tame it, than they do to Noah's patient obedience to God's will. With their focus on domestic strife, the Towneley and Chester pageants reveal an emergent theatrical interest in the precariousness of contemporary marriage codes.

In the portrayal of domestic conduct neither the Towneley nor the Chester Noah idealizes marriage or the patriarchal family. While the wife's rebelliousness in the Towneley *Processus Noe cum filiis* conforms to patristic diatribes against the inferiority and perfidy of woman and the dangers of marriage, her spirited combats with Noah deflect the solemnity of the moralizing.[43]

> VXOR. We women may wary
> All ill husbandys;
> I haue oone, bi Mary,
> That lowsyd me of my bandys! ...
> Bot yit otherwhile,
> What with gam and with gyle,
> I shall smyte and smyle,
> And qwite hym his mede.
>
> NOE. We! hold thi tong, ram-skyt,
> Or I shall the still.
> VXOR. By my thryft, if thou smyte,
> I shal turne the vntill.
> NOE. We shall assay as tyte.
> Haue at the, Gill!   (Play 3, ll. 300–3, 309–18)

Whereas Noah in the York and Chester versions responds to but does not initiate the combat, his counterpart in the Towneley pageant is the first to strike. The wife's rebellion, moreover, lacks biblical precedent; and her contemptuous disregard of the stock appeal to wifely patience – 'Therto say I nay' (l. 557) – is never attenuated. After a long farcical episode of conjugal wrangling in the Chester Noyes Fludd, Uxor still prefers to be with her 'gosseppes all' (Play 3, l. 242) rather than to obey Noah's call to enter the ark. Uxor is so set against joining her family that her children must forcibly carry her on board:

> SEM. In fayth, mother, yett thow shall,
> whether thou will or nought.   (ll. 243–4)

Nor is domestic amity ensured once Uxor enters the boat. The episode ends with Noah's greeting of his wife, who, having been overcome, replies by striking him (l. 246).

Moving beyond conventional sermonizing, the broad humour in the Noah plays periodically gives way to scenes with tragic overtones. When Uxor in the Towneley pageant importunes the women in the audience who 'Wold thare husbandys were dede' (l. 570), her altercation with Noah assumes a more serious tone, underscoring the instability attending the marriage:

VXOR. Lord, I were at ese
And hertely full hoylle,
Might I onys haue a messe
Of wedows coyll. ...

NOE. I shall make þe still as stone,
Begynnar of blunder!
I shall bete the bak and bone,
And breke all in sonder.   (ll. 560–3, 586–9)

In her analysis of Uxor's role in the Chester, York, and Towneley plays, Sarah Sutherland suggests that the wife's ultimate 'refusal to enter the ark betrays an independence intolerable to Noah and the audience alike.'[44] At the same time that these texts define Uxor as a prototype of Eve, however, they permit the supposition that a major factor of Uxor's popularity with medieval audiences is the absence of any divine punishment of her rebellion. Coupled with her independence, Uxor's rebellion, as Anthony Gash argues, enables her to evade 'the polarised roles assigned to women in the Bible and in medieval patriarchy.'[45] The unresolved conjugal conflict, I would suggest, yields the equally important inference that patriarchy can no longer be taken for granted.

Direct Renaissance analogues to the Noah plays are a group of domestic comedies written near the beginning of the seventeenth century, in which Noah's suffering is displaced by the trials of the patient wife.[46] Here the cruelty is entirely one-sided, the conflict being between a virtuous wife and her husband whose violence almost kills her. In four domestic comedies written between 1600 and 1607 – How a Man May Choose a Good Wife from a Bad, The London Prodigal, The Fair Maid of Bristow, and 2 Honest Whore – the patient wife's trials bring about the punishment and repentance of her prodigal husband. Arthur Quinn has delineated these plays' common dramatic strategies: all contain 'a rake and spendthrift who deserts his wife for gain or the love of a courtesan, maltreats the wife who remains faithful to him, and after he has sinned sufficiently, is taken into grace again and even rewarded.'[47] The plots are also indebted to the Prodigal Son plays dating from c. 1530–75, in which non-allegorical characters act out the biblical parable amid homiletic scenes.[48] Although the dramatic focus of the Prodigal Son plays is on the raising and education of children, Ingelend's *The Disobedient Child* (c. 1569) also alerts the spectator to the vicissitudes of marriage. The 'disobedient child' is an unruly, pampered prodigal who disobeys his wealthy and permissive father, borrowing money to marry a shrew who forces him to sell sticks on street corners; when he returns contrite to his father the latter refuses to pay his debts and sends him back to his wife. Although the prodigal eventually learns to abide by the biblical injunction of filial obedience, marriage is only tentatively advocated. The prodigal stalwartly commiserates with other men in the audience whose wives have usurped their husbands' natural authority:

> O Lord! ... how miserable men be those,
> Which to their wives as wretches be wedded,
> And have them continually their mortal foes,
> Serving them thus, as slaves that be hired![49]

'Experience,' moreover, teaches him the 'tru[th]' of his father's critique of marriage: 'My father did say, declaring his mind, / That in matrimony was pain evermore' (p. 303). A similar *topos* informs later domestic comedies: although the wife's endurance in the end brings about her husband's reformation, the spectator is warned that an even greater danger than a husband's backsliding is a wife's recalcitrance, a danger that must be checked at the outset of the marriage through vigilant testing. Thus the reformed prodigal-husband in the final scene of *How a Man May Choose a Good Wife from a Bad* instructs the audience in the differences between good and bad wives: 'A good wife' will be 'apt to do her husband's will,' whereas 'a bad wife' will be 'cross, spiteful and madding, / Never keep home ... / corrupt[ing] chaste wedlock's vow.'[50]

The gesture whereby an actor steps out of a role to address the audience has its roots in Roman drama, and was readily adapted to the medieval and early modern stage. During these intervals the actor is not a character in his or her own right but a type whose didactic gesture unifies actor and spectator in a mutual problem or experience. In medieval plays with seriocomic themes the actors' liaisons with the audience invoke contemporary social norms. In the Coventry Corpus Christi Pageant of the Weavers and the Pageant of the Shearman and Taylors the solemnity of Joseph and Mary's union is temporarily displaced when Joseph commiserates with the men in the audience about the woes of marriage:

> JOSOFF. How sey ye all this cumpany
> Thatt be weddid asse well asse I?
>   I wene *that* ye suffur moche woo; ...
>   And thatt all you do knoo. ...
> Now ys nott this a cumburs lyff?
> Loo! sirs, whatt ytt ys to haue a wyff!
>
> (Pageant of the Weavers, ll. 463–5, 470, 569–70)[51]

> JOSOFF. All olde men, insampull take be me, –
> How I am be-gylid here may you see! –
> To wed soo yong a chyld.
>
> (Pageant of the Shearmen and Taylors, ll. 133–5)

In the Towneley *Processus Noe cum filiis* Noah advises men to be quick to curb their wives' garrulousness in order to prevent future unruliness:

> NOE. Yee men that has wifys,
> Whyls they ar yong,
> If ye luf youre lifys,
> Chastice thare tong.
> Me thynk my hert ryfys,
> Both levyr and long,
> To se sich stryfys
> Wedmen emong ...   (ll. 573–80)

The actor's exhortation to husbands to maintain their socially sanctioned authority over their wives is consonant with the widespread need in late medieval society for betrayed husbands to punish intransigent wives, and corroborates historical evidence that some men, despite the natural authority invested in them, required society's assistance in controlling their spouses.[52]

In the domestic comedies and tragedies of the sixteenth and seventeenth centuries, the actors' expository gestures become widely synthesized as part of an entrenched ideology of secular and typological injunctions surrounding spousal obligations. The climactic scene of *A Woman Killed with Kindness*, in which the husband discovers his wife committing adultery, requires the actor playing the role of the erring wife to importune the women in the theatre:

> O women, women, you that have yet kept
> Your holy matrimonial vow unstain'd,
> Make me your instance: when you tread awry,
> Your sins like mine will on your conscience lie.   (xiii.141–4)

Although often treated ambivalently in domestic drama, this form of injunction belongs to a growing body of literary and extra-literary paradigms: the patient wife; the motif of selecting a 'good' wife; the value of marriage based on choice.

IV

A major emphasis in the early modern domestic play, especially the tragedies, is on the suffering brought about by marital dissolution, which is usually precipitated by the wife's adultery. Two medieval comedies which anticipate the later genre's preoccupation with the subject of woman's promiscuity are the N-town *Woman Taken in Adultery* and John Heywood's *Johan Johan* (printed 1533).

With the exception of the Towneley plays, all of the medieval cycles include versions of *The Woman Taken in Adultery*; the N-town adaptation, however, is the most dramatically poignant. Within a realistic comic structure, the play emphasizes not the woman's sin but the cruelty and hypocrisy of her accusers (the scribes and Pharisees) and the woman's dignified responses to them. The action revolves around the prostitute's house 'or simply a doorway to it, and an open space.'[53] The accusers' raid on the house is rendered in bold, realistic strokes that highlight the degradation and violence to which the woman is subjected:

> PHARISEUS. Fy on þe, scowte, þe devyl þe qwelle!
> Ageyn þe lawe xul we þe kyll?
> Fyrst xal hange þe þe devyl of helle
> Or we such folyes xulde fulfyll. ...
> ACCUSATOR. Come forth apase, þu stynkynge scowte,
> Before þe prophete þu were þis day,
> Or I xal ʒeve þe such a clowte
> Þat þu xalt fall down evyn in þe way.   (Play 24, ll. 177–80, 185–8)

While the play does not condone the woman's sexual offences, it points out that her real crime in the eyes of her detractors is public shame. Society's hypocrisy is juxtaposed with the woman's courage and her charity toward the friends and kin to whom her accusation will bring dishonour:

> MULIER. ... for my synne þat I xal dye,
> I pray 3ow kylle me here in þis place
>   And lete not þe pepyl upon me crye.
> If I be sclaundryd opynly,
>   To all my frendys it xul be shame.　　　　　　　　　　(ll. 170–4)

The action is bracketed by Jesus' insistence that the woman be treated mercifully: in the opening scene he tells the spectator, 'Iff þu aske mercy, I sey nevyr nay' (l. 16); in his closing address he reminds the audience that 'Whan man is contrite and hath wonne grace, / God wele not kepe olde wreth in mynde' (ll. 289–90), that God loves even 'bettyr' those sinners who, like the prostitute, are 'Very contryte' (ll. 291–2).

Heywood's *Johan Johan* in part recalls the Noah plays in its direct and satirical treatment of domestic themes. The play is significant to the development of domestic drama for its evocation of specifically English locations, its reliance on functional domestic space, and its satirical treatment of marriage. Like many Tudor interludes *Johan Johan* was likely performed between courses during a banquet or other large feast. In keeping with the fabliau structure of its French source, the *Farce du Pasté*, the plot revolves around a typical triangle-situation, the characters consisting of a lecherous shrew, a timid cuckold, and a profligate priest. As the play's recent editors remark, in relation to other Tudor interludes *Johan Johan* 'is closer to ordinary domestic circumstance ... it depends far more on physical objects and actions and is unique in its sustained representation of narrative.'[54] Heywood departs from his source by locating the play in Tudor London, altering a number of minute details in the fabliau, including the addition of London streets and districts, and English oaths. The staging requires a hall, a room in Johan and Tyb's house, and a door to the priest's residence. Most of the action takes place in a room which functions as the couple's kitchen and living area. At the back of the room stands a stone fireplace where a coal fire is burning. Other props required are trestles, a table top, place-settings, a stool, mugs, a keg of ale, and bread. Against a background of recognizable geographical locations and homely activities such as candle-chafing, dish-scrubbing, and pie-burning, Heywood achieves a vivid burlesque of contemporary domesticity.

He follows the fabliau in distancing the audience from the characters (we are invited to sympathize with none of them), but goes beyond the French source by giving Johan, the cuckolded husband, and the priest (Sir Johan) the same name, thereby blurring moral distinctions between them. Both the wife and the priest are, as Howard Norland observes, 'bolder and more cynical in the English version,'[55] and neither repents the adultery nor is punished for it. The play is also unusual in the way that it graphically describes the adultery to the audience:

SYR JOHAN. But I shall tell the what I have done, Johan
For that matter: she [Tyb] and I be sometyme aloft,
And I do lye uppon her, many a tyme and oft
To prove her, yet could I never espy
That ever any dyd wors with her than I.   (ll. 348–52)[56]

As in the Towneley and Chester Noah plays, marital discord is not resolved in the final scene. Remaining alone on stage following the brawl with Tyb and the priest, Johan turns to address the spectators with a question – 'But yet can ye tell / Whether they be go?' (ll. 668–9) – echoing his question at the beginning of the play, 'Wote ye not whyther my wyfe is gone?' (l. 2). Johan's decision to look for Tyb in the priest's bedchamber 'To se yf they do me any vylany' (l. 677) indicates that domestic conflict is about to resume.

V

During the gradual shift towards a representational theatre in England, the hybrid moralities of the mid-sixteenth century are crucial to the development of domestic drama. It is axiomatic that the transition from medieval to early modern dramaturgy coalesces in the hybrid moralities. In his widely influential study of what he called '*hybrid*, or *transitional*' plays, Bernard Spivack defined these texts, which comprise over a dozen extant works, as 'products of interaction between the old convention and the new'; the plots involve 'the *open* fusion of two radically different dramatic methods, the abstract and the concrete,' a fusion which becomes 'the customary method of the playwright and the unremarkable experience' of the playgoer.[57] Written primarily for London audiences, the transitional plays anticipate the Elizabethan drama's emphasis on individuality and idiosyncrasy. For Spivack, the dramaturgy of the hybrid moralities is still crude in that while 'the unity is homiletic' the plays lack formal 'coherence.'[58] More recently, Catherine Belsey has suggested that the absence of organic unity in these plays is a significant aesthetic feature creating for the audience 'a place of uncertainty or of unresolved debate'; and Frances Dolan has argued that the dramatic inconsistencies 'provide particularly rich evidence of social change and its relationship to changing literary forms.'[59] Revealing a strong authorial interest in intellectual debate and in the dynamics of shifting social structures, the exposition in these transitional plays is not always homiletically consistent or transparent.

Among the extant hybrid moralities that blur homiletic and naturalistic elements, Thomas Garter's *The Most Virtuous and Godly Susanna* (pub. 1578) and John Phillip's *Comedy of Patient and Meek Grissell* (c. 1558–66) are particularly significant to the evolution of domestic drama. Like many hybrid moralities, the two plays modify their source material by celebrating romantic love in marriage.[60] Other scenes depict the mutual affection of parents and children, and the action is set within clearly defined domestic spaces. In both plays the romantic theme is subsumed under the formula of the trials of the virtuous and patient wife, and the staging creates a distinct sense of time and place.

The importance of *Susanna*, which is based on the apocryphal book of Susanna, lies chiefly in its portrayal of the ideal wife and family within intimate domestic tableaux. During Susanna's initial appearance on stage, we view a heroine who speaks and acts according to the ideal of wifely behaviour described in the conduct literature. Susanna's language evokes a world of mundane time and space, whose preservation is the wife's duty:

> *Here entreth Susanna and her two maydes.*
> I cannot but must marueyle much, of Joachim my Lorde,
> And why he commeth not home to dyne, according to his worde.
> Was it not at xij. a Clock that he sayd he would dyne,
> Now thinke you both in fayth is it not, a little past that tyme.   (ll. 344–7)[61]

Before the Vice, Ill Report, sets in motion his devilish plot, Susanna and Joachim are a model wife and husband: she is loyal and submissive, while he is cheerful and good natured:

> IOACH. ... Susan come let vs go home, the sooner shall we dyne,
> As I doe you, so shall you me, obay another tyme.
> SUSANNA. And reason good in fayth my Lorde, both now and alwayes to,
> That I should follow your behestes, as reason wills me do.   (ll. 376–9)

The play also treats the parent-child bond with a poignancy similar to that which we saw in the medieval pageants of Abraham and Isaac and in the staging of the *planctus Mariae*. The domestic pathos that underwrites Susanna's interactions with her parents supersedes in intensity the expressions of feeling between Susanna and Joachim. A new development is the protracted role of the mother, whose tenderness towards her child and her anguish over Susanna's pending execution are juxtaposed with her husband's more stoic (and sceptical) response.

> ... *Helchia and his wyfe enter.*
> HELCHIA. Uertuous euer me thought the wenche, ...
> And therefore Lord if our offence, or else her owne desarte,
> Haue bene the cause of this her fall, yet quallify her smarte,
> And graunt that with her lyfe, her fame may also dye,
> And that we heare no more her fault ...
> VXOR. The losse of goods sometyme doth moue, a man his hart to breake,
> But of his childe: Ah, me alas, my sobs nill let me speake,
> These brests my Spouse, with tender milke, proceeding from my hart
> Did giue her suck, did nouish her, ...
> And sure I am those wicked men that doe accuse her still,
> Doe it because that she her selfe, would not obay their will.
>
> (ll. 859, 862–9, 872–3)

Helchia is quickly won over by his wife's impassioned words, and he too defends and comforts Susanna.

In addition to these homely vignettes, the action, as David Bevington points out, 'calls for an arrangement in staging unlike anything known to have been in use by popular troupes. Separated from its "stage" is an "orchard" with trees from which Susanna and her maids can be heard and probably seen as she prepares for her bath, and which has a functional gate that can be shut when her maids return to the main stage.'[62] While continuing to reproduce the narrative of female patience and fortitude, the play delineates the heroine's extra-moral perfections in language typical of love sonnets. 'Her cheekes,' declares Voluptas,

> that are so chery red, her lippes so red and thin, ...
> Her brestes that are so round and fayre, her armes that are so long, ...
> Her middle small, her body long, her buttockes broade and round,
> Her legges so straight, her foote so small, the like treades not on
>   ground ...
>
> (ll. 413, 415, 417–18)

The dramatic tension between the homiletic exposition of female virtue and Susanna's erotic appeal is only tentatively sketched. Although the Vice figure and Susanna's other detractors, Voluptas and Sensualitas, are theatrically intriguing in their clever and energetic scheming, and in their slanderous communications with the spectator, the purpose of the modifications to the apocryphal story is chiefly to enhance its appeal to diverse contemporary audiences.

The tension between homiletic and naturalistic impulses in the portrayal of the patient wife is more fully realized in Phillip's *Patient Grissell*, which belongs to a body of literature whose influence on domestic drama is fundamental, namely the Elizabethan versions of the Griselda story.

2

Fashioning Marriage Codes: Sixteenth-Century Griseldas

The sixteenth-century adaptations of the Griselda legend combine a number of features that are central to the domestic play; these include the trials of the patient wife, the theme of romantic love in marriage, and the tension between private life and public authority.[1] Among the extant sixteenth-century versions, Phillip's hybrid morality,[2] the ballad 'Of Patient Grissel,' and the 1599 *Patient Grissil* by Dekker, Chettle, and Haughton retain only marginally the symbolic structures of their medieval analogues. Rather than allegorizing the afflicted soul's progression towards virtue, Griselda's trials assume a broader social and political significance. The new emphasis is introduced by Phillip and absorbed by the ballad; in both texts the marquess's testing of his wife's patience is portrayed chiefly as a response to society's disapproval of a sovereign's marriage to a subordinate. A related theme, introduced by Phillip, is the desirability of marriage based on choice, a development coinciding with the humanist emphasis on romantic wedlock. In both Phillip's comedy and the ballad, the marquess's marriage to Griselda and his tests of her patience have an overtly didactic purpose: to instruct the audience in the Protestant code of marriage as the expression of active virtue, with the attendant expectation that a dutiful wife will eradicate marital conflict through patience, self-denial, and humility. The 1599 play complicates these themes, sustaining a greater interest in domestic strife and relating it to the broader problematic of patriarchal authority in marriage and society. The extremity of the marquess's cruelty, together with Griselda's rebellion against his abuse of power in his role as both husband and sovereign, qualifies the homiletic superstructure of the main plot. In a significant departure from its analogues, the 1599 *Patient Grissil* also employs a multiple plot which interrogates the male-female/sovereign-subject hierarchies. Focusing on the instability rather than the romance of marriage, the play speaks to the changes in the social fabric of early modern England which were creating sharp conflicts within social and gender hierarchies, destabilizing traditional ideals of a harmonious, divinely sanctioned social order.[3]

The major points of departure between the medieval and the early modern versions of the Griselda legend revolve around the presentation of marriage. During the Middle Ages the story of Griselda's marriage to a marquess, her subsequent trials and banishment, and her eventual reunion with her husband had a strong allegorical appeal. In Petrarch's *De Insigni Obedientia et Fide Uxoris* Griselda's ordeal serves as an *exemplum* of the Christian soul which submits to earthly suffering, eventually uniting with its divine Lord. In a letter to Boccaccio praising the tale of Griselda as the finest in *The Decameron*, Petrarch emphasized the allegorical significance of Griselda's suffering. His objective in rewriting the story 'was not to induce the women of our time to imitate the patience of this wife,' which he believed to be 'beyond imitation'; rather, his aim was 'to lead my readers to emulate the example of feminine constancy, and to submit themselves to God with the same courage as did this woman to her husband.'[4] In translating Boccaccio's narrative, Petrarch was also revising and correcting an ideology of readership. As Carolyn Dinshaw points out, 'what is most striking ... in Petrarch's explanation is his distinct and deliberate redefinition of the literary community, from *matronas nostri temporis* (for whom, as Boccaccio happily declares, the *Decameron* was written) to *legentes*, readers of Latin, a brotherhood of literate men of all times and all places.' Petrarch's narrative is written neither for nor about women – the allegorization of Griselda's trials as a paradigm of Christian suffering 'precisely thematizes what Petrarch's *translatio* in general does: as interlingual substitution, it excludes women from the audience of the tale; as a trope ... it eliminates the particular concerns of women and subsumes them into a larger vision of mankind.'[5] Although in translating Petrarch's tale Chaucer's Clerk in turn distances the woman, representing 'literary activity as gendered – as a masculine activity that is performed on a feminine body,'[6] the portrayal of Griselda's trials by Chaucer, and before him by Boccaccio, is not without an attendant interest in the origin of female suffering and subjection in secular hierarchies, especially the hierarchies of gender and class.

In *The Decameron* there is pronounced ambivalence in the presentation of Gualtieri's testing of Griselda. During the course of the narrative, the storyteller refrains from intervening with direct moral judgments. Instead, he records the strong disapproval of Gualtieri's subjects, all of whom love Griselda deeply: 'His subjects, believing he had killed his children, criticized him bitterly and regarded him as a cruel man, and they had the greatest compassion for the lady.'[7] Yet from the outset the storyteller's tone leads the reader to expect a happy resolution. Although Gualtieri's tests cause a great deal of suffering, we infer that he is only ostensibly cruel, his actions causing pain even to himself: 'Gualtieri, who felt closer to tears than anyone else there, stood nevertheless with a stern face' (p. 139). In his closing remarks, the narrator assures his listeners that 'Everyone was most delighted about how everything had turned out, and Griselda with her husband and children celebrated in great style,' that 'Gualtieri lived a long and happy life with Griselda, always honoring her as much as he could' (p. 142). Yet this assurance is immediately followed with a sharp rebuke of Gualtieri's former behaviour: 'What more can be said here, except that godlike spirits do sometimes rain down from heaven into poor homes, just as those more suited to governing pigs than to ruling over men make their appearances in royal palaces' (p. 142). And in his concluding remarks the narrator expresses doubt about the efficacy of the *exemplum* of Griselda's suffering: 'Who besides Griselda could have endured the severe and unheard-of trials that Gualtieri imposed upon her and remained with a not only tearless but happy face?' (p. 142).

Chaucer's *Clerk's Tale*, even more so than Boccaccio's novella, inscribes contradictory messages about the significance of Griselda's trials.[8] On one hand, the Clerk strongly condemns Walter's actions as cruel, unnecessary, and 'yvele,' pointing out that they are not atypical:

> He hadde assayed hire ynogh bifore,
> And foond hire evere good; what neded it
> Hire for to tempte, and alwey moore and moore,
> Though som men preise it for a subtil wit?
> But as for me, I seye that yvele it sit
> To assaye a wyf whan that it is no nede,
> And putten hire in angwyssh and in drede.   (ll. 456–62)[9]

On the other hand, although the Clerk sympathizes with Griselda's mistreatment by her husband, he ultimately offers the tale as an *exemplum* for all wives, implicitly admonishing modern women. While

lamenting that 'It were ful hard to fynde now-a-dayes / In al a toun
Grisildis thre or two' (ll. 1164–5), and that modern women would surely
fail 'if that they were put to swiche assayes,' (l. 1166) he urges them
nonetheless to try to emulate Griselda. At the same time that Chaucer
and Boccaccio problematize the marquess's cruelty towards Griselda,
their narratives, like Petrarch's, reauthorize the patriarchal imperative
of female silence and subordination.

In the sixteenth century the Griselda story is refashioned to emphasize the secular significance of the marriage. Whereas in the Italian
analogues the vassals, and in Chaucer the townspeople, advise a reluc-
tant marquess to marry Griselda so that her virtue will be passed on
through the generations, in the early modern versions it is the marquess
who chooses to marry the poor but virtuous maiden, a choice which
meets with public disapproval. His marriage to Griselda and his subsequent tests of her patience teach his subjects an important lesson: the
value of romantic wedlock, together with its attendant spousal duties
– the husband's to command wisely, the wife's to be patient and obedient. The *topos* of companionate marriage is introduced by Phillip and is
treated more extensively by the ballad. In their comedy of *Patient Grissil*
Dekker and his collaborators complicate even further the allegorical
structures of the tale: while marriage based on choice remains a fundamental issue, the play relates marriage to a broader framework which
encompasses the individual's tenuous relationship to authority.[10]

Although de-emphasizing the allegorical structures of the Griselda
story, the sixteenth-century versions retain the fairy-tale scheme whereby a poor maiden marries a prince, a scheme that contradicts contemporary social practices. Whereas the ideal marriage in Tudor and Elizabethan England for merchants, artisans, peasants, and those of the
professional classes was one based on choice, the practice of arranged
marriages was still the norm for the aristocracy. Furthermore, marriages
between members of the aristocracy and the gentry or the artisan classes
were still extremely rare. The children of nobles overwhelmingly
married the sons and daughters of other noble families or of non-titled
aristocrats, and very few married the children of merchants or artisans.
The marriage of a marquess to a peasant would thus have been viewed
as fantastic by contemporary audiences. The early modern redactions of
the Griselda legend, however, are not interested in fairy-tale marriages
per se; in an age when companionate marriage is being increasingly
sanctioned for the non-aristocratic classes, the story of the marriage
between a marquess and a peasant becomes a vehicle for the instruction

of contemporary audiences in the merits of romantic wedlock and reciprocity in marriage. In Phillip's comedy and in the *Patient Grissil* of Dekker and his collaborators, Gwalter often behaves more like a gentleman than a marquess. As Edward Pechter observes of Gwalter in the 1599 play, 'he is technically a Marquess, but for the most part ... Gwalter and Grissil live like people of the middling sort, centered in domesticity and family life.'[11] The fact that a marquess needs to learn the value of companionate wedlock would emphasize for the early modern spectator the enormous importance of this particular code of marriage. In the *Encomium Matrimonii* Erasmus had extolled marriage as the original sacrament on the basis that it preceded the Fall, disclaiming the monastic vow of celibacy because it contradicted the divine instruction to procreate.[12] And Juan Luis Vives had dedicated book two of *Instruction of a Christen Woman* to the state of marriage. Over a century later Jeremy Taylor, echoing the early humanists, warned that any 'disparagement of marriage ... scandal[ized] ... religion,' for 'marriage was ordained by God, instituted in paradise, was the relief of natural necessity and the first blessing from the Lord'; William Perkins described marriage as 'a state in itself far more excellent than the condition of a single life,' and observed that in order for marriage to be a true 'action of spirituall nature' it must be founded on 'mutuall love and agreement.'[13] The importance of marriage based on mutual consent is a common trope in the literature of the late sixteenth and early seventeenth centuries. George Puttenham, in his commentary on epithalamic poetry, describes matrimony as 'the highest & holiest' of human bonds; Spenser's *Amoretti* culminates in a marriage of choice: 'Sweet be the bands, the which true loue doth tye, / without constraynt or dread of any ill' (Sonnet LXV).[14] In the same sonnet we learn that marriage should be ruled by 'simple truth and mutuall good will' and founded on 'fayth' and 'spotlesse pleasure.'

The growing emphasis on romantic wedlock, however, was not indicative of a gradual disintegration of social hierarchies. On the contrary, early modern England witnessed an increase in inequality of wealth and status, which worked to reinforce hierarchy.[15] What the new emphasis on reciprocity and the mutual obligations of spouses decried was the practice of forced marriage. Between 1600 and 1650 a large number of plays and treatises criticize forced marriage as a major cause of domestic disorder.[16] In George Wilkins's domestic tragicomedy *The Miseries of Enforced Marriage* (c. 1607) the protagonist's bigamy, his abandonment to a profligate life, and his chosen wife's suicide are portrayed as the tragic consequences of enforcement. William Scarborow, the young hero, articulates the didactic message when he foretells the tragic outcome of his guardian's coercion: 'Fate, pity me, because I am enforc'd: / For I have heard those matches have cost blood, / Where love is once begun, and then withstood.'[17] In *A Curtaine Lecture* (c. 1637) Thomas Heywood denounces 'forced contracts,' singling them out as a principal cause of domestic violence: 'How often have forced contracts been made to add land to land not love to love? and to unite houses to houses, not hearts to hearts? which hath beene the occasion that men haue turned monsters ... '[18]

The notion of romantic wedlock as the expression and 'exercise of virtue'[19] is introduced into the Griselda legend by Phillip and is absorbed by Deloney in his 1593 version of the ballad. The quarto's subtitle of Phillip's play alerts us to the new schematic function of Griselda's trials, namely to instruct citizen audiences in domestic decorum: *The Commodye of pacient and meeke Grissill, Whearin is declared, the good example, of her patience towardes her husband ... '*[20] In addition to highlighting Grissell's and Gautier's roles as wife and husband, Phillip gives Grissell a mother and a nursemaid, and creates intimate family vignettes prior to the marriage proposal.[21] The additional female characters are types whose function is to underscore the virtues of perseverance and obedience. Where Phillip makes more extensive alterations to the medieval versions' allegorical design is in his portrayal of the marriage debate between the marquess and his subjects as a *psychomachia* in which Gautier protests against Fidence and Reason who are entreating him to marry. The marquess bases his objections on St Paul's preference for the single life, and the scene builds on the debate between virginity and marriage until the latter, which combines the practical consideration of offspring with earthly joy, is accepted by the marquess as the preferable condition. Like his medieval counterparts, Gautier chooses to marry Grissell for her virtue, but while he claims not to be 'Venus darlinge' he admits to loving Grissell deeply: 'from profound hart, doth perfit loue procead' (l. 664). Fidence and Reason, however, must win over the Vice Politicke Perswasion before the marriage can be accepted by society.

The Vice-figure, which is unique to Phillip's play, articulates social opposition to the marquess's choice of bride, altering the medieval *topos* which portrays public hostility to the marriage as merely an excuse invented by the marquess to justify to Griselda his testing of her virtue. In his role as public messenger, the Vice has a powerful effect upon the marquess, who only reluctantly yields to the entreaty to test Grissell:

'Oh cruell wightes, that cause my care, oh stonie harts of flint, / Can neuer teares nor dolfull paints, cause rigor for to stynt, / But that ye will procead to worke your curssed will' (ll. 1081–3). A significant development is the marquess's explanation to his wife of his intention in carrying out the tests: public pressure, he confesses, makes them necessary (ll. 1089–96). While the explanation abates the marquess's coercive conduct, the Vice's presence creates an awkward equivocation with respect to the marquess's motivation. Cyrus Hoy has noted the 'psychologically ambiguous ground' occupied by Politicke Perswasion: while the Vice 'moves independently' in this play, 'represent[ing] a force in the world that gives credence to what in Boccaccio and Chaucer have been but pretexts concerning voices in society that grumble at Griselda's rise,' Politicke is also 'the external voice of an inner evil, the overt manifestation of all the Marquess' efforts to deceive himself with specious arguments for Griselda's disgrace.'[22] By stressing the Vice's public role, Phillip evades the unsettling possibility that the marquess's cruelty stems from within. The play does not build on the realistic presentation of character, anticipating the ballad's portrayal of the tests as the marquess's conscious ploy to win public support for the marriage.

The ballad 'Of Patient Grissel and a Noble Marquesse' moves rapidly to the courtship between the marquess and Grissel, dispensing altogether with the marquess's initial doubts about marriage. In Deloney's version the romantic intrigue is brought into relief, and the emphasis is as much on the marquess's passion as it is on Grissel's virtue:

> She sang most sweetly, with pleasant voice melodiously,
> Which set the Lord's heart on fire.
> The more he lookt, the more he might,
> Beauty bred, his heart's delight.[23]

While retaining the testing motif, Deloney treats Grissel's trials as a means to prove her merits to the sceptics at court, the marquess expressing the hope that his cruel behaviour will make others pity Grissel and 'her foes ... disgrace' (stanza 5). Upon the successful completion of the tests, the ballad proceeds to celebrate the virtues of patience and constancy.

Both the ballad and Phillip's comedy, then, downplay the marquess's cruelty during the tests. In both texts characterization is subordinated to the critique of unjust social practices and to the presentation of wifely patience as a means of securing domestic harmony and social stability. The opposing voices are quickly persuaded of Griselda's merits, and society is transformed by the marriage which it celebrates.

In the *Patient Grissil* by Dekker, Chettle, and Haughton the romantic union of Grissil and Gwalter is counterbalanced by the various conflicts – personal, moral, social, and political – attending the marriage. Although the main plot revolves around the theme of the desirability of marriage based on choice, our attention is drawn to the marquess's violence against Grissil. One trajectory of the action affirms the growing belief that a husband's coercive behaviour generally stemmed from outmoded social values. The causal relation is presented with considerable psychological poignancy, highlighting an issue which is only implied by Phillip, namely the marquess's personal need to humiliate his wife. In the opening scene a courtier reminds Gwalter of his duty to marry an equal in order to maintain political stability within the kingdom (I.i.22–8).[24] But the marquess, who has been pretending to scorn love and marriage in order to deflect the court's suspicion, has secretly fallen in love with a poor maiden who has evoked romantic feelings in him. Upon his introduction of Grissil to the court, the marquess openly admits his romantic interest: 'I tell ye Lords, / ... Beautie first made me loue, and vertue woe' (I.ii.251–5). Shocked at Grissil's poverty, the courtiers become forceful opponents, publicly deriding Gwalter's choice of bride and warning him that 'the world' will be shocked 'when the trump of fame / Shall sound your high birth with a beggers name' (I.ii.279–80). The courtiers' persistent taunts evoke in the marquess feelings of anger, doubt, and shame, which lead to a sudden 'burn[ing] ... desire' (II.ii.20) to mortify his wife. During his ruthless tests of Grissil's patience we perceive a genuine internal struggle, so that for the first time in the evolution of the Griselda story the marquess's cruelty approaches psychological depth.[25] On one level, then, the play subscribes to the widespread view that denying marriages based on choice was the cause of personal grief and domestic instability. Sensitive to the public outcry, the marquess blames Grissil for his dishonour, bitterly regretting the joy he has found in marriage: '(oh my soule) / Why didst thou builde this mountaine of my shame, / Why lye my ioyes buried in *Grissills* name?' (II.ii.59–61). That Gwalter has internalized his opponents' hostility is suggested by the operative phrase 'mountaine of my shame' and by his striking admission that his defence against public dishonour is a source of personal anguish:

... oh my *Grissill*,
How dearely should I loue thee,
Yea die to doe thee good, but that my subiects
Vpbraid me with thy birth, and call it base.   (II.ii.115–18)

Under profound emotional strain, the marquess turns Grissil into an
object for the court's pleasure, hoping her servility will impress her
detractors:

MARQ. [to the courtiers] ... I grieue
To see you grieue that I haue wrong'd my state,
By louing one whose basenes now I hate.
Enter Grissill with wine.
Come faster if you can, forbeare *Mario*,
Tis but her office: what shee does to mee,
She shall performe to any of you three.   (II.ii.133–8)

The strongly subjective nature of Gwalter's cruelty is emphasized in the
climactic moment of the denouement when the marquess admits, 'My
selfe haue done most wrong, for I did try / To breake the temper of
true constancie' (V.ii.204–5).

While the audience is moved to sympathize with Gwalter's emotional
struggle, the scene builds in such a way that our pity is blocked by the
excessiveness of the tests. The inordinate nature of the trials is first suggested in a brief vignette depicting Gwalter's cruelty as a manifestation
of a dark inner impulse, its catalyst being not only repressive social
claims and temporary moral weakness but also the marquess's brutal
exploitation of his power. Removed from the suspicious gaze of the
courtiers, Grissil is shown beseeching her husband to share with her the
'burden of all sorrowes' (II.ii.43), to which Gwalter responds with a
spectacular insult: 'I am not beholding to your loue for this, / Woman I
loue thee not, thine eyes to mine / Are eyes of Basiliskes, they murder
me' (lines 45–7). Given the absence of the courtly faction at this moment,
the spectator may well wonder why the marquess resorts to such degrad-
ing epithets, comparing his wife with a mythological reptile that destroys
with its gaze. As Grissil quietly acquiesces to her husband's insults,
Gwalter's abusive language gives way to sadistic behaviour:

MARQ. Cast downe my gloue ... ,
Stoope you for it, for I will haue you stoope,

And kneele euen to the meanest groome I keepe.
GRIS. Tis but my duetie: if youle haue me stoope,
Euen to your meanest groome my Lord ile stoope.   (II.ii.78–82)

Grissil's humiliation is exacerbated when the marquess commands her
to tie an attendant's shoes, after which he 'rail[s] at her' and 'burst[s]
her heart with sorrow' (ll. 132–3). Although cruelty towards women is
not unusual in Renaissance plays, the convention of the patient wife in
the Griselda tales and in domestic drama requires only the wife's qui-
escence, not her submission to self-deprecating tasks. Even in *A Yorkshire Tragedy*, in which the Husband's treatment of his wife and children
is wild and uncontrollable, the Wife's patience is never tried in the same
grotesque fashion as is Grissil's.

The 1599 play thus metes out the rewards for patience with a cynical
excess of concession to the ethic of female submission. The shifting
dramatic perspective attests to the tension at the heart of the play
between the dramatic interest in the psychology of power on the one
hand, and the dictates of literary and social conventions on the other.
While the portrayal of Gwalter's excessive behaviour introduces a
psychological dimension rooted in the tensions generated by the ideologies of gender and class, the psychological interest is eclipsed by the
commonplace denunciation of violent husbands found in the conduct
books and other discourses. In treatises written between 1560 and 1660,
a period when 'marital conflict and marital breakdown' consistently
receive the attention of both church and secular courts,[26] a widely sanctioned solution to marital strife holds that while reciprocity should
serve as a natural solution for all marital disputes, wives are ultimately
subject to the authority of their husbands on the biblical grounds that
the husband was created in the likeness of God. While the conduct
literature exposes numerous contradictions and inconsistencies with
respect to contemporary ideas about marriage, it is unequivocal on the
need for the wife's quietness and obedience. However, a large body of
literature also offers advice to abusive husbands. In 1653 Jeremy Taylor,
while preaching that a husband must consider his wife 'as himself' and
'must love her equally,' follows a long tradition in asserting that a
'husband's power over his wife ... is not a power of coercion but a
power of advice' equal to 'that government that wise men have over
those who are fit to be conducted by them.'[27] The stipulation that a
wife's quietness is to be matched by her husband's leniency underscores the secret betrothal scene in Wilkins's *The Miseries of Enforced*

Marriage, where the couple's vows are preceded by a list of mutual responsibilities:

> SCARBOROW. Their [wives'] very thoughts they cannot term their
>   own.
> Maids, being once made wives, can nothing call
> Rightly their own; they are their husbands' all ...
> CLARE. Men must be like the branch and bark to trees,
> Which doth defend them from tempestuous rage, ...
> If it appear to them they've stray'd amiss,
> They only must rebuke them with a kiss ...   (Act I, p. 480)

While husbands are generally advised to temper violence with reason, the issue of male dominance is treated more problematically. Wilkins's play, like the main plot of the 1599 *Patient Grissil* and many of the marriage manuals, equivocates about the definition of the normative wife as a sign of her husband's possession. In his analysis of early modern representations of the female body, Peter Stallybrass has observed that in legal, economic, and political treatises woman, as a sign, 'unlike man, is produced as a *property* category.' The construction of woman as 'land or possession' has a long historical tradition: cases in point are the biblical description of a wife as part of 'a man's assets,' and the Jewish classification of betrothal 'as a form of masculine acquisition, related to the acquisition of slaves, cattle, and other belongings.' As an economic category, woman 'is the fenced-in enclosure of the landlord, her father, or husband.'[28] Once women have been 'made wives,' declares Scarborow in *The Miseries of Enforced Marriage,* they are the possession of their husbands. An unacknowledged discontinuity, however, informs Wilkins's play: although wives may be 'their husbands' all,' husbands have a duty to correct but not to coerce – 'They only must rebuke them [wives] with a kiss' (Act I, p. 480). The discontinuity echoes the often ambivalent claims of contemporary attitudes towards marriage, especially with regard to male dominance and female inferiority. In Edmund Tilney's *Flower of Friendship* the traditional misogynist claim that wifely subordination is beneficial to women because men share more 'capacity to comprehende, wisdome to understand, strength to execute, solicitude to prosecute, pacience to suffer ... and above all a great courage to accomplishe, all which are ... in a woman verye rare,' is contradicted by what Valerie Wayne has called Lady Isabella's 'emergent, egalitarian ideology of marriage';[29] elsewhere in the treatise, matrimony is at once described as the 'perfite love' that 'knitteth loving heartes, in an insoluble knot of amitie,' and a 'long, and troublesome journey.'[30]

The main plot of the 1599 *Patient Grissil*, we have seen, prevaricates about the issue of male dominance and female inferiority by at once individualizing Gwalter's cruelty and exaggerating Grissil's subservience. In addition, the play includes scenes in which Grissil voices a bold critique of the marquess as an unjust husband and sovereign. In Act II the stock gesture whereby an actor self-consciously reminds the men in the audience of their role in marriage, namely to sustain the male-female hierarchy, is invoked when the marquess, after subjecting Grissil to a series of trials designed to try her patience, interrupts the testing with his injunction: 'men men trie your wiues, / Loue that abides sharpe tempests, sweeteley thriues' (II.ii.32–3). But Gwalter's bombastic solution to domestic conflict is sharply attenuated when Grissil steps out of her patient-wife role to contest her husband's cruelty. Upon being banished from court, Grissil, in an uncharacteristic display of anger, bitterly inveighs against her husband's ruthless behaviour, which conflicts with his public duty to uphold justice: 'Thus tyranny oppresseth innocence, / Thy lookes seeme heauy, but thy heart is light, / For villaines laugh when wrong oppresseth right' (IV.i.191–3). Grissil's rebellion clashes with the homiletic overtones of the testing. While her outburst against tyranny upholds the traditional notion that power should be used wisely, and that sovereigns must exercise benign paternalism just as much as subjects must exercise obedience, her words expose a principal cause of domestic strife, namely the hierarchical structure of marriage and society, which threatens the powerless. When the marquess orders her to part from her children, Grissil lashes out against the status hierarchy which sanctions injustice: 'I must oh God I must, must is for Kings, / And loe obedience, for loe vnderlings' (IV.ii.142–3). Instances of Grissil's insubordination continue into the denouement where she responds with both relief and doubt to her husband's reformation:

MARQ. Why stands my wronged *Grissil* thus amazed?
GRIS. Ioy feare, loue hate, hope doubts incompasse me.   (V.ii.192–3)

Grissil's bold outbursts notwithstanding, the comic resolution of the main plot deflects the significance of her 'feare' and 'doubts,' capitulating to the orthodox assumption that harmony and reciprocity under-write the relationship between rulers and subjects and between hus-bands and wives. Once the sceptics have been convinced of Grissil's merits, Gwalter rejoices in the reunion with his wife. While admitting that he has been chiefly to blame for Grissil's humiliation – 'My selfe haue done most wrong' (V.ii.204) – he stresses that a 'multitude' of 'many headed beastes' is also blameworthy: 'With wrongs, with bitter wrongs, al you haue wrong'd her' (l. 203).

The problem of dominance is more forcefully explored in the two minor plots, both of which are new additions to the Griselda story. These plots bring into relief the tensions underlying Grissil's tentative rebelliousness in the main plot. The longer of the two minor plots focuses on the passions, rivalries, and conflicts attending the explosive relationship of the marquess's cousin Gwenthyan and Sir Owen, a Welsh knight. Gwenthyan's cruelty towards Sir Owen is rooted in her precarious situation with respect to the hierarchies of gender and class. The cousin of a prince, married to a knight, Gwenthyan provides an example of the threat faced by the woman who marries beneath her in social class. Although the ideal of companionate marriage upheld the couple's spiritual equality, in practice equality was denied to partners of unequal social rank. William Gouge, in his *Domesticall Duties*, ration-alizes the contradiction by appealing to the traditional idea of marriage as the fusion of two identities into one, namely the husband's: if 'a woman of eminent place' is married to a man of low social rank, 'It booteth nothing what either of them were before mariage ... for in giuing her selfe to be his wife, and taking him to be her husband, she aduanceth him aboue her selfe, and subiecteth her selfe unto him.'[31] Gwenthyan's refusal to comply with Sir Owen's attempts to tame her is an abrogation of her socially prescribed duty to place him 'aboue her selfe.' Yet just as the marquess's violence towards Grissil is clarified in the denouement as merely a testing ploy, Gwenthyan's abuse of Sir Owen yields her surprising announcement that just 'as her cozen has tryed *Grissill*, so *Gwenthian* has Sir *Owen*' (V.ii.262–3). In equating her abuse of Sir Owen with the marquess's testing of Grissil, however, Gwenthyan both appropriates the prerogative of (male) action and retains her intellectual superiority over Sir Owen. Gwenthyan's claim that she was only pretending thus only ostensibly mitigates her former transgressions.

Gwenthyan's claim to pretence amounts to a parody of the marquess's tests of Grissil. Following Gwenthyan's pronouncement, Sir Owen and Gwenthyan debate the extent to which women should be 'pul'd downe':

> SIR OW. Owe, by Cod is thought should pull her downe, ah ha.
> GWEN. Is not pul'd downe neither, but sir *Owen* shal be her head, and
> is sorry has anger her head and mag it ake, but pray good Knight
> be not proude and triumph too much and tread her Latie downe,
> God vdge mee will tag her will againe doe what her can ...   (V.ii.264–9)

Gwenthyan's capitulation to Sir Owen's natural superiority is only momentary, for she quickly begins to qualify her subjection: 'but pray good Knight be not proude and triumph too much and treade her Latie downe' (ll. 266–8). Finally, in defiance of Sir Owen's suggestion that '*Gwenthian* shall no more be call'd *Gwenthian* but patient *Grissill*,' (ll. 270–1) Gwenthyan rejects Grissil's example of wifely humility, viewing it as a means to keep women in subjection, and warning the women in the audience to resist their husbands' authority:

> GWEN. ... awl you then that haue husbands that you would pridle,
> set your hands to *Gwenthians* pill, for tis not fid that poore womens
> should be kept alwaies under.   (V.ii.290–2)

Richard Levin, arguing for unevenness in the play's multiple-plot structure, is uneasy with the structural and thematic incongruities that it generates: 'the values of the folktale source of the main plot dictate that Grissil's utter self-abnegation be treated as the wifely ideal,' but the morality structure 'places Gwalter in an ambiguous position, for while his persecution of Grissil ... is defined by the double structure as a gross distortion of proper husbandly behavior at the opposite pole from Sir Owen, the folk doctrine would have us accept it as the prerogative of his sex (and rank)'; because the plots combine two polarities, 'the comedy of the subplot actually works at cross-purposes with the idealization of the main-plot heroine, whose claim to perfection is undercut both by its *reductio ad absurdum* in the henpecked Sir Owen and by Gwenthyan's spirited refusal to emulate ... Grissil.'[32] The disjunctions created by the Gwenthyan-Sir Owen plot, I propose, do not constitute dramatic failure; rather, they confirm the impossibility, already intimated in the main plot, of fully assimilating homiletic structures with the play's realistic impulses.

Gwenthyan's critique of gender and class hierarchies is reinforced in the action dealing with the misogamy of Gwalter's sister Julia. After observing the behaviour of the married couples, Julia rejects marriage altogether, preferring the freedom of maidenhood. Gwalter's assertion that 'Patience hath won the prize and now is blest' (V.ii.274) is counterpointed by Julia's expectation that others besides herself are sceptical of the tidy resolution:

> ... amongst this company I trust there are some mayden batchelers,
> and virgin maydens, those that liue in that freedome and loue it,
> those that know the war of mariage and hate it, set their hands to
> my bill, which is rather to dye a mayde and leade Apes in hell, then
> to liue a wife and be continually in hell.　　　　　　(V.ii.278–83)

Julia is suspicious of the peace which has been won: marriage, she concludes, is an ongoing war.

The 1599 play's prevarication with respect to the problem of sovereignty in marriage extends to its treatment of sovereignty in society at large. The play's modifications to the Griselda story, we have seen, define the conjugal ideal as an extension of a broader hierarchical power structure. The relation is merely implied during those moments when we witness Grissil's surprising critique of the marquess's abuse of his role as both husband and sovereign; it is more fully developed in the contrast between the marquess and Grissil's father, Janicola, who serves as a model of wisdom and Christian steadfastness. Although Janicola's occupation as a basket-maker renders survival in a money economy a hardship, his serenity and fortitude give succour to the members of his household: 'thogh I am poore / My loue shall not be so ...' (I.ii.151–2).[33] An ideal father and master, Janicola rules his household like a benevolent patriarch. An early modern audience would have recognized that Janicola's role as head of a household includes moral responsibilities that are similar to those of his sovereign, who is ultimately accountable to God. Dekker, for one, is fond of the analogy between sovereign and father: in *Foure Birds of Noahs Arke* (1609) he writes that a ruler's moral obligation to his subjects, like a father's to his children, is to guide and comfort them, and to teach them 'brotherly affection one towards another ... in loyaltie to him that is their Soueraigne.'[34] In the same year James I declared that 'Kings are ... compared to Fathers of families: for a King is trewly *Parens patriae*, the politique father of his people.'[35]

For William Perkins, 'the superiour' who fails 'in his charge, will prooue uncapable of publike imployment; so the inferiour, who is not framed to a course of economicall subiection, wil hardly vndergoe the yoake of Ciuill obedience.'[36] Janicola's frequent speeches on the need to eradicate conflict with steadfastness provide a litany on the action, underscoring Gwalter's tyrannical behaviour towards not only his wife but his subjects as well. In a significant departure from its sources, the 1599 play extends the marquess's cruelty to Grissil's entire family: hoping to appease the courtiers, Gwalter orders that Janicola and the members of his household, who have been brought to court with Grissil, be humiliated and banished with her (III.i.69–100). The juxtaposition of Janicola (the wise, temperate father) and Gwalter (the impulsive, punishing ruler) as characters and as philosophical polarities is an abstract statement on the necessity of benevolent authority, both in the home and in the kingdom. In the denouement Janicola's family is reunited at court once the marquess appears to have learned the lesson of good rulership. Asked by the marquess whether he will sanction Grissil's marriage, Janicola laconically replies, 'I say but thus, / Great men are Gods, and they haue power ore vs' (V.ii.177–8), echoing King James's assertion that 'Kings are iustly called Gods, for that they exercise a manner or resemblance of Diuine power vpon earth.'[37] The preceding action, however, attenuates the dramatically orthodox resolution. Janicola has remained a morality figure while the cruel marquess has been the more plausible character, indicating the diminishing capacity of earthly authority to imitate divine benevolence. As well, because Janicola is largely a character type, the shift in focus to the ideal patriarch in the denouement does not entirely defuse the impact of the misogamy and female insubordination so forcefully expressed in the two minor plots.

In the 1619 chapbook, the story of Griselda becomes an instruction piece in status-seeking and economic survival for women of the lower classes. As the title suggests, the story is a lesson in expediency: The / Ancient True and Admirable / History of / Patient Grisel, / A Poore Mans Daughter in France: / Shewing / How Maides, By Her Example, In Their Good Behaviour / May Marrie Rich Husbands; / And Likewise Wives By Their Patience And Obedience / May Gaine Much Glorie.[38] In contrast to the bold wish-fulfilment expressed by the chapbook, Dekker, Chettle, and Haughton, in their grappling with the disturbing relation of marriage and power, register a high degree of scepticism towards the cult of domesticity, a scepticism that becomes pervasive in domestic tragedy.

3

Domestic Tragedy and Private Life

Civility and the Crisis of Order

Domestic tragedy flourished during a time when early modern England was undergoing a severe crisis of order. The 1599 *Patient Grissil*, we have seen, speaks to the tensions that contradicted the dominant view of the well-regulated family sustained by companionate marriage. 'Marital disharmony and unhappiness,' writes Ralph Houlbrooke, 'were very widespread according to contemporary observers, indeed commoner than mutual affection or contentment in the view of some.'[1] Disorder in the family was also evinced by numerous case histories of adultery and bigamy; the rise in the number of illegitimate children, which reached a peak between 1590 and 1610; the increasing problem of infanticide; and the desertion and murder of spouses and children. In 1633 Matthew Griffith, in his tract 'To the Christian Reader,' declared that pervasive unruliness originated in the disorderly family:

Why are our children so disobedient and our servants so disordered? Why are some wives so unfaithfull, and some husbands so unprofitable members both of *Church*, and *Common-wealth*? ... [Because they are] not part of God's building ... [that is, of a] well-ordered family ... That which hath both an orderly head, and orderly members, having mutuall relations with each other.[2]

On one hand, disorder was anticipated, given the prevailing doctrine of original sin, which led contemporaries to expect everyone to disobey to some degree both divine and secular commands. What the authorities feared, however, was that the intentional commission of sin and continued law-breaking without punishment would undermine the civil order. As Cynthia Herrup points out, individuals' 'attempts to control' their propensity for sin 'became as important a measure of criminality as success or failure in such attempts,' the chief distinction between criminals and offenders being that, 'unlike other sinners, criminals had abandoned even the quest for self-discipline.'[3] Because the retention of rigid laws 'alongside flexible applications' was deemed necessary for the enforcement of law 'to reflect both human potential and human frailty,'[4] it is difficult to determine whether the rise in crime represented an increase in actual criminal activity or a stronger enforcement of the law. The doctrine of original sin and the qualification of intention notwithstanding, by 1610 the fragmentation of families was seen as a problem of national urgency, and a vagrancy statute declared that individuals guilty of deserting their families would suffer the punishment of rogues and criminals.

The five surviving domestic tragedies written between 1590 and 1610, the period that witnessed the flowering of the genre, are all preoccupied with the dissolution of the contemporary household.[5] Among these, all but Yarrington's *Two Lamentable Tragedies* focus on marital strife. Domestic tragedy is brought about by the infidelity or other refractory behaviour of one of the spouses (the wife's in *Arden of Feversham*, *A Warning for Fair Women*, and *A Woman Killed*; the husband's in *A Yorkshire Tragedy*), whose suffering, repentance, and punishment expiate the crime. The tragedies' interest in the contemporary crisis of order coextends with their scrutiny of the early modern concept of civility as a collective obligation which promises to ensure social cohesion and continuity. In all of these plots, tragic suffering stems from the protagonists' inability to abide by the ideologies of civility and private life.

In early modern definitions of 'civility' the political and social applications of the term are conflated. As a political category, 'civility' refers to the divinely sanctioned polity or orderly state, together with the citizens' conformity to the principles of social order; as a social category, it signifies the condition of being 'civilized,' including 'good breeding,' 'refinement,' and 'ordinary courtesy or politeness' (*Oxford English Dictionary*, 2nd edn. [*OED*]). In the concept's political application, civil society rests on the hierarchical arrangement of the body politic and of the family. For Thomas Hobbes, civility occurs when the instinct for self-preservation acquired in the state of nature is abandoned in favour of 'government under *one*,' namely a sovereign in whose 'will' 'the wills of many are contained'; just as a society of individuals 'is compacted ...

under a common lord,' so in families 'the will of each servant [i.e., member] is contained in the will of his lord.'⁶ Although for Hobbes and other political theorists of the later seventeenth century the analogy between the commonwealth and the patriarchal household is not a requisite to the actual governance of society as it is in the sixteenth century, civility is still considered intrinsic to the patriarchal order. The civil state, explains Hobbes, is a mirror of 'the *whole* universe,' which 'is governed by *one* God'; it is a contractual association ruled over by a patriarchal head who retains power over subordinates – women, children, and servants – who possess no political rights.⁷ The concept of the family as a divinely ordained hierarchy reflective of the civil order is inscribed in sixteenth-century treatises such as Hooker's *Laws of Ecclesiastical Polity* and Smith's *De Republica Anglorum*. 'To fathers within their private families,' writes Hooker, 'Nature hath given a supreme power; for which cause ... all men have ever been taken as lords and lawful kings in their own houses.' Smith describes the family as a 'private' institution whose governance replicates that of the kingdom: 'in the house and familie is the first and most naturall (but private) appearance of one of the best kindes of a common wealth, that is called *Aristocratia* where a few and the best doe governe ... '⁸

Because wedlock is a divinely ordained manifestation of the civil order, it must be carefully maintained through the power of the householder, who is defined as male. Just as the monarch governs by divine sanction, notes Smith, so 'God hath given to the man great wit, bigger strength, and more courage to compell the woman to obey by reason ...' And in *The Lawes Resolutions of Womens Rights* (1632), which the title page describes as a 'Collection of such Statutes and *Customes* ... as doe properly concerne Women,' T.E. explains why women must be ruled and why they have no political rights: husbands 'shall rule over' their wives in punishment for Eve's transgression in Eden; Eve's sin is also 'the reason' why 'Women have no voyse in Parliament, They make no Lawes, they consent to none, they abrogate none. All of them are understood either married or to bee married and their desires as subject to their husband ... The common Law here shaketh hand with Divinitie ... '⁹

Underwriting the political organization of the body politic, civility in the early modern period, as a concept pertaining to the behaviour of individuals who share common goals, becomes inextricably associated with courtesy and manners. Because 'there is no meaning,' write Medvedev and Bakhtin, 'outside the social communication of understanding, i.e., outside the united and mutually coordinated reactions of people to a given sign,' ideology 'first acquires its specific existence ... its semiotic nature' in social interaction.[10] Erasmus's treatise *On Good Manners for Boys* (*De civilitate morum puerilium*; pub. 1530), in which he declares that his intention is 'in moulding a boy,'[11] is one of the first to codify public and private behaviour. The treatise in effect reconceptualizes for the early modern period the definition of civil conduct. According to Erasmus, 'the external decorum of the body' – gestures, posture, clothing – attests to one's innate 'nobility,' so that one of the chief 'tasks of fashioning the young' must be the 'training in good manners right from the earliest years.'[12] A similar view is expressed in the 1603 English translation of Montaigne's *Essayes*. 'Of the Institution and Education of Children' describes the ideal tutor as one who exhibits 'wisdome, judgement, civill customes, and modest behaviour, than bare and meere literall learning.' Instruction in 'civill customes' is necessary, notes Montaigne, because there is no gesture that is not grounded in 'a public language.'[13]

A fundamental aspect of the association of civility with manners is the equation of civil conduct with virtue. The equation is articulated in numerous discourses, including the treatises which dispute the value of the theatre. Both the pro- and anti-theatrical tracts of early modern England promote civility as a moral obligation. For Thomas Heywood, the chief function of the public stage is to inculcate civilized values and behaviour in its audiences. *An Apology for Actors* reconstitutes the morality play through a pivotal early modern perspective: the purpose of drama is not only 'to perswade men to humanity and good life,' but also to 'instruct them in ciuility and good manners, shewing them the fruits of honesty, and the end of villany.'[14] The theatre's detractors also invoke civility in their claims that stage plays advocate reprobate behaviour. The author of *A Refutation of the Apology for Actors* decries the theatre's roots in vice and 'sundry impieties,' by means of which it 'turn[s] vpside downe all discipline and good manners.'[15] The link between civility and virtue remains commonplace as late as the 1690s when Henry More, in his *Account of Virtue*, defines civil conduct as 'a Virtue that minds us of our Tye to all Men in the common Link of Humanity; and bids us with such Chearfulness of Voice, Countenance, and Gesture, to salute whom we meet; as that when we ask them How they do, they may think themselves even the better for our asking.'[16]

Domestic tragedy neither uniformly nor unequivocally upholds the cults of civility and domesticity. In *A Woman Killed with Kindness* Heywood tentatively problematizes Anne Frankford's abrogation of domestic hierarchy and decorum as rooted in the hierarchies of gender and status; and while in *A Warning for Fair Women* Anne Sanders's transgressions are not authorially condoned, the character never makes an easy adjustment to the civil order. *Arden of Feversham* and *A Yorkshire Tragedy* militate more forcefully against the apparent inevitability and naturalness of the patriarchal order and the civilizing process.

A Woman Killed with Kindness

Raymond Williams, in speaking of the relation of art to society, refers to 'a particular sense of life, a particular community of experience' that is generated by art.[17] Our habitual question – 'what is the relation of this art to this society?' – construes society as an artificial, 'specious whole': if a text 'is part of the society, there is no solid whole, outside it, to which, by the form of our question, we concede priority.' Instead, texts inscribe a 'structure of feeling' which 'is as firm and definite as "structure" suggests, yet it operates in the ... least tangible parts of our activity.'[18] In some respects, the 'structure of feeling' is synonymous with culture. In this context, the artistic production of a given historical period, which includes 'characteristic approaches and tones in argument,' is especially important, for in it the structure of feeling is likely to be encoded, although it will not be 'possessed in the same way' by all cultural artifacts.[19] In *A Woman Killed with Kindness* this structure, as exemplified by the rhetorical patterns of setting, action, and dialogue, adheres to dominant ideologies. The play, however, ambivalently legitimizes the formal hierarchies that inform the institutions of marriage, civility, and private life, the action's deeper structures alerting the spectator to the contradictions that render those institutions vulnerable.

From the outset, John Frankford's affluent household in *A Woman Killed* is a model of civility and order. Sumptuous private spaces, elaborate stage properties, and leisurely activities create an atmosphere suggestive of English prosperity and gentility: the Yorkshire country house; the subdivided home; the retinue of servants; expensive furnishings (tables and chairs, doors, stools, beds, and other household objects);[20] sporting and other amusements. From 1570–1640 England witnessed a period of 'Great Rebuilding,' which included the augmentation of private space and domestic furnishings. The widespread emphasis on private space coincided with the transformation from the feudal great household dominated by the hall to the smaller houses of the gentry, citizens, and yeomen, in which rooms and their domestic functions were sharply differentiated. A related phenomenon was the popular indulgence in the large-scale consumption of goods. For the houses of the gentry in particular great amounts of capital were expended on edifices, ornate gardens, and luxurious living spaces.[21] In *The Description of England* (1577) William Harrison clarifies the link between wealth, ornament, and civility. For Harrison, the salubrious household is a quintessential sign of 'delicacy.' Among the most notable structures 'to be marvelously altered in England' is the widespread 'amendment of lodging,' the 'manors and houses of our gentlemen' having been built by 'workmen' who 'excel and are in manner comparable in skill' with the great Italian engineers, designers, and architects – 'old Vitruvius, Leon Battista, and Serlio.'[22] Although critical of the ostentation that sometimes surrounds 'the furniture of our houses,' Harrison provides a detailed inventory (including estimated costs) of the luxurious furnishings that adorn the houses of the nobility and gentry:

Certes in noblemen's houses it is not rare to see abundance of arras, rich hangings of tapestry, silver vessel, and so much other plate as may furnish sundry cupboards, to the sum oftentimes of £1,000 or £2,000 at the least, whereby the value of this and the rest of their stuff doth grow to be almost inestimable. Likewise in the houses of knights, gentlemen, merchantmen, and some other wealthy citizens, it is not geason [uncommon] to behold generally their great provision of tapestry ... pewter, brass, fine linen, and thereto costly cupboards of plate, worth £500 or £600 or £1,000, to be deemed by estimation.[23]

Harrison further observes that the 'costly furniture' which in the past had remained the exclusive property of the elite classes has presently 'descended yet lower, even unto the inferior artificers and many farmers,' who have 'learned also to garnish their cupboards with plate, their joint beds [beds made by joiners] with tapestry and silk hangings, and their tables with carpets and fine napery, whereby the wealth of our country ... doth infinitely appear.'[24]

The staging of *A Woman Killed with Kindness* emphasizes the interactions and rituals that signify what another contemporary, Henry Wotton, describes in *The Elements of Architecture* (1624) as the 'proper' household, namely one that, 'according to the degree of the *Master*,' is 'decently and *delightfully* adorned.'[25] Scene viii opens as '*3 or 4 Servingmen*' are preparing for the after-supper game of cards. The servants' activities and the stage properties bring into relief important signs of social status and domestic decorum: *one [servant] with a voider and wooden knife to take away all, another the salt and bread, another the tablecloth and napkins, another the carpet. JENKIN with two lights after them* (viii, s.d.). His master's company having dined, Jenkin observes degree by commanding his fellow-servants to 'march in order' (l. 1) while they now 'spread for the servingmen in the hall' (l. 3). Before the company sits down to the card-game, Jenkin further instructs the servants to 'spread the carpet in the parlour and stand ready to snuff the lights' (viii.13–14). When Frankford enters he is *as it were brushing the crumbs from his clothes with a napkin, as newly risen from supper* (s.d.). A parallel scene (xi) emphasizes Frankford's reputation as a host with a generous 'heart' (l. 17), and it does so by emphasizing the commodities and activities that contribute to the preparation of another evening meal.

> *Enter Anne, Cranwell, Wendoll, and Jenkin.*
> ANNE. Sirra, 'tis six o'clock already stroke;
> Go bid them spread the cloth and serve in supper.
> JENK[IN]. It shall be done forsooth, mistress.
> Where is Spiggot the butler to give us our salt and trenchers?
> [*Exit.*]
> WEN[DOLL]. We that have been a-hunting all the day
> Come with prepar'd stomachs, Master Frankford;
> We wish'd you at our sport.
> FRANK[FORD]. My heart was with you, and my heart was on you; ...
> A stool, a stool! Where's Jenkin, and where's Nick?
> 'Tis supper time at least an hour ago. ...
> *Enter [Spiggot the] Butler and Jenkin with a*
> *tablecloth, bread, trenchers, and salt [, then exeunt].*   (xi.10–17, 19–20)

As early as 1577 Harrison had observed that 'dinner and supper' had become important indicators of domestic propriety.[26] The taking of meals assumed a ritualistic form reflecting the growing emphasis on manners. At the beginning of the sixteenth century changes in English cuisine coincided with changes in social stratification. A significant development was the growing influence of the emerging professional and merchant classes, whose obsession with status and degree was abetted by the use of printed books prescribing domestic behaviour. These manuals included, as Jack Goody observes, 'the ubiquitous cookbook,' which helped the households of the middling sort 'to breach the hierarchical organisation of cuisine.' The '"secrets" of rich households were now revealed and sumptuary laws prohibiting imitation were no longer effective.'[27] Salt, for example, which is mentioned twice in the above-cited passage from *A Woman Killed*, was considered the most significant component of every meal, the ceremonial salter having a special ritualistic significance in that grace was said in front of it. Ornate salters were associated with families of consequence, as were tablecloths and silver or pewter trenchers such as those that adorn Frankford's dinner table.[28]

The early modern house, notes Felicity Heal, 'was no mere assemblage of rooms: instead, it served to embody the qualities of its owner.'[29] Throughout the play we witness Frankford's abundant hospitality to his friends and neighbours. To Wendoll, Frankford pledges his friendship by providing him with a servant, horse, and 'table,' all at his 'own charge' (iv.71–2). Frankford's courtesy accords with the prevalent image in the conduct books of the English gentleman's home as the place in which he practises civility towards others. In his celebration of the 'proper' home as a 'theatre' of hospitality, Henry Wotton emphasizes the benefits that hospitality can accrue for the civilized householder:

Every Mans proper *Mansion* House and *Home*, being the *Theater* of his *Hospitality*, the *Seate* of *Selfe-fruition*, the *Comfortablest part* of his owne *Life*, the *Noblest* of his Sonnes *Inheritance*, a kinde of priuate *Princedome*; Nay, to the *Possessors* thereof, an *Epitomie* of the whole *World* ... [30]

The ritual of hospitality is a coded language, its purpose being to express the householder's inherent nobility, which invests the home as 'a kinde of priuate *Princedome*,' effecting the mediation between the home and 'the whole *World*.' In this context it is significant that Frankford's courtesy is underscored not only by his hospitality towards his house guests but also by his charity to the debt-ridden aristocrat Charles Mountford (xi.28–35). Nobility is no longer strictly a matter of class; it is a virtue practised by gentlemen of innate distinction.

Frankford's civility is bolstered by another conspicuous sign, namely his bride Anne, whom 'many' others have 'sought' (i.24). During the marriage celebration Anne is perceived by the community not as a subject in her own right but as an 'ornament' complementing her husband's civility:

SIR CHARLES. Master Frankford,
You are a happy man, sir; and much joy

Succeed your marriage mirth, you have a wife
So qualify'd and with such ornaments
Both of the mind and body.   (i.12–16)

Anne's 'qualif[ications]' to be Frankford's bride include 'noble' birth (ll. 16–17) and an 'education such / As might become the daughter of a prince' (ll. 18–19): she is well versed in 'all tongues' and has taught 'all' stringed instruments 'to speak in their best grace' (ll. 19–20). Anne's accomplishments fulfil the injunction of English and continental humanists that women should be educated as long as their instruction enhances their natural tendency towards humility and does not infringe upon their domestic responsibilities.[31]

Anne is well qualified for the role of civilized woman not only by birth, beauty, and education but also by her considerable wealth. That Anne's wealth is an important signifier of value is underscored by the acting company's large payment for the actor's dress, which came to more than the cost of the play.[32] At the same time that Anne qualifies to be Frankford's wife, the ostentatiousness of her dress, which invokes the long-standing misogynist catalogue denigrating women for their 'extravagant adornment,'[33] alerts the spectator to her vanity.

Anne is both an ostentatious, vain woman and a possession. Her other 'ornaments,' for example, amount to a series of prosthetic parts of her husband's body – 'She doth become you like a well-made suit' (i.59); 'she's a chain of gold to adorn your neck' (i.64). The references to Anne as an extension of Frankford reaffirm the prevalent Renaissance view of women as hoardable property, a view which derives from the definition of the husband and wife as one flesh.[34] Although Heywood seems to be exploiting this commonplace trope for comic effect, the action only tentatively qualifies the system of signification on which Anne's characterization relies.

The relation between Anne and property is sustained in the scenes following her fall. The most serious consequence of Anne's adultery is that her 'spotted body' (xiii.124), as Frankford tells her, has not only 'stained' her children's 'names with stripe of bastardy' (l. 125) but has also 'blemish[ed]' Frankford's 'house' (l. 118) and 'infect[ed]' his property (l. 127). That the contamination of Anne's body is one and the same with her 'infect[ion]' of Frankford's property is clarified during the suspenseful episode in which Frankford discovers her transgression. In the moments leading up to the exposure of the lovers, Heywood carefully maps the refuges of civility and privacy that have been corrupted,

Frankford's entrance of his house paralleling Wendoll's penetration of Anne's body. The scene opens outside the house where the distraught Frankford takes 'the key that opes ... [the] outward gate' (xiii.8). The action of unlocking the 'gate' invokes a sexual pun, 'gate' being a common Elizabethan slang term for the vulva,[35] and corresponds with Wendoll's first sexual overture to Anne, in which he describes Anne's mouth as 'The path of pleasure and the gate to bliss, / Which ... I knock at with a kiss' (vi.162–3). After Frankford unlocks the gate, he leads the audience through an intricate setting framed by passageways and doors until he arrives at the innermost bedchamber – the heart of 'sanctity' (xiii.13) and privacy:

> This is the hall door, this my withdrawing chamber.
> But this, that door that's bawd unto my shame,
> Fountain and spring of all my bleeding thoughts,
> Where the most hallowed order and true knot
> Of nuptial sanctity hath been profan'd.
> It leads to my polluted bedchamber,
> Once my terrestrial heaven, now my earth's hell,
> The place where sins in all their ripeness dwell –
> But I forget myself; now to my gate.   (xiii.9–17)

During the late sixteenth century, the new emphasis on subdivided homes represented a significant move towards the concept of individuality and privacy, including sexual privacy. A common motif in the iconography of the period was 'the newly married couple joined in the [bed]chamber in a ceremonious celebration of their new intimacy,'[36] a motif which resonates in Frankford's description of his 'bedchamber' as 'Once my terrestrial heaven' (l. 14). After Frankford unlocks 'the last door' (l. 23) to find the lovers 'lying / Close in each other's arms, and fast asleep' (ll. 42–3) he momentarily exits, re-enters the bedroom, exposes the adulterers, and 'retire[s] awhile into ... [his] study' (l. 130) to contemplate Anne's punishment.

Frankford's seclusion in his study at this critical moment has been interpreted as an instance either of callous detachment or of moderation and reason.[37] Frankford's action, I would suggest, has two values: one religious, the other social. The action derives in part from the pious gesture of withdrawing 'inwardly' that is employed extensively in the literature of the period. In her analysis of 'inward experience' in English Renaissance poetry, Anne Ferry has observed that a prevalent metaphor for 'examining one's internal state' is the entrance of 'a room in a house: a chamber, closet, or cabinet,' spaces which 'had specific architectural reference.'[38] In addition to self-examination, other activities undertaken in private quarters include confession and prayer, activities conforming to the biblical injunction: 'when thou prayest, enter into thy closet, and when thou hast shut thy door, pray to thy Father which is in secret; and thy father which seeth in secret shall reward thee openly' (AV, Matthew 6:6). In this context, Frankford's seclusion is in keeping with the practice of withdrawing to a private space in order to take account of one's spiritual condition. Frankford's retreat into solitude and contemplation at this critical juncture indicates his need to examine his conscience, an act which mitigates his apparent failing as a husband. Although Anne's moral transgression has disrupted the orderly household, domestic conflict was viewed as the husband's serious abrogation of his duty to rule his family. 'What a comfort,' exclaims the author of *The Good Hows-holder*,

must it needs to be to thee, who art a Master of a Family, to see thy houshold (through the blessing of God on thy care and pains) to be walking Heaven-ward? ... For where God is served with perfect purity, there is perfect peace: But where God is not served, there is no peace, but jars and contentions, strife and debate.[39]

Frankford's movements through the house, however, also highlight the semiotic function of private space as an indicator of status and privilege. The movements are profoundly social acts deriving from the cultural meanings assigned to the forms of privatization that proliferated during the sixteenth and early seventeenth centuries. As we follow Frankford through the numerous passageways of the house to his study, Heywood accentuates the door and the private chambers. In order to facilitate the movement in this scene, there must have been, as George Reynolds points out, a 'curtained space' on stage, together with a number of side and front entrances acting as doors.[40] The special importance both of the doors and of the study would not have been lost on Heywood's audience. In important rooms and chambers of late sixteenth-century English houses, the door became a signal decorative feature and indicator of social rank.[41] Orest Ranum has observed that by the sixteenth century 'souvenir-space[s]' enclosed by walls or doors (the 'walled garden, bedroom, *ruelle*, study, or oratory') had become 'quite private, having been possessed by an individual unique in time and space.' Doors and other forms of enclosure were especially significant for the gentry, merchants, and nobles, whose houses and mansions were identifiable by their demarcation of public and private spaces: public rooms were for entertaining visitors and engaging in business affairs; private rooms were 'center[s] of emotional life and intimate relations.'[42]

By 1600, to 'withdraw' came to mean 'to go away, depart' or 'retire' not only from 'a place or position' but also from 'someone's presence, to another room or a private place' (*OED*). The most private space was the chamber or inner room, which could serve as either bedroom or study and which was separated from the rest of the dwelling 'by a door with a lock.'[43] The 'chamber,' writes Montaigne, is 'where I often lie, because I would be alone.'[44] And in *The Diary of Sir Simonds D'Ewes*, the private chamber is a site of welcome isolation to a busy gentleman like D'Ewes: '[i]n the morning I went to the Starr-chamber and ther profited prettilye well, and after dinner, to my great comforte, followed my studye.'[45] In this most personal of quarters, the private chamber, were stored various treasures and objects that reflected one's social status and taste. One entered in order to gaze on these objects in solitude, to contemplate, or to enjoy a conversation with intimate friends. Before Anne Frankford's fall, the study is for Frankford a site of peaceful seclusion, where he can reflect upon the sources of his 'content[ment]': his enviable status in the world, his extensive 'possess[ions],' a civil education, and above all a 'perfect' wife:

> *Enter Master Frankford in a study.*
> How happy am I amongst other men
> That in my mean estate embrace content.
> I am a gentleman, and by my birth
> Companion with a king; a king's no more.
> I am possess'd of many fair revenues,
> Sufficient to maintain a gentleman.
> Touching my mind, I am study'd in all arts,
> The riches of my thoughts, and of my time
> Have been a good proficient. But the chief
> Of all the sweet felicities on earth,
> I have a fair, a chaste, and loving wife,
> Perfection all, all truth, all ornament.
> If man on earth may truly happy be,
> Of these at once possess'd, sure I am he.   (iv.1–14)

The action of withdrawing to one's private chamber is an indicator not only of status and civility but also of masculine privilege. The uniquely masculine access to solitude permitted by the withdrawal to a private space is inscribed in much of the literature of the period. The 1581 edition of *The Civile Conversation of M. Steeven Guazzo,* made widely popular in England by George Pettie's translation, describes the 'pleasant,' masculine activities which are performed exclusively in private areas:

... solitariness of place, is the chamber or privat dwelling which everie one chooseth of purpose to sequester him selfe from the companie and conversation of others. Here we have to consider that men settle themselves in this solitarinesse of place for divers respects, some to the intent to raise their thoughts from worldly vanities to the contempla tion of God ... some to get with studie and speculation the fruit of learn- ing, some to discourse with them selves publike or private affaires.[46]

Montaigne also extols the pleasure that men derive from seclusion within a chamber or private dwelling:

... [there] I may the better seclude my selfe from companie, and keepe incrochers from me: There is my seat, there is my throne. *I endevour to make my rule therein absolute, and to sequester that only corner from the communitie of wife, of children and of acquaintance.*[47]

In his biography of Sir Thomas More, William Roper writes in a similar vein that More, needing

for godly purposes sometimes *to be solitary and sequester himself* from worldly company, *a good distance from his mansion-house* builded he a place called the New Building, wherein there was a chapel, a library, and a gallery. In which, as his use was upon other days to occupy himself in prayer and study together, so on the Friday, there usually continued he from morning till evening, spending his time only in devout prayers and spiritual exercises.[48]

In *The Diary of Sir Simonds D'Ewes,* the partition of chambers into public and private spaces promotes homosocial bonding: 'after supper I went into one of my acquaintance chamber where with some other gentlemen wee had much good discourse.'[49]

A Woman Killed similarly portrays Frankford's friendship with Wen-doll, which prior to the adultery is a source of contentment for both men, as facilitated by the private spaces, commodities, and comforts provided by Frankford's house:

FRANK [to Wendoll]. Choose of my men which shall attend on you,
And he is yours. I will allow you, sir,
Your man, your gelding, and your table, all
At my own charge; be my companion. ...
To dinner. Come, sir, from this present day
Welcome to me for ever ...   (iv.69–72, 83–84)

When Frankford is alone in his study, he muses on the qualities that make Wendoll such 'a good companion':

This Wendoll I have noted, and his carriage
Hath pleas'd me much; by observation
I have noted many good deserts in him –
He's affable and seen in many things,
Discourses well, a good companion,
And though of small means, yet a gentleman
Of a good house, somewhat press'd by want.
I have preferr'd him to a second place
In my opinion and my best regard.   (iv.27–35)

Immediately following the discovery scene, Frankford's retreat to his private, unpolluted study counterpoints the corruption of the two men's friendship and of the household's other private spaces, in particular the bedchamber. After exposing the adulterers, Frankford informs the audience that the two rooms – the withdrawing chamber and the bed-room – are now competing spaces, one inviting private meditation, the other intimate but sinful contact: 'this my withdrawing chamber. / But this, that door that's bawd unto my shame, / ... It leads to my polluted bedchamber' (xiii.9–10, 14). Frankford's withdrawal to his study counter-balances Anne and Wendoll's betrayal not only through the association of the study with prayer, but more importantly through the study's relation to masculine privilege.

It is significant that the audience never views Anne in a space in which she is entirely alone. Frankford's recourse to solitude reaffirms the defini-tion of virtue as vested in male subjectivity and action,[50] seclusion being a privilege afforded by Frankford's gender and rank in a world inhabited by others. Anne's (female) lack of a private self, on the other hand, merely underscores her otherness, even in an intimate situation.

Anne's alterity is further defined by her symbolic function as adulteress. Although Heywood, by scrutinizing the structures of private life that have been disrupted by Anne's transgression, exposes the cracks in the cults of civility and domesticity, he evades a radical critique of those structures by capitulating to the stereotype of the fallen woman.[51] Anne's tragedy is largely a lesson in female pride, in which vanity and lust figure prominently. The 'Homily of the State of Matrimony,' which in 1562 had been designated by the state as required reading in English churches, declares that women are 'lighter ... and more vain in their fantasies and opinions' than men; and in *The Scole House of Women* (c. 1542, 1560) Edward Gosynhyll warns that woman is 'farre more lecherous' and vain than man,[52] a warning which remains commonplace in Renaissance literature. The platitude informs Anne Frankford's only request following the public exposure of her sin. When Anne pleads with Frankford not to 'mark' any part of her body, the spectator perceives that vanity, the quintessential female vice, has been a principal cause of her undoing:

> For womanhood – to which I am a shame,
> Though once an ornament – even for His sake
> That hath redeem'd our souls, mark not my face
> Nor hack me with your sword, but let me go
> Perfect and undeformed to my tomb.   (xiii.96–100)

Anticipating a cruel punishment, Anne would prefer that her physical beauty remain intact, firstly for the sake of 'womanhood' and only secondly for her meeting with the redeemer.

The play's emphasis on woman's vanity is underscored by the contrast between Heywood's presentation of a vain, temptable woman and the portrayal of the adulteress in the medieval versions of The Woman Taken in Adultery. In the N-town adaptation we have seen that the woman accepts her guilt with courage and dignity; rather than pleading with her accusers to spare her beauty, she asks that they 'kylle' her secretly (l. 175) in order that her friends and kin will be spared her 'shame' (l. 174).

The ease with which the initially ideal wife succumbs to seduction in *A Woman Killed* has been variously defended as an instance of Heywood's fidelity to his sources, as the inevitable expression of a wider misogynist tradition, or as the symbolic portrayal of human susceptibility to error.[53] Citing as unavoidable the minimal attention given to causation in the portrayal of Anne's motivation, many commentators further conclude that the reason for Anne's fall is unimportant.[54] What has been ignored is how the play elicits the response that the heroine's actions are not worth scrutinizing. Anne is cowardly, untrustworthy, and lacking in 'intellectual resources' precisely because she is a woman. Her transgression, rather than stemming from a conscious choice, is precipitated not only by vanity and lust but also by her corrupt feminine understanding. Anne herself explains her initial submission to Wendoll as the result of her 'want of wit' (xi.112), and her subsequent 'yield[ing]' as the consequence of 'fear' (xi.113). Heywood's depiction of the fallen woman vindicates his injunction, in An Apology for Actors, that 'Women ... that are chaste, are by vs [i.e., playwrights] extolled, and encouraged in their vertues ... The vnchaste are by vs shewed their errors ... ' Anne's demise also prefigures Heywood's advice, in his own book of manners Gunaikeion (1624), that women 'demeane themselves in all Conjugall love towards their Husbands.'[55]

The homiletic resonance attending Anne Frankford's fall and repentance is sustained in the presentation of female chastity in the subplot. One of the chief purposes of the subplot, as Freda Townsend has suggested, is to effect 'the dramatic contrast between the chaste Susan and the unchaste Anne, between the honorable Sir Charles and the dishonorable Wendoll, between the rewards of virtue and the wages of sin.'[56] The contrast between the chaste and unchaste woman deflects both the spectator's interest in Anne's motivation and the tragic implications of her inability to abide by a patriarchal code of marriage.

Whereas Heywood's depiction of female virtue generally conforms to homiletic discourses, his treatment of the wronged husband is more ambiguous. On one hand, Heywood's portrait of the forgiving husband has a precedent in homiletic discourses: noting that 'woman is a weak creature, not endued with like strength and constancy of mind ... and the more prone to all weak affections and dispositions of mind, more than men be,' the 'Homily of the State of Matrimony' urges the husband 'to be the leader and author of love in cherishing and encreasing concord,' which shall come about 'if he will use measurableness and not tyranny' in 'expound[ing] all things.'[57] Frankford is thus apparently enacting what would be expected of a rational, constant husband.[58] Yet Frankford's 'kindness' is not portrayed without qualification. His initial response to the adultery is to undertake the 'bloody sacrifice' of his wife's seducer (xiii.69), but a maid-servant *stay[s] the hand of her master* (s.d.), forestalling his vengeance.[59] Later in the same scene, Frankford's 'judgement' of Anne (xiii.157) is interrupted by his house guest, Cranwell:

> FRANK. ... I'll not martyr thee
> Nor mark thee for a strumpet, but with usage
> Of more humility torment thy soul
> And kill thee even with kindness.
> CRAN. Master Frankford –
> FRANK. Good Master Cranwell – woman, hear thy
>   judgement ...   (xiii.153–7)

Although the reason for Cranwell's sudden interruption is never explained, Frankford's verbal dismissal of his guest indicates that Cranwell considers the punishment severe. Indeed, while Frankford's choice of punishment complies with the homiletic literature advising husbands to instruct their wives in 'their duty rather by gentle words than by ... extremity and severity,'[60] Heywood's audience would recognize that Anne's punishment – exile – is psychologically more effective than outright physical violence. Heywood's model, as Waldo McNeir has shown, is Cicero's preference for psychological over corporeal punishment on the grounds that 'it is not sufficient [revenge] for the person who has injured you to repent of the wrong done, so that he may never be guilty of the like in future.'[61]

Frankford's choice of punishment ensures that Anne has no future.[62] That Frankford is less forgiving than has sometimes been supposed is also suggested by the fact that he publicly forgives Anne only after she has starved herself to the point of death (xvii.83–95). Once again, a comparison with the N-town Woman Taken in Adultery reveals the 'unkindness' of Frankford's choice of punishment. In the medieval play the action is bracketed by Christ's injunctions to the spectator on the necessity of mercy and forgiveness: 'Whoso aske mercy,' he reminds the audience, 'he xal haue grace' (l. 38); Christ further explains that the truly 'contryte,' like the woman who has committed adultery, are 'bettyr loue[d]' than all other sinners (ll. 289, 291).

The denouement of *A Woman Killed*, however, deflects the spectator's discomfort with the form of Anne's punishment. Anne's starvation, which her punishment precipitates, would have been interpreted by early modern audiences as a form of purification of the soul, a practice synonymous with the suppression of lust. In *The Christian Man's Closet* (1581), Bartholomeus Battus, echoing the widely held view that a young woman should be instructed only in a moral education, advises that she be underfed to prevent lustful impulses: 'Let her not eate openly ... in the feastes and banquetes of her parents, lest shee see such meats as shee might desire ... Let her so eate as that shee may alwayes be un-hungred.'[63] Although Anne's starvation indicates that she has chosen her final punishment, her demise upholds a conservative ideology of gender, as is suggested by her brother Sir Francis Acton's response to her piteous condition:

> SIR FRA. I came to chide you, but my words of hate
> Are turn'd to pity and compassionate grief;
> I came to rate you, but my brawls, you see,
> Melt into tears, and I must weep by thee.   (xvii.63–6)

Whereas Anne's former vanity, selfishness, and wildness were the enemies of feminine self-denial, her self-punishment has successfully suppressed power, self-assertion, and autonomy, all forms of control forbidden to women.

Anne's punishment also adheres to the early modern conflation of morality and civility. Anne's exile and repentance are circumscribed by two important stage properties – the lute and the bed. After Frankford's discovery of the adultery, he dispatches Anne to his 'manor seven mile off,' (xiii.165) ordering her to 'Leave nothing' behind that would attest to her having been 'mistress' of 'the house' (xiii.160–1). In cleansing the house of all vestiges of his wife's presence, Frankford specifies two objects that are to be dispatched with Anne – her '*lute*' (xvi.17) and 'a bed and hangings for a chamber' (xiii.163). During Anne's journey to her place of banishment, her voice merges with the mournful sounds of the lute:

> ANNE. I know the lute. Oft have I sung to thee;
> We both are out of tune, both out of time. ...
> ... My lute shall groan;
> It cannot weep, but shall lament my moan.
> [*She plays.*]
>   (xvi.18–19, 30–1)

Anne's apostrophe to the lute clarifies the 'loss' (xvi.28) attending her fall: the transgressive wife has sacrificed not only the 'joy' of matrimony (xvi.74) but also civility and refinement, values symbolized in Renaissance iconography by the playing of a musical instrument. In the denouement (xvii.39–140) Anne's entrance is prefaced by the stage direction, *Enter* ANNE *in her bed*. Early modern staging practices would have required the bed to be '"thrust out" from one of the rear-stage doors.'[64] At the critical moment when Anne repents her sin and is pardoned by Frankford, the bed functions as the central visual icon:

> ANNE. Raise me a little higher in my bed.
> Blush I not, brother Acton? Blush I not, Sir Charles?
> Can you not read my fault writ in my cheek?
> Is not my crime there? Tell me, gentlemen.   (xvii.54–7)

On one level, the bed, as a vestige of medieval symbolism, is associated with the protagonist's soul. Just as in *The Castle of Perseverance* Mankind's soul is hidden under his bed until death, so Anne Frankford's soul, we infer, will soon be released from the mutable sphere of the body. In *An Apology for Actors*, however, we saw that Heywood redefines the morality play from an early modern vantage point: 'a morall [play] ... is to perswade men to humanity and good life, *to instruct them in ciuility* and good manners, shewing them the fruits of honesty, and the end of villany.'[65] In its early modern context, the bed is a supreme sign of civility. Since the late Middle Ages the bed had been valued as among the most important of household objects, even by the poorest members of society. From the fifteenth through to the seventeenth centuries, the bed assumed an increasingly semiotic function, the number of beds in a household indicating the latter's size as well as the civility and social standing of its owner.[66] The bed, like the lute, clarifies the enormous forfeiture that attends Anne's violation of the civil order.

Ideology, writes Jonathan Dollimore, 'typically legitimates the social order by representing it as a spurious unity, metaphysically ordained, and thereby forestalls knowledge of the contradictions which in fact constitute that order.'[67] Although Heywood, in his equivocal portrait of the avenging husband, only ambivalently upholds the power of ideology to restrain subversive desire, *A Woman Killed with Kindness* constructs the social order in such a way that none of the characters fears its power to root out contradiction and instability.

Arden of Feversham

Whereas *A Woman Killed with Kindness* resists a radical scrutiny of early modern ideologies of the family, civility, and private life, *The Tragedy of Master Arden of Feversham* invites the spectator to confront the possibility that, as collective obligations, civility and domestic patriarchy are neither unchangeable nor metaphysically ordained.

The play is based on a crime committed around 1550 and documented in Holinshed's *Chronicles*, Stow's *Annals*, the Wardmote Book of Faversham, and other local histories and records.[68] Arden, a gentleman, is murdered by his unfaithful wife Alice who employs various men, including her lover, to slay him. The murderers unwittingly leave their footprints in the snow while dragging Arden's corpse to the fields. In the denouement Alice repents before dying at the stake while all but one of her accomplices meet their deaths.

Arden, however, is more than an instruction piece on 'the domestic virtues,' as has been suggested, or on 'the inexorable workings of Providence in detecting the perpetrators of crimes and ... the inevitable punishment of sin and the efficacy of repentance in achieving salvation.'[69] Although the text incorporates a loose homiletic design, the structures of authority – textual, moral, and patriarchal – are treated problematically. Arden tries desperately to make his house the seat of civility and conjugal contentment, understanding marriage chiefly in terms of his role as master of the household and Alice's as helpmate. For Arden, it is only natural for the husband to assert his privilege of possession and dominance, as is evident in his habitual stress of the first-person possessive pronoun when referring to his domicile:

> To warn him [Mosby] on the sudden from *my house*
> Were to confirm the rumour that is grown.   (i.351–2)

> ... Come I once at home,
> I'll rouse her [Susan, Mosby's sister and Alice's maid] from
>   remaining in *my house*.   (iii.31–2)

> ARDEN. *My house* is irksome; there I cannot rest.
> FRANKLIN. Then stay with me in London; go not home.
> ARDEN. Then that base Mosby doth usurp *my room* ...
>   (iv.27–9; emphases added)

Arden's exertion of total control over the household blinds him to Alice's passion and desperation, so that initially he considers his wife merely a victim in her trespass against his conjugal rights and privileges:

> ARDEN. ... that injurious ribald that attempts
> To violate my dear wife's chastity ...
> Shall on the bed which he [Mosby] thinks to defile
> See his dissevered joints and sinews torn ...
> (i.37–8, 40–1)

'The central characters in *Arden*,' observes Alexander Leggatt, 'cannot separate their passions from the social world in which those passions arise. Arden is offended not just because Alice is dishonouring him but because she is doing so with a social climber.'[70] Yet the play's portrayal of marriage, class, and property goes beyond mere sociological interest, elucidating the tension between the characters' public selves and their personal desires. It also achieves a more complex psychology than is afforded by the source material.[71]

The play exploits the prevailing ideology of private life in part by subjecting to close scrutiny its insistence upon uniformity and hierarchy. Arden's obsession with order creates a world of time and space that generates clear, predictable choices. A recurring motif is Arden's pleasure in feeding. Arden conceptualizes time according to its proximity to dinner, his communication with Alice revolving largely around the subject of meals:

> ARDEN. ... prepare our breakfast, gentle Alice,
> For yet ere noon we'll take horse and away.
> (i.91–2)

> ARDEN. Alice, make my breakfast; I must hence.
> (i.299)

> ARDEN. Come, Alice, is our supper ready yet?
> ALICE. It will by then you have played a game at tables.
> (xiv.221–2)

The basic role of the economy of feeding is to encode social values and customs. By the late sixteenth century, an established routine of socially acceptable times and places for dining signified one's place in the status hierarchy. As was noted in the feasting episodes of *A Woman Killed with Kindness*, food is a code expressed in a pattern of social relations. The encoded message, as Mary Douglas suggests, is 'about different degrees of hierarchy, inclusion and exclusion, boundaries and transactions across the boundaries.'[72] In *The Description of England* Harrison describes the 'order of repast' by citing the appropriate times at which meals are to be taken. His examples of civilized dining are typically derived from the top and middle rungs of the social ladder, the 'order of repast' for the 'poorest sort' being 'but a needless matter.'

> With us the nobility, gentry, and students do ordinarily go to dinner
> at eleven before noon and to supper at five, or between five and six at
> afternoon. The merchants dine and sup seldom before twelve at noon
> and six at night, especially in London. The husbandmen dine also at
> high noon ... and sup at seven or eight; but out of the term in our
> universities the scholars dine at ten.[73]

At the same time that *Arden of Feversham* inscribes the codes of civility that would have been familiar to an Elizabethan audience, it brings into focus the displacement of desire that underwrites those codes.

A simple quotidian ritual like feeding comes to indicate a deeper hunger that Arden never recognizes but which is reified in his obsessive discourse about meals as signifiers of order and decorum. Arden proves to Alice 'that I hold thee dearer than my life' (x.31) by promising to be home in time to dine with her (x.33–4); he alleviates anxiety about his troubled dreams through an invitation of Franklin to supper (vi.41–5); and to Franklin's expectation of Alice's 'griev[ing]' over not being included in her husband's public activities (xiii.71) Arden laconically replies, 'let us strain to mend our pace / And take her unawares, playing the cook' (xiii.72–3). The role of cook is one which, Arden believes, Alice will perform well in order 'to mend our cheer' (xiii.74). The syntactical formulas 'if A ... then B' and 'do this ... for that effect' dominate Arden's discourse, stressing ostensibly logical alternatives and creating a world in which cause predictably follows effect. It is also a world in which language is a smokescreen concealing ennui.

Realizing that the codes of civility will not prevent domestic discontent, Arden declares 'My house is irksome; there I cannot rest' (iv.27). The tragic irony culminates in the murder scene where, after pursuing Arden unsuccessfully within the community at large, Arden's assassins stab him when he is seated at a card table following a dinner party within his own home (xiv.232–8). The murder assumes a grotesque dimension when considered in light of the physiological nature of dining, which since the sixteenth century has been 'known to induce a state of rest and relaxation, especially following ingestion in genial company.'[74] Commenting on the propensity among Elizabethan 'nobility, gentlemen, and merchantmen' to 'long sitting' at meals, Harrison observes with some misgiving the pleasure derived by the 'common' practice of 'sit[ting] ... till two or three of the clock at afternoon, so that with many is an hard matter, to rise from the table to go to Evening Prayer and return from thence to come time enough to supper.'[75] Feeding as a ritualized activity induces tranquillity, a state which the semiotician James Brown refers to as the 'serenity syndrome.'[76] The syndrome already begins to assume a grotesque dimension in Alice's earlier attempt to murder her husband by poisoning his broth. The episode exploits the emphasis in domestic drama on both the ritual of feeding and spatial concreteness, a familiar stage property becoming an instrument of rage:

> ALICE. Husband, sit down; your breakfast will be cold.
> ARDEN. Come, Master Mosby, will you sit with us?
> MOSBY. I cannot eat, but I'll sit for company.
> ARDEN. Sirrah Michael, see our horse be ready.
> [*Exit Michael but returns soon after.*]
> ALICE. Husband, why pause ye? Why eat you not?
> ARDEN. I am not well. There's something in this broth
> That is not wholesome. Didst thou make it Alice?
> ALICE. I did, and that's the cause it likes not you.
> [*Then she throws down the broth on the ground.*]
>
> (i.360–7)

The syndrome is once again destabilized moments before Arden's death in the combination of the predictable linguistic formula, the anxiety about feeding, and the *topos* of the after-dinner game of cards:

> ARDEN. Come, Alice, is our supper ready yet?
> ALICE. It will by then you have played a game at tables.   (xiv.221–2)

The home is a castle only from the outside. Alice Arden's wistful reflection upon a former, more pleasurable time attests to how profoundly she feels the absence of conjugal joy:

> ALICE. Home is a wild cat to a wand'ring wit.
> The time hath been – would God it were not past! –
> That honour's title nor a lord's command

Could once have drawn you [Arden] from these arms of mine.
But my deserts or your desires decay ...   (x.13–17)

Lamenting the devolution of married love into a union that is now 'but words' (i.101), Alice determines to have Mosby 'In spite of him [Arden], of Hymen, and of rites' (i.104). Yet to claim that Alice murders her husband simply out of love for Mosby,[77] or that her unruly behaviour is chiefly the result of an irreconcilable tension between her current social position and her aristocratic breeding,[78] is to ignore the play's engagement with the contemporary crisis of domesticity. Although in committing adultery Alice Arden openly defies a sacrosanct code, the audience is invited to sympathize with her need to create a more desirable private space. Unlike Anne Frankford's passive capitulation to her seducer in *A Woman Killed with Kindness*, which in effect upholds the notion of woman's feeble-mindedness and innate tendency to vanity and concupiscence, Alice Arden's rejection of female subordination gives voice to a radical discourse of desire.[79]

Alice's defiance of the stereotypical female role is expressed in language that is charged with longing for deliverance from bondage: 'Might I without control / Enjoy thee [Mosby] still, then Arden should not die' (i.274–5). Douglas Bruster has observed that 'the social thematics of women's language' during this period, 'though sometimes working to portray female speakers in favorable, even privileged positions ... most often emerged in terms of negative images, of prejudicial, scornful commonplaces and stereotyped versions of female speech and speakers.'[80] In his description of the ideal marriage, the Venetian humanist Francesco Barbaro defines silence as the quintessential female virtue:

women should believe they have achieved glory of eloquence if they
will honor themselves with the outstanding ornament of silence.
Neither the applause of a declamatory play nor the glory and ado-
ration of an assembly is required of them, but all that is desired of
them is eloquent, well-considered, and dignified silence.[81]

Barbaro's injunction to women to be silent echoes the early modern anxiety about female wit. A case in point is Thomas Gainsford's warning to men that 'if witty,' a woman will be 'impudent to shame thee or make thee weary.'[82] A comparison with *A Woman Killed with Kindness* clarifies the *Arden* playwright's more complex treatment of female speech and desire. During her second seduction by Wendoll, Anne Frankford's mental disorientation is indicated by her confused, cliché-ridden language:

> ANNE. You have tempted me to mischief, Master Wendoll;
> I have done I know not what. Well, you plead custom;
> That which for want of wit I granted erst
> I now must yield through fear ...
> Once o'er shoes, we are straight o'er head in sin.
>
> (*A Woman Killed with Kindness*, xi.110–14)

Anne's bewilderment – 'I have done I know not what' – contrasts sharply with Alice Arden's wilful encroachment upon the male prerogatives of desire and resoluteness:

> ALICE. Nay, Mosby, let me still enjoy thy love;
> And, happen what will, I am resolute.   (i.218–19)

Alice's forbidden speech reverses the commonplace that man only is by nature audacious and therefore better suited to command the household, whereas woman, who is naturally weak-minded and timorous, is better equipped for the role of helpmate.[83] In this context, Alice's behaviour negates the neo-Aristotelian construct of the *mulier economica*, which defines woman strictly according to the order of marriage. All women, writes T.E. in *The Lawes Resolutions of Womens Rights*, 'are understood either married or to bee married and their desires as subject to their husband,' the 'common Law here shak[ing] hand with Divinitie'; that is why women have no political 'voyse,' and why they do not 'make,' 'consent to' or 'abrogate' any laws.[84] Throughout the play Alice struggles with a rigid system of male dominance which denies agency and freedom to women. The Protestant wife, remarks Lisa Jardine, was granted 'freedom' only on the condition that she perform 'a number of clearly allotted tasks,' at the same time that 'the quality of the [marital] relationship lay only minimally within her control.' Protestant discourses confirm 'the absence of any actual means of altering' the wife's situation, 'however piously her entitlement to such alteration was affirmed.'[85]

As a rebellious wife, Alice Arden shares the recalcitrance of early modern women who questioned the hierarchy of gender. D.E. Underdown has argued that widespread attempts by authorities to enforce patriarchal dominance in late sixteenth- and early seventeenth-century

England were largely a response to women's insubordination: 'Women scolding and brawling with their neighbours, single women refusing to enter service, wives dominating or even beating their husbands: all seem to surface more frequently than in the periods immediately before and afterwards ... [t]his is also the period during which witchcraft accusations reach their peak.'[86] Alice Arden's transgressions also coincide with recently discovered writings of recusant and other English women of the Stuart period, many of whom were disillusioned with orthodox prescriptions of female behaviour. The diaries, memoirs, and other forms of personal memoranda of women from the gentry and nobility reveal that the writers, while generally accepting the conduct literature's division of female experience and duties into the three stages of virginity, marriage, and widowhood, did not always welcome the second stage with enthusiasm. Sara Mendelson observes that 'marriage could represent a major trauma for women, and various sources reveal that they regarded it as the crucial turning-point in life'; among the unmarried women's diaries a consensus emerges that maidenhood is 'the most carefree and enjoyable' of the three female states, with the prospect of marriage often eliciting 'a tense and anxious period,' and an 'unwillingness to abandon ... liberty.'[87] As for the outcome of actual marriages, the diaries and memoirs record a variety of responses to marital relations and domestic duties, ranging from conjugal bliss to bitterness, strife, and desertion.

The alternative voices to dominant ideologies of marriage include various female literary conventions. In her analysis of women's anti-marriage poems of the seventeenth century, Margaret Ezell has illustrated that marriage is depicted as 'a "snare" or "trap" where the true, unpleasant character of the spouse is revealed. Love acts as "fetters" which "enslave" those foolish enough to get caught. The particular danger from love, however, which is cited only in women's poems, is that once married, women fall under the legal authority of their spouses.'[88] In her study of women writers of Jacobean England, Barbara Kiefer Lewalski has found that while 'women did not ... float free of the ideology and institutions that structured Jacobean society,' a 'strong resistance' is nevertheless 'mounted in all these women's texts to the patriarchal construct of women as chaste, silent, and obedient, and their overt rewriting of women's status and roles.'[89]

Like her real-life and fictional counterparts, Alice Arden breaks silence and in doing so challenges not only the external trappings of order, but also the very basis of society which denies a married woman's right to agency and self-expression. In so doing, Alice Arden prefigures characters such as Elizabeth Cary's Mariam and Webster's Duchess of Malfi and Vittoria Corombona, who, as Lisa Jardine contends, represent 'a consistent and believable female heroic persona.'[90]

In another trajectory of the plot, Arden's business practices reveal a character with whom the audience cannot make a comfortable, let alone heroic, identification. During the early scenes Arden flouts the principle of charity through covetousness and gain of his neighbours' lands. Although Arden's actions have legal sanction, his expropriation of land having been made possible through the state's privatization of church property during the seizure of church revenues, his status seeking blinds him to the suffering of those who have become dispossessed through the free land market:

> GREENE. Desire of wealth is endless in his mind,
> And he is greedy-gaping still for gain;
> Nor cares he though young gentlemen do beg,
> So he may scrape and hoard up in his pouch.   (i.474–7)

Arden's civilized position in the status hierarchy is made possible by his exploitative business dealings.[91] In a stroke of dramatic irony, Arden's murderers conceal themselves in his 'countinghouse' (xiv.101), a 'private chamber, closet, or cabinet appropriated to business and correspondence' (OED), before stabbing him. Immediately preceding the murder, another quintessential sign of civility and social rank – the door – is brought into relief when the killers, in order to reach their target, must pass through a series of doors: 'When this door opens next, look for his death' (xiv.141). As we saw in A Woman Killed with Kindness, it was common practice in the homes of the gentry for the head of the household to withdraw by himself to a separate space where he could meditate in private; it was also the place where he engaged in the reckoning of household accounts, an activity often employed in literary and other discourses as a metaphor for taking stock of one's spiritual condition.[92] Arden, however, never has time to repent his cupidity, and he dies oblivious to the retribution for his sins which Providence has presumably effected.

The plot is further complicated by the involvement of Bradshaw, Arden's innocent victim in the land deal, who, through a series of bizarre, coincidental events, is implicated in Arden's murder and suffers the same fate as the assassins. And although two of the murderers,

Black Will and Shakebag, function in part as providential agents who
are requited with death, the other assassin, Clarke, escapes and is never
heard from again ('how he died we know not' [Epilogue, l. 8]). His
disappearance is a deliberate departure from Holinshed's account, in
which none of the assassins escapes.[93] Clarke is allowed to go free, we
infer, because his profession – painter – is ranked among 'the poets'
favourites' (i.255) and because he has participated in Arden's demise
strictly out of love for Alice's servant Susan, 'Love' being 'the painter's
Muse' (i.256). The denouement also prevaricates about Alice's repentance and eventual redemption; although Alice shows some contrition
for her crime, her remorse is not entirely credible since it closely follows
her arrest.[94] The providentialist narrative is forestalled, signalling
authorial uneasiness with homiletic closure.

A Warning for Fair Women

Like *Arden of Feversham*, *A Warning for Fair Women* (a murder play in
which an unfaithful wife's accomplices murder her merchant-husband
so that she can marry a gentleman) only tentatively upholds the homiletic pattern of action. The play, however, has received little critical
attention, the standard interpretation being that it accomplishes its
'goals of warning and moral conversion through a system of rewards
and punishments.'[95] Recently, a more careful reading has been proposed by Frances Dolan, who locates the play within the tradition of
the hybrid moralities, which, 'in their oscillation between the old and
the new,' are 'vehicles for competing, irreconciled interpretations of the
events depicted.' A 'late example' of a hybrid play, *A Warning for Fair
Women*, argues Dolan, 'vividly dramatizes' Anne Sanders's 'thwarted
desires for status and independence,' at the same time that it 'censures
ambition and social change by immediately associating social climbing
with adultery and murder.'[96] Lena Cowen Orlin demonstrates that the
play 'participate[s]' in 'the late-Elizabethan dialogue of rule and order';
elsewhere Orlin argues that Anne Sanders's transgression 'arises from
the ambiguities and contradictions of the woman's coterminous roles
in the household hierarchy. And the fundamental premise of her
seduction is the fabrication of a crisis of patriarchal authority,'
although in its portrayal of 'the wife who is ... ethically manipulable
and defraudable' because she is 'oeconomically tractable,' the play
'reauthorizes patriarchal control.'[97] The play's deeper structures, I
would suggest, force the spectator to recognize the contradictions

inherent in the cults of civility and domestic patriarchy, at times challenging in dramatically subtle ways the premises on which those structures rely.

The play opens by invoking the signifiers of early modern civility:

Enter Anne Sanders with her little sonne, and sit at her doore.
BOY. Praie ye mother when shal we goe to supper?
A. SAN. Why, when your father comes from the Exchange,
Ye are not hungrie since ye came from schoole.
BOY. Not hungrie (mother,) but I would faine eate.
A. SAN. Forbeare a while until your father come,
I sit here to expect his quicke returne.
BOY. Mother, shal not I have new bow and shafts,
Against our schoole go a feasting?
A. SAN. Yes if ye learn,
And against Easter new apparel too.
BOY. Youle lend me all your scarfes, and al your rings,
And buy me a white feather for my velvet cappe,
Wil ye mother? yea say, praie ye say so.
A. SAN. Goe pratling boy, go bid your sister see
My Closet lockt when she takes out the fruite.   (ii.323–37)

The vignette is bracketed by two important signs of status and prosperity: the 'doore' (s.d.) by which Anne and her son are sitting, and Anne's private 'Closet' (l. 337). Anne's closet, as the dialogue indicates, would have been 'a small side-room or recess for storing utensils, provisions,' and delicacies (*OED*). Although as a private repository Anne's closet would not have been considered as valuable a space as was the study or chamber normally reserved for the private activities of men, the closet, together with the other itemized objects and goods (the door, Anne's scarves and rings, the boy's 'velvet cappe,' and the fruit), point to Anne's considerable wealth. The material pleasures are made possible, we infer, by George Sanders's business at 'the Exchange' (l. 324). But while the dialogue and stage properties draw on the convention of the salubrious household setting, the subsequent action destabilizes the ideology of the familiar. Anne Sanders's wealth is unable to forestall the dissolution of her marriage. Her tragedy is precipitated not by her adultery with George Browne, but by a domestic squabble over her husband's deferral of payment of her debt to the Draper and Milliner, for the reason that his 'great affaires / Must not be hindred by such trifling wares' (iv.578–9). Anne does not overtly repudiate the wife's natural subordination to her husband, but she does express her anguish at her subjugation as a woman:

> I am a woman, and in that respect,
> Am well content my husband shal controule me,
> But that my man should over-awe me too,
> And in the sight of strangers ...
> I tell you true, do's grieve me to the heart. (iv.655–9)

Like Alice Arden, Anne comes to realize that a public self is unavailable to a married woman beyond her identity as someone's wife. Anne's subordinate status not only requires her husband to 'controule' her (l. 656) but also permits her male servant to 'over-awe' her (l. 657). The submissiveness required of women conflicts with Anne's strong sense of autonomy and personal integrity:

> So that my breach of credite, in the while
> Is not regarded: I have brought these men,
> To have their mony for such necessaries,
> As I have bought, and they have honestly
> Delivered to my hands, and now forsooth,
> I must be thought so bare and beggarly,
> As they must be put of until to morrow. (iv.629–35)

Anne's refusal to 'goe on credite' (l. 645) startles the two merchants, who are not used to such behaviour in a woman (ll. 636–53). More significantly, although Anne's rebelliousness is not as fully drawn as Alice Arden's, her decision to flout her husband's disapproval is a tacit negation of domestic hierarchy.

Anne Sanders's crimes are rendered in bold allegorical strokes in the play's three dumb shows. The allegorical structures of the dumb shows have been generally deemed incongruous with the rest of the plot, which is usually considered more realistic.[98] On closer inspection, however, one senses that the dramatist is conscious of the limitations of the allegorical structures of the dumb show, structures which by 1600 would be largely outmoded,[99] employing them mainly to illustrate the simplism of stock moral formulas. The insufficiency of moral exegesis in explaining tragic action is crystallized in the third dumb show, in which Tragedy anticipates the moral consequences of the crimes which have been committed:

Thus lawles actions and prodigious crimes
Drinke not the bloud alone of them they hate,
But even their ministers, when they have done
Al that they can, must help to fil the Sceane,
And yeeld their guilty neckes unto the blocke.   (ll. 1811–15)

The moral is undermined by two striking complications: (1) Tragedy's
self-consciousness as a figure in a drama who is aware of the need for
other characters who 'must help to fil the Sceane,' that is, who is concerned with theatrical rather than moral imperatives; (2) the dense,
laborious quality of the syntax, which prevents the smooth articulation
of a crisp moral lesson.[100]

The unique features of the first dumb show, that of the 'bloody banquet,' resist facile allegorizing in an especially complex way. The conspicuous function of the 'bloody banquet' is to alert the audience to
Anne's seduction by Browne and to foreshadow Browne's murder of
George Sanders. A more unsettling effect is the dramatization of the
household not as the seat of civility, as it appears to be in the play's
opening scenes, but of distortion and incongruity. Citing A Warning for
Fair Women as an example, Muriel Bradbrook has noted 'a dumb show
of particular horror known as "the bloody banquet,"' which 'was rather
like the Thyestean feast: the table was set with black candles, drink set
out in skulls and the Furies served it up. ... The realism of the mutila-
tions was helped by bladders of red ink and the use of animal's
blood.'[101] The 'bloody banquet' in A Warning for Fair Women complicates
the connection, commonly found in medieval and Renaissance alle-
gories, between the appetites for food and lust; it does so by linking
quotidian pleasures with the grotesque and the uncanny.

The dumb show depicts a 'deadly banquet' (iv.780) and 'bloudy feast'
(l. 788) given in a 'fatal house' (l. 785) in which familiar domestic props
are transformed into grotesque iconographic signs: a 'table' spread with
blood (l. 788); 'Ebon tapers' (l. 781); 'lustfull wine,' (l. 793); 'pale mazors
[wooden drinking bowls]' (l. 794); and a 'fatall doore' through which
the Furies enter (l. 796). 'In the grotesque,' writes Bakhtin, 'all that was
for us familiar and friendly suddenly becomes hostile. It is our own
world that undergoes this change.'[102] A similar destabilization of the
familiar underlies the uncanny. Sigmund Freud defines 'the uncanny'
(in German, das unheimlich) as 'that class of the frightening which leads
back to what is known of old and long familiar.'[103] Linking unheimlich
to its opposite, heimlich, Freud locates the uncanny within a structure,

namely the home, which at once comforts and conceals. '*Heimlich*,' that which is 'familiar, tame, intimate,' and which 'belong[s] to the house or the family,' refers to 'the enjoyment of quiet content ... arousing a sense of agreeable restfulness and security as in one within the four walls of his house.'[104] '*Unheimlich*,' on the other hand, is terrifying 'precisely because it is *not* known and familiar.' But not all that is unfamiliar is terrifying. In its more specific association with a 'feeling' of 'horror,' or of 'gruesome[ness],' *unheimlich* is that which makes one 'uncomfortable, uneasy,' so that 'everything is *unheimlich* that ought to have remained secret and hidden but has come to light.'[105] Especially significant here is the ambiguity inherent in the term *heimlich*: 'among its different shades of meaning,' notes Freud, 'the word "*heimlich*" exhibits one which is identical with its opposite, "*unheimlich*". What is *heimlich* thus comes to be *unheimlich*.' The word *heimlich*, then, 'belongs to two sets of ideas, which, without being contradictory, are yet very different: on the one hand it means what is familiar and agreeable, and on the other, what is concealed and kept out of sight.'[106] In his translation of Freud's essay, James Strachey points out that 'a similar ambiguity attaches to the English "canny", which may mean not only "cosy" but also "endowed with occult or magical powers".'[107] The eerie 'banquet' in *A Warning for Fair Women* reveals that the structures of feeling which have come to light were hitherto not absent in the Sanders's home; they were merely repressed.

In the portrayal of Anne's repentance and execution, the conventional structures that conceal disorder and ennui are themselves depicted as contributing to the devolution of civility and domestic order. The playwright deliberately departs from the predictable solutions found in the chief source for the denouement, Arthur Golding's *A Briefe Discourse* (1573).[108] Golding's Calvinist pamphlet emphasizes the adulterous wife's contrition, her prayers before her execution, and Browne's scaffold speech, all of which are attended by the Doctor of Divinity who 'instruct[s]' the sinners 'aright.'[109] The wife prefaces her lengthy confession with the recognition of and lament for her former domestic bliss, which has included material prosperity – 'I had a good husband, by whom I had manie children, *with whom I lived in wealth, & might have done stil*, had not the devill kindled in my hearte ... unlawfull lust & ... a murtherous intent' – and she dies uttering a 'godly Prayer out of the Service boke which is used to be said at the hour of death.'[110]

Anne Sanders's words echo the sixteenth-century commonplace that spiritual riches constitute true wealth. But in breaking with Golding's emphasis on the wife's forfeited 'wealth,' the play also points to the spiritual bankruptcy of the ethos of civility. Anne's repentance speech is compressed to approximately thirty lines (2664–93) in which she calls on heaven's mercy and society's pardon, but never mentions her former material comforts. Her only pious act is to bestow on her children a gift in the form of 'a booke / Of holy meditations' known as 'Bradfords workes' (xxi.2702–3), namely the Protestant martyr John Bradford's *Godlie Meditations upon the Lordes Prayer, the Beleefe, and the Ten Commandements* (1562). This gift, Anne tells the children, shall make them 'richer than with gold, / *Safer than in faire buildings*: happyer / Than al the pleasures of this world can make you' (xxi.2705–7; emphasis added). Anne's disparagement of 'gold' and of 'faire buildings,' edifices which presumably would include the proper house which she managed at the beginning of the play, recalls Bradford's definition of the spiritual role of the *domus*: 'Houses are ordained for us, that we might get into them from the injury of weather, from the cruelty of beasts, from disquietness of people, and from the toils of the world'; they are not to be enjoyed for secular pleasures, but rather for the 'rest and peace' and 'quiet mind' which they should provide.[111] Bradford is also invoking the prevalent medieval *topos* of the house as, in the words of St Augustine, a gauge of one's spiritual condition: 'Then in that great quarrel of my spirituall house, which I had stifly made against my selfe, in the chamber and closet of my hart.'[112] Bradford's advice is even more critical of material prosperity than the sermon preached approximately one hundred years later at Paul's Cross by John Gore, who warns that 'It is a blessing to have the wealth of the world and to prosper outwardly; but it is a greater blessing to have the grace of the Spirit and to prosper inwardly.'[113]

The contradictions that militate against the ideology of civility and private life in *A Warning for Fair Women* are only partially deflected by Anne Sanders's acquiescence to an earlier Christianity in which the world and the soul are polarized. The facile solution to 'unlawfull' conduct prescribed in Golding's homiletic tract is qualified in the play by Anne's rejection of a world in which agency is entirely determined by gender, class, and status.

A Yorkshire Tragedy

A late murder play, *A Yorkshire Tragedy* is based on the arrest and execution of Walter Calverley (or Caverley), a Yorkshire gentleman, for crimes which he committed against his family and other members of his household on 20 April 1605. The play was entered in the Stationers' Register on 2 May 1608. The general consensus has been that the play is based on an anonymous pamphlet entered three years earlier, on 12 June 1605, entitled *Two most vnnaturall and bloodie Murthers: The one by Maister Cauerley, A Yorkshire Gentleman, practised vpon his wife, and committed vppon his two Children, the three and twentie of Aprill 1605. The other, by Mistris Browne, and her seruant Peter, vpon her husband, who were executed in Lent last past at Bury in Suffolke. 1605.* Recently, however, it has been proposed that 'the play was in fact written *before* the pamphlet,' and that 'the pamphlet is based on the play ... '[114] Both texts follow a similar plot line: Walter Calverley, a gentleman whose parents bequeath him a fortune of approximately eight hundred pounds per year, becomes the ward of a venerable guardian. Calverley, a minor, falls in love with and privately betroths himself to a gentlewoman; after some time, he departs for London where he agrees to a marriage arranged by his guardian. The honourableness of the new wife notwithstanding, the arranged union is for Calverley the source of profound distress. The disappointment with his marriage, and his burdensome role as a married gentleman and dependent ward, lead to profligacy, waste, the abuse of his wife, and the murder of his children. In the pamphlet Calverley spends the remainder of his life in prison, where he daily repents his crimes. The play, on the other hand, suggests that he is subject to 'a deadl[y] execution' (x.75).[115] In addition to the anonymous play and the pamphlet, George Wilkins's *The Miseries of Enforced Marriage* (c. 1607) is also based on the Calverley incident. Wilkins, however, completely disregards the subject of child murder. As we have already seen, the play focuses instead on the hero William Scarborow's prodigality and his first wife's suicide as the pernicious effects of forced marriage.[116]

Both the pamphlet of *Two Most Vnnatural and Bloodie Murthers* and *A Yorkshire Tragedy* appropriate the prevalent sixteenth-century trope of the murderous husband/father. Frances Dolan has observed that towards mid-century, popular literature such as ballads and pamphlets 'shift their focus from insubordinate dependents to the murderous husband, depicting his abuse of his authority as petty tyranny.' These texts 'demoniz[e] the murderous husband as a lunatic exception ... deny[ing] his relationship to other husbands, refusing to reflect on the potential for abuse built into marriage or the imbalance of power within the household.'[117] The stated purpose of the pamphlet is to present for 'Christian heart[s]' a

'murther so detestable, that ... it desires record for example sake ... '[118]
Although it occasionally invests Calverley's crimes with a complex
causation – having brought his family to poverty, Calverley sets out to
murder his infant child because, 'prickt by his preposterous fate, [he] had
a desire to roote out all his owne generation: and onely intending to
murther it, was carelesse what became of himselfe ... ' (p. 108) – the
pamphlet quickly capitulates to the homiletic significance of the crimes:

Maister *Caverley*, though God permitted the Sunne to blush at his un-
naturall acts, yet he suffered him not to escape without his revenge:
for when he was at the townes ende, within a bowshoote where his
childe sucked, that hee came to murther ... he was soone overtaken ...
and indeede ceazde on by those, did both lament his fall, and pitty
his folly.   (pp. 108–9)

A Yorkshire Tragedy explores in a more systematic way both the psychology of the murderous husband and the social dimensions of his crimes.
Like *Arden of Feversham* and *A Warning for Fair Women* the play shows
how the ideology of private life is unable to withstand contradictions
and challenges, so that it inevitably effaces them.

The plot of *A Yorkshire Tragedy* traces how the 'ancient honour ... and
name' of a house (ii.9) is desecrated by the Husband's aloofness and his
'voluptuous' and 'ill beseeming' habits (ii.7–8). The principal characters
are named according to their domestic or social roles (Husband, Wife,
Maid, Gentleman, and so on) and the action takes place within the various private rooms of Calverley Hall. Among the scenes set outside the
house, two take place on the grounds, the other 'right against ... [the]
house' (x.1) where the Husband is arraigned for killing his children and
wounding his wife and servant. The words 'home' or 'house,' the latter
referring both to one's household and lineage, appear more than fifteen
times during the course of the play. The dramatist, however, avoids the
usual practice in domestic tragedy of delineating, in the opening scenes,
the comforts and pleasures of the civilized house; and although much of
the action is set within private spaces, there are no wholesome scenes of
family life. Instead, the plot moves quickly to the presentation of the
Husband's crimes, and to his arrest and punishment.

Early modern England, we have seen, was a society in which one's
identity and survival were defined according to one's membership in
a family. A person alienated from his or her family and place in the
social hierarchy was, Michael Macdonald observes, 'socially extinct';

conduct 'that threatened to destroy the relationships and objects that defined a person's social identity was gravely irrational,' and was among the 'signs of alienation from the fundamental values of ... society.'[119] Affirming the ideology of collective obligations and rights, the choric figures in A Yorkshire Tragedy define the civilized house as the foundation from which an individual gains an honourable identity, and to which he or she owes absolute allegiance:

> GENTLEMAN [to Husband]. Y'are of a virtuous house; show virtuous
>   deeds.
> 'Tis not your honour, 'tis your folly bleeds.
> Much good has been expected in your life ...   (ii.170–2)

> KNIGHT [a justice of the peace]. ... Ruinous man,
> The desolation of his house, the blot
> Upon his predecessors' honoured name.   (ix.32–4)

Blaming the Husband's 'scandal[ous]' crimes (ii.110) on madness, the members of the community are deeply disturbed by his consequent loss of reputation and property. Nothing, they caution, must ever be done to forfeit others' esteem.

The link between social alienation and madness is introduced in the First Gentleman's warning:

> ... Those whom men call mad
> Endanger others; but he's more than mad
> That wounds himself, whose own words do proclaim
> Scandals unjust to soil his better name.
> It is not fit; I pray forsake it.   (ii.107–11)

The Husband himself, during one of his raving speeches, recognizes madness and social suicide as inescapable consequences of the abandonment of honour and civility:

> ... Down goes the house of us; down, down it sinks. Now is the name
> a beggar, begs in me. That name, which hundreds of years has made
> this shire famous, in me and my posterity runs out ... My riot is now
> my brother's jailor, my wife's sighing, my three boys' penury, and my
> own confusion!   (iv.73–9)
> Tears his hair.

Although the Husband's addiction to gambling and whoring brings him 'inexorably to the crimes which form the catastrophe of the drama,'[120] his refractory behaviour throws into relief the insufficiency of civility and domesticity in forestalling either his madness or malaise.[121] Before the Husband's arraignment his despondency, like Alice Arden's and Anne Sanders's, is directly linked to the *domus*, the institution against which these characters hurl themselves, denouncing the confinement it represents. The Husband's transgressions are linked to a stultifying domesticity, his colourful metaphors not only underscoring his wildness but also counterpointing the flat injunctions of the choric characters. Ridiculing the latter's linguistic propriety and decorum – 'God den, I thank you, sir; how do you? adieu, I'm glad to see you. Farewell instructions, admonitions!' (ii.114–15) – the Husband decries hospitality and neighbourliness. Refusing to be 'Curbed in' (ii.79), he admits to having married strictly 'for fashion' (ii.74), that is, 'out of regard for convention,'[122] and to 'hat[ing] the very hour I chose a wife, a trouble, trouble. Three children like three evils hang upon me, fie, fie, fie ... ' (ii.101–3).

The 'world of the seventeenth century,' writes Michel Foucault, 'is strangely hospitable ... to madness. Madness is here ... an ironic sign that misplaces the guideposts between the real and the chimerical ... an absurd agitation in society ... '[123] The Husband's riotousness is counterpointed by the Wife's 'Kind[ness],' her 'obedien[ce]' (ii.174), and altogether exemplary behaviour within the community of Yorkshire. On the surface, the Wife's conduct is two-dimensional: the Wife, suggests Henry Tyrrell, 'is all tears, morality, and crouching submission. She is not an interesting, but a painful character.'[124] And although A.C. Cawley and Barry Gaines show that in contrast to her 'wordy, pious and submissive' counterpart in the pamphlet, the Wife is 'endowed with much more sense and spirit,' they nevertheless argue for a character defined strictly according to homiletics: 'The language of the emotions comes naturally to her; in contrast to her husband, she constantly uses words like *heart, soul, heaven* because they express the Christian and human values that matter most to her.'[125] The Wife's sterling reputation in the community accords with the early modern idea that civilized conduct in the home is supposed to make individuals better disposed to act honourably outside of its confines. Yet the Wife's virtue is inextricable from her concern with matters of property and pecuniary liability. The complication is reinforced by a development which is not found in the pamphlet, namely the Wife's humble visit to her rich uncle in London, a visit which she undertakes to secure 'some office / And place at court' for her husband (iii.19–20). The visit has a dual purpose: (1) to preserve the reputation of the Wife's immediate family – 'Why should our faults at home be spread abroad? / 'Tis grief enough within doors' (iii.5–6); and (2) to sustain her landed status.

> WIFE. ... 'Twill be a means, I hope,
> To make new league between us and redeem
> His [the Husband's] virtues with his lands. (iii.21–3)

> By this good means I shall preserve my lands ...
> Now there is no need of sale ... (iii.29, 31)

The Wife's self-interest in preserving both the family's honour and property explains her puzzling behaviour in the final scene, the purpose of which has eluded commentators. Given her spirited sententiousness until now, the Wife's meagre response to the Husband's murder of their children has been viewed as surprisingly out of character.[126] Her only reference to the murder occurs when the children are *'laid out'* (s.d.) before their parents:

> WIFE. O, our two bleeding boys,
> Laid forth upon the threshold! (x.33–4)

While the emphasis on 'the threshold' brings back into relief the domestic space which has been defiled by the Husband's crime, the Wife's limp outburst abates the crime's enormity. Her attention is entirely focused on her hope for her husband's repentance and his forgiveness by the court. In a rhetorically effective strategy, the Wife publicly hesitates in expressing complete assurance in the court's pardon: 'O my repentant husband! / ... Thou shouldst not, be assured, for these faults die / *If the law could forgive as soon as I*' (x.28, 31–2; emphasis added). The Husband's contrition restores his 'father's and forefathers' worthy honours' (ii.137). Likewise, the Wife's forgiveness of the Husband, a virtue noted twice by the presiding justice (x.62–5, 70–1), preserves her reputation. More to the point, in a society in which a woman's property became her husband's upon marriage, and could be confiscated in punishment for his crimes, the Wife's public expression of unqualified forgiveness of her husband's crimes preserves not only her reputation but also her lands.

The Menial Household and the Politics of Plenty

Two Lamentable Tragedies

In Robert Yarrington's *Two Lamentable Tragedies* the subject is once again domestic murder. The text consists of two alternating plots: the first, 'of the murther of Maister Beech,'[127] is set in London, and was likely written as early as 1594 'to take advantage of the notoriety of the murder of Thomas Beech,' which took place on 23 August 1594;[128] the second, of the murder of a young child by his uncle, is set in Padua. The two plots are loosely connected through the Induction and Choruses, a connection which enhances the homiletic pattern: in both plots Homicide, Avarice, and Truth oversee the crimes, and both end with the conviction, repentance, and execution of the murderers Merry and Fallerio. The two plots are otherwise dramatically distinct. As in *A Warning for Fair Women* the characters in the English plot inhabit identifiable geographical spaces while allegorical figures are relegated to the periphery of the action. And as in all other domestic plays, the site of conflict is the English household, with an important difference: the subject of scrutiny is now the menial rather than the gentrified household. 'The murther of Maister Beech' interrogates the ideology of order and civility by considering the menial household's role in the money economy.[129] At the same time that the English plot stresses moral and theological edification, it forces the spectator to take note of a disturbing paradox: the root of Thomas Merry's crime is the sin of covetousness, but the problem of sin is complicated by the widespread social and economic instability that typifies Merry's world.

The topical events, the village atmosphere, and the society of neighbours locate the action in late sixteenth-century England. As in a number of other domestic-murder plays, however, 'The murther of Maister Beech' goes beyond journalistic reportage. Although based on actual contemporary events, the action is not reducible to a mere interplay of conventional discourses and praxes; rather, it intervenes in the narrative of the familiar by transforming it. Puzzled as to why 'none of the persons murdered shows any moral guilt,' Henry Adams perceptively suggested that 'the fate of the innocents may possibly be laid to blind chance operating even in a world controlled by Providence.'[130] Yet blind chance is only one factor that displaces the homiletic design. Attending blind chance are severe fluctuations in a money economy that give rise to poverty, disorientation, and discontent, problems acutely felt by the villagers who populate the play.

Unlike most domestic tragedies, in which the protagonists are well-to-do landholders, 'the murther of Maister Beech' deals with townspeople who are for the most part poor. The characters consist of small merchants or retailers, smallholders (who owned fields), cottagers (who for the most part did not own even smallholdings), day labourers, and servants. Although small retailers, cottagers, and smallholders in late sixteenth-century England sometimes held offices such as that of churchwarden, juror, pig and ale warden, and other local positions, the other characters in the play belong to the majority of the population, the group that William Harrison lumped together as 'the fourth and last sort of people,' and that Thomas Smith described as 'hav[ing] no voice nor authoritie in our common wealth ... no account [being] made of them but onelie to be ruled ... '[131]

The plot brings into relief the tension between the ideal orderly society drawn in homiletic and other discourses, and village life as experienced by the majority of the population who felt the brunt of the economic crisis that, since the 1590s, had disrupted English villages. During the decade in which the events of the play take place, England had experienced a number of poor harvests which caused adversity to the point of starvation in many communities, precipitating an economic crisis that drove many small landholders into a lifetime of debt. The crisis was especially hard on the poor, many of whom were forced to rely on parish relief.[132] During the early sixteenth century possibly as much as 50 per cent of the population had been unable to live without assistance, a situation that worsened during the 1590s. The problem was even more severe in the towns, where poverty had emerged as a fundamental problem in the 1520s and 1530s; despite the rise in economic prosperity during the later part of the century, the number of poor people in towns grew, 'many of them with little hope of finding permanent employment or adequate housing for themselves and their families.'[133] The hardships led to an increase in crime and in the numbers of vagrants and vagabonds, as well as to widespread discontent, which in turn led to riots.[134]

At the outset of the play Yarrington stresses that Thomas Merry, an alehouse-keeper, has managed in spite of indigence to fulfil the role of ideal householder: although his house is simple, he is a model of civility. His 'conversation, / Is full of honest ... curtesie,' and he is 'belou'd' by his family and neighbours; he has a 'louing sister, and a carefull man,' both of whom strive to please him (sig. A3v); his 'little house' is 'well frequented,' his neighbours preferring it because, in addition to serving the best beer 'in all this towne,' Merry 'keepes good rule and orders in his house' (sig. A3v). The emphasis on Merry's orderly, civilized household and business establishment contradicts the popular assumption about alehouses, which were deemed to appeal to the desperate and the dispossessed. Drinking establishments in pre-industrial England consisted of three types: 'in declining order of size and status, the inn, the tavern and the alehouse.' Inns were normally 'large, fashionable' premises that offered expensive food and lodging to the well-to-do; taverns provided wine and limited accommodation to prosperous customers. Alehouses were usually smaller establishments selling beer and basic food and lodging to those from the bottom of the social hierarchy, including vagrants.[135] By the 1580s alehouses had proliferated to include as many as one establishment for every fifty persons in some towns, their chief function being to minister to the needs of the vagrant and labouring poor, providing them with food, drink, and shelter. Those who kept alehouses did so either because they wished to supplement a meagre income or because they could find no other source of employment.[136] Rather than being a site of misconduct, Merry's 'house' attracts patrons whose reputations are unsullied and whose conversation revolves around the subjects of trade and employment. Merry and his customers habitually refer to one another as 'neighbor,' recalling the advice in contemporary homilies and conduct books that courtesy and fellowship will shield one from hardship.

In the prologue, Homicide laments the scarcity of crime in this 'happie' and prosperous English town:

> I Haue in vaine past through each stately streete,
> And blinde-fold turning of this happie towne,
> For wealth, for peace, and goodlie gouernement,
> Yet can I not finde out a minde, a heart
> For blood and causelesse death to harbour in;
> They all are bent with vertuous gainefull trade,
> To get their needmentes for this mortall life,
> And will not soile their well addicted harts:
> With rape, extortion, murther, or the death,
> Of friend or foe, to gaine an Empery.   (sig. A2r)

The town's peacefulness is soon disrupted by Merry's crime. Overhearing his loyal patron, Thomas Beech (a thrifty chandler), discussing his financial stability, Merry resolves 'To bring his coyne to my possession' (sig. A4v). Luring Beech to an upper room of the alehouse, Merry strikes him fifteen times with a hammer. Merry's faithful sister Rachel and his man-servant Harry Williams are aware of the murder and promise to conceal it. Although he does not break his promise, Harry takes refuge at the Three Cranes Inn, trusting that 'God will reuenge' the 'iniquitie' (sig. C1r). Rachel, on the other hand, who is still a 'Maide,' (D2v) must remain in her brother's household, and she vows to be his 'true and faithfull comforter' (sig. D2v). Rather than 'mend-[ing]' his and Rachel's 'pouertie,' (sig. B3v) as he had hoped to do, Merry is forced to devote all of his time to concealing the crime. In the process, he strikes Beech's assistant, young Thomas Winchester, who later dies from the wound, and he dismembers Beech's corpse in an attempt to rid the alehouse of any evidence of murder.

But the portrait of 'vertuous gainefull trade' (sig. A2r) is undercut not only by Merry's obsession with 'wealth and reputation' (sig. A3v) but also by the uncertainty that dominates the lives of all the villagers. The contradiction between the quiet prosperity noted in the prologue on one hand and the historical record on the other is brought into focus by the rhetorical emphasis on discontent, which dominates the first hundred lines of the dialogue. Although the town appears to be a model of 'goodlie gouernement,' a certain uneasiness is shared by the inhabitants. Although Thomas Beech is 'not much in debt' (sig. A4v) and boasts that he 'liue[s] contentedlie' (sig. A4v), he seems to need Merry's liquor in order to dull a nameless apprehension:

> BEECH. Now fill two cans of your ould strongest beare:
> That make so manie loose their little wits,
> And make indentures as they go along. (sig. A3v)

Merry's man Harry Williams is described as 'not verie well' as he 'sitteth sleeping by the kitchen fier' (sig. A4). In his first appearance on stage, Merry is perplexed by his own 'meane and discontented' life: 'But wherefore should I thinke of discontent,' he ponders in soliloquy, when 'I am belou'd' by many? (sig. A3v).

At the same time that Merry is portrayed as covetous, the spectator is forced to take note of the precariousness of his livelihood. Merry's character is not drawn as crudely or as naïvely as has sometimes been suggested;[137] rather, Yarrington carefully explores the conflict between the character's conscience and his desire to escape a life of extreme indigence. Merry's poverty is part and parcel with one of the most serious social problems of late sixteenth- and seventeenth-century England – dearth amid plenty.[138] In *The Anatomy of Abuses* (1583) Philip Stubbs had voiced the widespread complaint 'that in plentie of all things, there is great scarsitie and dearth of all thinges ... that which might haue been bought heretofor within this twentie, or fourtie Years, for twentie shillings, is now worth twentie nobles ... That which was worth twentie pound, is now worth a. C. pound, and more.'[139] Although Merry is employed, he lacks the bare necessities of life: 'I cannot buy ... my bread, my meate' (sig. A4v); and although his 'little [ale]house' is 'well frequented' (sig. A3v) he himself 'cannot buy ... beare'; nor can he afford 'fagots' or 'coales' and other 'necessaries' (sig. A4v). Despite the fellowship promised by Merry's patrons, none can afford to assist him. All they can do is advise patience:

> NEIGH[BOR]. In time no doubt, why man you are but young,
> And God assure your selfe hath wealth in store,
> If you awaight his will with patience.   (sig. A4r)

Until now, Merry declares, he has been satisfied to 'content my selfe, / Till God amend my poore abilitie' (sig. A4r). But patience ultimately gives way to despair and crime.

The paradox of scarcity amid plenty was puzzling to many of Yarrington's contemporaries. Responding to the metaphysical questions raised by the prevalence of dearth, Protestant divines appealed to the doctrine of judgments. Seeking to explain the three national burdens – famine, plague, and war – William Gouge and other clerics interpreted them as judgments of divine wrath, the 'consequents of sinne.'[140] Among the sins blamed for these burdens were gluttony, drunkenness, and in particular covetousness. According to Stubbs, 'scarsitie and dearth' amid 'plentie' were largely caused by 'the rich Men' who had

so balaunced their shelfs with Gold and siluer, as they cracke againe. And, to such excesse is this couetousnes growne, as ... many a poore man, with his wyfe, childe, and whole famelie, are forced to begge their bread all their dayes after. Another sorte who flow in welth, if a poore man haue eyther house or Land, they [i.e., the rich] will neuer rest untill they haue purchased it, giuing him not the thirde parte, of that it is worth.[141]

God's punitive measures, however, were not interpreted as a sign of divine disapproval of an exploitative class system, but as hardships to be endured as part of a divine strategy for bringing about spiritual reform and regeneration. To many theologians and commentators this succinct explanation clarified and therefore made more tolerable an ominous situation. Others were more sceptical about the theory of divine retribution. In the 1549 edition of Thomas Smith's *Discourse of the Common Weal*, written in response to the economic crisis of the late 1540s when, in spite of good harvests, prices were inflating, a character expresses amazement at the 'scarcitie of thinges' among so much wealth:

I mervayll much ... what should be the cause of this dearth; seinge all
thinges are (thanckes be to Gode) so plentifull. There was never more
plentie of cattell then there is nowe, and yet it is scarcitie of thinges
which commonly maketh dearth. This is a mervelous dearthe, that in
such plentie cometh, contrary to his kynd.[142]

Faced with a heretofore unknown development, other characters provide moral answers to the problem, determining that cupidity is the cause. The Doctor, however, persuades them that the causes are monetary. Dearth, he explains, causes rising prices and underemployment, a problem which he attributes to the debasement of the coinage, the effect of which is that individuals now have to pay more in coins to obtain the same number of goods.[143]

In the 1590s the problem of dearth was occasioned by a series of poor harvests which diminished supply, thereby raising the price of grain.[144] Like a number of his contemporaries, Yarrington construes the root cause of the paradox of dearth amid plenty as extending beyond morality. Aware that the merchants on the wealthier side of town are involved in 'gainefull trade,' (sig. A2r) Merry's patrons attribute the disparity to widespread covetousness (sig. A4r); but Merry's patrons also decry the impact of expensive imports on the national economy:

NEIGH[BOR]. ... I had rather drinke,
Such beare as this as any Gascoine wine:
But tis our English manner to affect
Strange things, and price them at a greater rate,
Then home-bred things of better consequence.
MER[RY]. Tis true indeede, if all were of your minde,
My poore estate would sooner be aduanc'd:
And our French Marchants seeke some other trade.   (sig. A4r)

In the exchange between the Neighbor and Merry, we overhear Yarrington's critique of unfair trade laws. Merry and his neighbours' resentment of the importation of luxuries like French wine was shared by Tudor and Elizabethan commentators who saw that English prosperity was being channelled into the conspicuous consumption of imports rather than into ensuring full employment. Thomas Starkey, in *A Dialogue between Pole and Lupset* (c. 1529–32), had criticized English merchants for exporting 'thyngys necessary to the use of our pepul' (food, metals, and cloth) in order to import 'vayn tryfullys & concetys'; 'all such marchantys ... be procurarys only of the vayn plesure of man ... of the wych sorte surely many we have here in our cuntrey, by whome we may se thys polytyke <body> ys ... grevusly dyseasyd ... ' In 1577 William Harrison had denounced in similar terms the practice of importing French wines in other than English ships: 'when every nation was permitted to bring in her own commodities, [the latter] were far better cheap and more plentifully to be had.'[145]

While Yarrington does not treat Merry's crimes solely as an effect of economic deprivation, 'the murther of Maister Beech' is more than a dramatized homily against the sin of covetousness. Robert Law has observed that in the denouement of both the English and Italian plots the murderers, 'in long laments, precisely in keeping with the style of the broadside ballad, acknowledge their sins, pray God for forgiveness, and announce their readiness for death.'[146] And in each plot a relative who has helped conceal the criminal's identity is also executed. In 'the murther of Maister Beech,' however, the limitations of the homiletic formula are once again revealed when Merry's sister Rachel, who has been guilty of concealment but not of murder, is executed, while Merry's servant Harry, who has also assisted in the concealment, pleads benefit of clergy and escapes with a branding, 'wretched Rachel's sexe den[ying] that grace' (sig. I2v). As in *Arden of Feversham* and *A Warning for Fair Women* the theological perspective is only tentatively upheld. Juxtaposing the homiletic narrative with a frank portrayal of hardship and discontent, Yarrington exposes moral, social, and economic codes as constructed by a money economy that benefits only a few.

4

'Retrograde and Preposterous': Staging the Witch/Wife Dyad

An important juncture in the evolution of domestic drama is the emergence of plays dealing with the effects of witchcraft on English communities and, more specifically, on English households.[1] The two extant examples of domestic witch plays are both tragicomedies: Dekker, Ford and Rowley's *The Witch of Edmonton* (1621) and Heywood and Brome's *The Late Lancashire Witches* (1634). In subject matter these texts share the domestic murder plays' interest in contemporary reportage and the cult of domesticity. The last of the surviving murder plays, *The Witch of Edmonton*, stages a recent contemporary event, namely the execution of Elizabeth Sawyer for witchcraft on 19 April 1621. The action surrounding the witch-figure fuses with the marriage plot, in which an English household is destabilized through the tragic consequences of forced marriage. *The Late Lancashire Witches*, a hastily contrived play performed at the Globe Theatre in 1634, exploits popular interest in the trial of several Lancashire women also charged with practising witchcraft. As Andrew Clark observes, the play contains other 'undeniable similarities to domestic drama': Mr Generous 'belongs entirely to Heywood's long line of magnanimous, forgiving husbands,' and the transgressive wife is a 'variation on her predecessors,' although the 'intrusive element in the marriage is not a lover, but the wife's involvement in witchcraft.'[2]

In addition to exploiting contemporary journalism and the tropes of domestic drama, both plays encode extensive cultural anxiety about witchcraft. In the popular culture of early modern England, including the theatre, the figure of the witch is a sign of disorder – in the body, the family, and the body politic – the causes of which are rooted in female insubordination. Witchcraft, as described in Protestant discourses, is first and foremost a subversive act, encouraged if not initiated by the devil, and intended to thwart the divine order. In *The Mystery of Witchcraft* (1617) the Protestant theologian Thomas Cooper declares that his treatise, in which he describes 'the truth, nature, occasions, growth and power' of witchcraft, is 'very necessary for the redeeming of these atheisticall and secure [i.e., careless, dangerous] times'; witchcraft is a threat to stability because it is a 'plaine *vsurpation* of the *diuine office*, and a flat peruersion & disgracing of the *diuine* Provide[n]ce.'[3] As with any behaviour that challenges the established order, the underlying cause of witchcraft is seen to be the desire for power. Those perceived as most likely to become witches, therefore, are those who are powerless. For early modern demonologists, women are especially susceptible to witchcraft not only because many are dispossessed materially, but also because, as Cooper's treatise concludes, women are 'vsually more *ambitious* and *desirous of Soueraignety*, the rather because they are bound to subiection.'[4] In other words, since women are disenfranchised under patriarchy they can be easily tempted to oppose it.

A common thread linking early modern discourses on the subject of witchcraft is the perception that witches, like the garrulous wives of the domestic plays discussed in previous chapters, negate the neo-Aristotelian construction of female subordination, namely the *mulier economica* or the belief that woman can be considered only in relation to the order of marriage. Against the construction of the ugly, vituperative witch, defenders of patriarchy promote the image of the virtuous housewife who remains subordinate to her husband's authority. 'Patriarchal hierarchy,' writes Allison Coudert, 'was not threatened by the celebration of women in subordinate roles, but at the beginning of the early modern period, forces were at work that challenged the established intellectual principle of male superiority. The witchcraze was one response to that challenge.'[5]

The link between women and witches had informed European discourses long before the witch hunts. The stereotype of the witch combines the Aristotelian view of women's souls as deficient in reason, rendering them more prone to credulity and superstition than men, with the Judaeo-Christian view of woman as the cause of original sin and the Fall from grace.[6] In the Middle Ages witchcraft was considered an act of heresy to which women, as a consequence of their frail intellects, were especially susceptible. The *Malleus Maleficarum* (1486), the first printed encyclopedia of witchcraft, describes women as 'more credulous' than men, 'naturally more impressionable,' and therefore 'more ready to receive the influence of a disembodied spirit.'[7] The charge of female credulity is reiterated by James I, who in *Daemonologie* (1597) explains why far more women than men are 'giuen' to witchcraft:

The reason is easie, for as that sexe is frailer then man is, so is it easier to be intrapped in these grosse snares of the Deuill, as was ... proued to be true, by the Serpents deceiuing of *Eua* at the beginning, which makes him the homelier with that sexe ... [8]

There is, however, a marked shift from the medieval definition of witchcraft as heresy to the early modern construction of witchcraft as a form of usurpation of the divine order. Whereas in the Middle Ages invectives against witchcraft are restricted for the most part to formal diatribes generated chiefly by patristic and scholastic authorities, in early modern Europe they shift to the persecution of the accused. This development has in part been located in the Reformation's literal obedience to the biblical injunction, 'Thou shalt not suffer a witch to live' (AV, Exodus 22:18). Alan Kors and Edward Peters contend that the strong Protestant emphasis on scripture and on the role of Satan 'only strengthened the already present fear of diabolism and witchcraft in the lands that reformed the Church.'[9] But the shift is also rooted in the early modern perception of witchcraft as an act of transgression against the orderly, stable commonwealth. Those accused of practising witchcraft, that is, those who posed the most severe threat to social cohesion, were not simply poor and aged women, but unassimilable women – old or diseased spinsters, widows, prostitutes, obstreperous wives, healers, and midwives. Merry Wiesner writes that although 'learned notions of witchcraft as demonology made some inroads into popular culture, the person most often initially accused of witchcraft in any village' was a woman 'who had a reputation as a healer, a scold, or a worker of both good and bad magic.'[10] Midwives, for example, were 'expert in methods of birth control, and most likely cooperated in abortions and infanticides' with families who were either too poor to sustain many children, or who 'did not wish to jeopardize their new prosperity.'[11] The early association of *maleficia* (the misfortunes, injuries, or calamities suffered by persons, animals, or property as the result of the witch's pact with the devil) with abortofacients and sterilizing potions, together with the almost universal assumption that the users of such potions would be women, helped to feminize the crime of witchcraft.[12] The danger attributed to all forms of *maleficia* was their association with a malevolent femininity that, if empowered, would engender chaos.

On the English Renaissance stage, the witch is a signifier of female insubordination, and witchcraft a powerful threat to patriarchal hierarchy and authority. In her association with negation and mutability, the witch-figure belongs to the literary trope of the *mundus inversus* (the world upside down).[13] A prevalent form of this trope is the construction of the witch as the inversion of the ideal Protestant wife, whose insubordination overturns the orderly household and, by extension, the social order.

I

The plays that treat the effects of witchcraft on the *domus* divide into two categories: (1) those such as Lyly's *Endimion* (c. 1591), Shakespeare's *Macbeth* (1606–7), Middleton's *The Witch* (c. 1610–6), and Marston's *The Wonder of Women or The Tragedy of Sophonisba* (c. 1604), which rely for their material primarily on English and European folk-lore, and in which the subject of witchcraft is influential but not central to the action; (2) the domestic tragicomedies that focus on the role of the witch.[14] Although *The Witch of Edmonton* and *The Late Lancashire Witches* deal more extensively with the witch's influence on the English household, considerable intertextuality exists between these plots and their non-topical counterparts, particularly in the portrayal of the witch/wife dyad.

Among the non-topical plays, Lyly's *Endimion* is the first to articulate a profound anxiety about perceived attempts by witches to subvert natural law within the state and the family. The anxiety is manifest in Lyly's treatment of Dipsas, who is partly modelled on classical witches. Dipsas's 'damnable Arte' has threatened the rulership of Cynthia (the allegorical representation of Queen Elizabeth), whose 'gouernment' is the 'possess[ion] ... [of] the eternall Gods' (V.iii.25–6).[15] Dipsas's challenge of Cynthia, a challenge which Cynthia easily dispels, conforms to the pervasive fear of witches as instruments against the monarchy, a fear which helped to mobilize the persecution of witches in Elizabethan England.[16] But Dipsas's ability to seduce unwitting males into ungodly marriages represents a more mundane danger: Dipsas is also an ignoble wife who in divorcing her husband and banishing him to the wilderness vindicates feminine frailty.

Like many early modern women punished for scolding, brawling, and dominating their spouses, Dipsas is a distortion of wifely grace and humility. When Sir Thopas (a young, half-witted knight) expresses his wish to marry Dipsas, three male choric figures reduce her to the stereotype of the witch as a repulsive, voracious shrew.

> SAM[IAS]. That vglie creature? Why shee is a foole, a
> scold, fat, without fashion, and quite without fauour. ...
> EPI[TON]. Why in marrying *Dipsas*, hee [Sir Topas] shall
> haue euerie day twelue dishes of meate to his
> dinner, though there be none but *Dipsas* with him.
>   Foure of flesh, four of fish, foure of fruite. ...
> SAM[IAS]. Excellent! for of my word, she is both
> crabbish, lumpish, and carping.   (III.iii.88–9, 93–5, 99–100)

Dipsas's grotesqueness is enhanced by her 'scold[ing]' speech (III.iii.88), a feature derived from the commonplace notion in medieval and early modern discourses that women's mental powers are weak and therefore susceptible to evil partly because, as the *Malleus* warns, 'they have slippery tongues.'[17] Dipsas is also guilty of reversing the notion that man only is by nature audacious and therefore better suited to rule the household, whereas woman, who is by nature defective, is better equipped for submission:

> [SIR THOPAS]. ... Doth *Dipsas* stoope? wyll shee yeeld? will she bende?
> DARES. O sir as much as you would wish, for her chin almost
>   toucheth her knees. ...
> Shee is a notable Witch ...   (V.ii.55–6, 78)

Yet the danger that Dipsas represents is comically contained by the broad humour in these episodes, which undercuts the force of the witch's professed threat to male sovereignty. In the final scene we witness the witch/shrew's unexpected repentance of her former 'wicked[ness]' (V.iii.40), central to which has been her irreverence towards her husband:

> DIPSAS. ... Yet among al the things that I committed, there is noth-
> ing so much tormenteth my rented and ransackt thoughts, as that
> in the prime of my husbands youth I diuorced him by my deuillish
> Arte; for which, if to die might be amendes, I would not liue till to
> morrowe.   (V.iii.41–5)

Following Dipsas's public confession, Cynthia permits her to return to society and to the husband whom she had divorced in order to practise sorcery (V.iii.258–68). Dipsas's forgiveness restores both social and domestic harmony; we also infer that her ugliness vanishes once she renounces black magic.

By the end of the sixteenth century, the association in the drama between witches and obstreperous wives is conceived as a more serious and less manageable deviation than it is portrayed by Lyly. Social renewal becomes contingent upon the witch's punishment rather than her repentance. The increasingly negative portrayal of the witch has a political underpinning in the accession of James I, whose *Daemonologie* denounces not only witches but also those who profess scepticism about their existence.[18] The notion of the witch as unworthy of redemption is also closely related to the pervasive concern in late sixteenth- and early seventeenth-century England with the growing insubordination of women. Those accused of being witches were often women who resisted patriarchal claims, and in Puritan circles especially the rebelliousness of many wives was often equated with witchcraft.[19]

In *The Witch*, a non-topical play set in seventeenth-century Italy, Middleton does not scrutinize the sociopolitical dimensions of witchcraft. Like Jonson's *Masque of Queens*, *The Witch* exploits traditional witch-lore for sensational effects, drawing on the standard view of witches as the embodiment of chaos;[20] like Shakespeare's *Macbeth*, for example, it employs the cauldron motif as part of the apparatus of the 'feast of death and essential disorder.'[21] In addition to Middleton's reliance on popular magical *topoi* is his depiction of the witch as the inversion of the 'honest duteous wife' (I.i.16).[22] Against a background of marriage celebrations, the opening scene of *The Witch* revolves around the returned soldier Sebastian's determination to honour his betrothal to Isabella in spite of her marriage to Antonio. Sebastian enlists the aid of Hecate, who creates a *maleficium* rendering Antonio selectively impotent, permitting him to continue sleeping with his whore but not to consummate his marriage to Isabella who has received false news of Sebastian's death. Middleton is exploiting the belief that witches could induce impotence even in the innocent. King James, for one, had proclaimed that the devil's 'filthy witchcraft' can make a man 'unable *versus hanc*' (that is, sexually dysfunctional towards a specific woman), that 'if the power of witchcraft may reach to our life, [so] much more to a member [i.e., sexual organ] ... wherein the Devil hath his principal operation.'[23] The mythical witches – Hecate, Stadlin, and

Hoppo – are complemented by the ordinary, recognizable woman who crosses traditional gender boundaries. Isabella's sister Francisca is unwed, pregnant, and in danger of being outcast because she has not been made 'sociable and honest' through 'the married life' (II.i.66, 67). A major source of anxiety for Isabella and the other married women is that Francisca is 'too long alone' (l. 65). Ironically, Francisca's autonomy permits her a certain freedom of expression that alarms the married women. She declares, for example, that there 'should ... be a statute against' all adulterous husbands (II.i.86), but her outburst is censored by Isabella who advises her sister that a husband and children would 'mend your discourse much' (II.i.102). Like many women accused of witchcraft, Francisca, in refusing to be silent, is threatened with the punishment of isolation from society.

A woman becomes a witch when she resists or refuses to conform to her prescribed social and religious role, negating both natural and divine law. Shakespeare's Lady Macbeth has much in common with Middleton's Francisca and Lyly's Dipsas and with those women labelled witches by early modern theologians who advocated that a wife's foremost desire was to be 'bound to subiection.'[24] Characterized by the newly created king Malcolm as a 'fiendlike queen' (V.viii.70),[25] Lady Macbeth is demonic, just as Lyly's Dipsas is 'deuillish' (V.iii.43), precisely because she subverts prescribed notions of femininity. Lady Macbeth's rejection of prescribed feminine behaviour has been widely observed. She and the 'secret, black, and midnight hags' (IV.i.48) who tempt Macbeth are invested with a certain 'wild[ness]' (I.iii.40) that, as Peter Stallybrass has observed, opposes an implied norm of womanliness.[26] Banquo is disturbed by the Witches' equivocal identity in much the same way that the spectator is invited to be disturbed by Lady Macbeth's: 'You should be women,' Banquo tells the Witches, 'And yet your beards forbid me to interpret / That you are so' (I.iii.45–7). In both action and speech Lady Macbeth also transgresses, and parodies, the normal roles of demure wife and hostess.[27] She undertakes all of the preparations for Duncan's murder, advising Macbeth to 'look up clear' and to 'Leave all the rest to me' (I.v.71, 73). She desires to 'chastise' Macbeth 'with the valor' of her 'tongue' (I.v.27), and she reproaches him for his guilt in a barrage of imperative utterances – 'Give me the daggers'; 'Retire we to our chamber'; 'Go get some water / And wash this filthy witness from thy hand' (II.ii.51, 64, 44–5). Rhetorically, Lady Macbeth's appropriation of masculine language fuses with the language of the three Witches, which is also dominated by imperatives: 'Give me'; 'Look what I have done'; 'Show me, show me' (I.iii.5, 26, 27). Like many women of the early modern period who were branded witches because, as Allison Coudert argues, they 'rejected the private world of female domesticity for the public world of men,'[28] Lady Macbeth appropriates male prerogatives and brings about domestic and social dissolution.

The construction of the witch/shrew by Shakespeare and other playwrights has a direct parallel in Luther's association of the witch with the impious Christian wife. Unlike medieval demonologists, for whom the antithesis of the witch is the virginal nun, Luther contrasts the deviant behaviour of the witch with the behaviour of the ideal housewife, whom he compares with the inner-directed snail:

... just as the snail carries its house with it, so the wife should stay at home and look after the affairs of the household, as one who has been deprived of the ability of administering those affairs that are outside and that concern the state. She does not go beyond her most personal duties.[29]

'Luther's remedy for the female vulnerability to witchcraft,' writes Sigrid Brauner, is 'a logical corollary of his views on marriage: women should accept their God-given place as housewives and use their inherent moral power.'[30] Luther's explanation for the female practice of witchcraft also coincides with English political discourses on the theological and social value of the family as, to quote Hobbes, 'a little Monarchy' in which 'the Father or Master is the Sovereign.'[31]

The fusion of Lady Macbeth and the Witches is further grounded, as Janet Adelman has argued, in their mutual 'perverse' maternity, Lady Macbeth's rejection of her natural domestic role signalling the 'unnatural abrogation' of motherhood: 'Calling [for her unsexing] on spirits ambiguously allied with the witches themselves, she phrases this unsexing as the undoing of her own bodily maternal function.'[32] 'Make thick my blood,' Lady Macbeth commands the spirits,

Stop up th' access and passage to remorse,
That no compunctious visitings of nature
Shake my fell purpose ...
... Come to my woman's breasts,
And take my milk for gall, you murdering ministers,
Wherever in your sightless substances
You wait on nature's mischief! ...

(I.v.43–50)

Lady Macbeth's equation of her maternal 'milk' with 'gall' is consonant with the identification found in contemporary treatises on colostrum (the first milk secreted after birth, sometimes called 'green milk' [*OED*]) with the milk of witches, an identification, notes Adelman, 'localiz[ing] the image of maternal danger.'[33]

The portrait of Lady Macbeth, however, also echoes a cross-cultural fear of women's bodies. Anthropological studies indicate that the issue of ritual pollution has been used in many cultures as evidence of women's inferiority. As James Brain observes, at the same time that 'all bodily emissions are considered polluting,' the physiology of women 'makes them appear more polluted and polluting than men.'[34] In a broad range of patriarchal cultures, women's bodily emissions are perceived as fundamentally dangerous because they are signifiers of death. Thus it is not coincidental that witches in various cultures have been accused of using their bodily excretions to bring about the death of their victims, a threat inscribed in Lady Macbeth's association of breast-feeding with murder (I.v.47–8).

Although Lady Macbeth is directly associated with the witches in 'direst cruelty' (I.v.43), the profound influence of her murderous ambitions and fantasies on her husband extends beyond even the witches' powers over the natural world. As the witches themselves admit, although they can severely tempt human beings to destruction, their power is in fact limited: 'Though his [the captain's] bark cannot be lost, / Yet it shall be tempest-tost' (I.iii.24–5). The failure of their temptation of Banquo underscores their role as mere catalysts to Macbeth's crimes. Lady Macbeth's influence, on the other hand, is destructive – the witch/wife is even more terrifying than her androgynous supernatural counterparts.

The conflation of witches and abusive wives, and the link between women's bodies and death, are more sensationally dramatized in Marston's *Wonder of Women*. Just as Lady Macbeth renounces the true calling of her womb in favour of a barren yet insatiable thirst for power, Marston's arch-witch Erichto displays a 'woman's greediness' (V.i.14)[35] for carnal pleasure and dominance. Erichto's terrifying powers are unleashed in the underworld where she performs necrophilic and necrophagous rites, arousing the spectator's dread of the female body's insatiable desires.[36]

> When her deep magic makes forced heaven quake
> And thunder spite of Jove, Erichto then
> From naked graves stalks out, heaves proud her head

With long unkempt hair loaden, and strives to snatch
The night's quick sulphur. Then she bursts up tombs,
From half-rot cerecloths then she scrapes dry gums
For her black rites. But when she finds a corse
New graved whose entrails yet not turn
To slimy filth, with greedy havoc then
She makes fierce spoil and swells with wicked triumph
To bury her lean knuckles in her eyes. ...
... But if she find some life
Yet lurking close, she bites his gelid lips,
And sticking her black tongue in his dry throat,
She breathes dire murmurs which enforce him bear
Her baneful secrets to the spirits of horror.   (IV.i.106–16, 118–22)

According to the *Malleus Maleficarum*, 'all witchcraft comes from carnal lust, which is in women insatiable ... '[37] Asserting that 'Love is the highest rebel to our [the witch's] art' (IV.1.170), Erichto, echoing Lady Macbeth's stealthy and lurid search for earthly power, seeks her pleasure in the beds of kings.

ERICHTO. Know we, Erichto, with a thirsty womb,
Have coveted full threescore suns for blood of kings. ...
We, in the pride and height of covetous lust,
Have wished with woman's greediness to fill
Our longing arms with Syphax' [the King of Libya's] well-strung
     limbs.   (V.i.8–9, 13–15)

Erichto's double is Sophonisba, a model of 'female glory, / The wonder of a constancy so fixed / That fate itself might well grow envious' (Prologue, ll. 20–2). Like the ideal wife of the conduct literature, Sophonisba is dutiful and submissive, promising her husband Massinissa 'that no low appetite / Of my sex' weakness can or shall o'ercome / Due grateful service unto you or virtue' (I.ii.175–7). Sophonisba's 'immense / ... virtue' (V.iii.110–11) enables her to accept the limits of female intelligence and the value of female silence:

... since affected wisdom in us women
Is our sex' highest folly, I am silent.
I cannot speak less well, unless I were
More void of goodness.   (II.i.136–9)

Because her husband and Carthage 'owe [i.e., own]' her 'body' (II.i.140), Sophonisba 'resolve[s]' out of a sense of 'honour and just faith' (V.iii.96–7) to 'save' her husband (l. 97) by sacrificing her life. She dies, she claims, 'most happy in my husband's arms' (l. 106).

II

In the domestic witch plays the danger posed by women who challenge patriarchal authority is perhaps most crudely articulated in *The Late Lancashire Witches*. In addition to staging topical events (two series of notorious Lancashire witch trials), the play shares the domestic drama's emphasis on conflict between predominantly English characters from the non-aristocratic ranks (in this case, merchants, housewives, a tailor, and a miller). Amid the accusations of and confessions to witchcraft, the dramatists treat farcically a number of folk beliefs about sorcery: magic bridles, a mill haunted by cats, and false apparitions. The *maleficia*, on the other hand, are portrayed as serious threats, and their supposed practitioners – women who have overthrown the 'wholesome order' and 'governance of ... a house' (IV.i.1866, 1861) – are judged as deserving of their punishments by 'lawfull Iustice' (Epilogue, l. 2803).[38] Although the Prologue lays claim to the familiar technique in domestic drama of 'ground[ing]' the action in scenes 'from our owne Nation' (ll. 6, 5), the play forsakes historical veracity for theatrical sensationalism. No reference is made to the actual accused women's recorded disavowals of witchcraft, which were credible enough to convince the assize authorities to defer sentencing, in turn prompting Charles I and the Privy Council to initiate an investigation. 'The play,' writes Herbert Berry, 'represents the case for the prosecution alone.'[39] In the final scenes, those who had voiced reasonable doubts about the actuality of witchcraft acknowledge their ignorance.

Cross-cultural studies of witchcraft have revealed that while the nature of witch beliefs will often vary from one society to another, two interrelated constants about these beliefs transcend cultural boundaries: 'witches,' argues James Brain, 'represent people's deepest fears about themselves and society, and they represent a reversal of all that is considered normal behavior in a particular society.'[40] Prominent among the Lancashire witches' *maleficia* are their supposed crimes against the orderly family: like Middleton's Hecate they employ 'a plaine *Maleficium versus hanc*' (III.i.1967) to emasculate men and to induce in wives the desire to behave with 'immodesty' (l. 1968). When the home of a 'respected ... master of a govern'd Family' is disrupted by the women's supposed 'sorcery' (I.i.266–8), the event is described by a neighbour as 'retrograde & preposterous' (l. 273) because it has 'turn'd topsie turvy' (l. 271) the natural hierarchy of relationships within the household:

> The good man, in all obedience kneels vnto his son,
> Hee with an austere brow commands his father.
> The wife presumes not in the daughters sight
> Without a prepared courtesie. The girle, shee
> Expects it as a dutie; chides her mother
> Who quakes and trembles at each word she speaks,
> And what's as strange, the Maid she dominiers
> O're her yong mistris, who is aw'd by her.
> The son to whom the Father creeps and bends,
> Stands in as much feare of the groome his man.   (ll. 276–85)

Observing that the 'foot' has usurped the 'head' (l. 306), another neighbour comments that 'such rare disorder ... / breeds pitty ... ' (ll. 286–7). The harshest judgment is reserved for the fictional Mistress Generous, the wife of the most pious and 'Hospita[ble]' neighbour in Lancashire (I.i.206). Despite her husband's forgiveness, Mistress Generous refuses to abandon witchcraft, whereupon her husband considers it his Christian duty to 'deliver' her 'Into the hand of Iustice' (V.i.2531–2). Although in the Epilogue the authors disclaim 'That we for Iustices and Judges sit' (l. 2812), asserting that 'Mercy' may still intervene on behalf of the accused (ll. 2807–9), Mistress Generous has been implicitly found guilty, and will presumably be damned.

   None of the plays discussed so far scrutinizes, through its representation of the witch-figure, the subordinate position of women in early modern England. *The Witch of Edmonton* is unusual in that the dramatists deliberately discredit supernatural causation by treating witchcraft as a complex social construction. With its undertone of pain and bewilderment, the play makes a radical statement about demonology: Elizabeth Sawyer is not an agent of supernatural powers but an individual confronting an entrenched social code that relegates old and poverty-ridden spinsters to the devil's company. Mother Sawyer's tragedy arises from an inextricable link between her persecution and her internalization of the community's brutality: 'Some call me Witch,' she declares, 'And being ignorant of my self, they go / About to teach me how to be one' (II.i.8–10).[41] Feeling 'shunn'd / And hated like a sickness: made a scorn

/ To all degrees and sexes' (II.i.95–7), she resolves to take revenge against an abusive world since ''Tis all one, / To be a Witch, as to be counted one' (ll. 113–14). When Mother Sawyer finally summons the 'Familiar' or 'devil,' her desire for revenge is a coherent response to the violence she can no longer endure.

The play's immediate source is *The Wonderfull Discouerie of Elizabeth Savvyer, a Witch*, a pamphlet entered in the Stationers' Register on 27 April 1621 in which Henry Goodcole, chaplain of Newgate prison, records his interviews with Elizabeth Sawyer shortly before her execution. The pamphlet is essentially a tract against the dangers traditionally associated with witchcraft. Elizabeth's answers form a conventional catalogue of the causes and effects of demonology, revealing little about the personality of the woman or the social roots of witchcraft. Dekker, Ford, and Rowley, on the other hand, initially portray Mother Sawyer as knowing nothing about witchcraft. Long before her pact with the Familiar, she is accused of 'Forespeak[ing]' her community's cattle and of 'bewitch[ing] their Corn' and 'their Babes at nurse' (II.i.12–13). The villagers blame demonology for the community's economic hardships and for behaviour which poses a disturbing challenge to the patriarchal order. Through desperation Mother Sawyer conforms to society's expectations to the point where she becomes consumed by 'madness' (IV.i.153). Her madness attests to what William Monter suggests witchcraft itself had become, that is, 'a *magical* form of violent revenge, practiced by exactly those persons who could not employ physical violence.'[42] Marginalized women especially suited this requirement: 'They had many grievances; they wanted revenge; yet recourse to the law often was beyond their economic power, and successful physical violence was beyond their physical power.'[43] They gained revenge by arousing their accusers' fear of magic. In response to her suffering and social dislocation, Elizabeth Sawyer adopts a strategy of survival that is also similar to that of early modern revenge heroes. In his study of radical revenge plays, Jonathan Dollimore remarks that 'the disintegrating effects of grief are resisted not through Christian or stoic renunciation of society,' but through 'a vengeful re-engagement with the society and those responsible for that grief.'[44]

The unorthodox structures of the Mother Sawyer plot locate the roots of witchcraft in the external conditions of class, misogyny, and poverty. The signs which identify Mother Sawyer as an outcast are her age, her gender, her physical deformity, and her poverty, her demise epitomizing what Frank Thorney claims awaits those in her world who 'feel /

The misery of beggery and want; / Two Devils that are occasions to enforce / A shameful end' (I.i.17–20). The dark side of rural England is represented by the villagers, including prominent citizens, all of whom exploit Mother Sawyer's outcast status. As Joseph Klaits has demonstrated, in the witch persecutions of the early modern period, 'members of the elites and ordinary folk found a common cause.'[45] The accusations against Mother Sawyer are initiated by her landlord, Old Banks, who calls her 'Witch' (II.i.17) and 'Hag' (l. 27) and beats her when she refuses to return the 'few rotten sticks' (l. 21) which she has gathered from his property. It is significant that the spectator first sees Mother Sawyer collecting bits of firewood from her landlord's grounds. In England witchcraft trials coincided with the enclosure laws, which 'broke up many of the old co-operative village communities,'[46] increasing the numbers of poor people, many of them widowed and elderly, and depriving them of any means of subsistence. When old women evoked the now-dying code of communal sharing by asking their neighbours for help, and were rebuffed, they responded, like Elizabeth Sawyer, with curses.

The play's boldest statement about witchcraft, however, is the Anne Ratcliff action, which exploits the popular construction of the witch as a rebellious wife. The episode deals with the supposed bewitchment of Old Ratcliff's wife Anne, which is used to explain her madness and death. The 'bewitchment' takes place moments after the villagers have burned Mother Sawyer's thatch. Exasperated and 'dri'd up / With cursing and with madness' (IV.i.152–3), Mother Sawyer reminds the Familiar about Anne Ratcliff, 'Who for a little Soap lick'd by ... [Mother Sawyer's] Sow, / Struck, and almost had lam'd it' (ll. 169–70). Having been refused charity by Anne Ratcliff, her neighbour, Mother Sawyer had instructed the Familiar to 'pinch that Quean to th' heart' (l. 171). The Dog's 'Look here else' (l. 172) is followed by the stage direction, *Enter* Anne Ratcliff *mad*. A number of critics have commented on the ambiguity surrounding Anne's estrangement. Etta Onat points out that Mother Sawyer's Familiar rubs Anne only after she has gone mad, and proposes that 'her suicide might very well have been caused by nothing more than a coincidental madness, not the result of demonic possession at all'; and Michael Hattaway notes that 'the text makes it legitimate to conjecture that ... [Anne's] madness arose independently of the devil's action,' the 'motives for action aris[ing] out of social transactions' while the 'chains of causation are left incomplete.'[47] The structural indeterminacy, I believe, crystallizes the interplay between the social and psychological construction of both Mother Sawyer's and Anne Ratcliff's madness. Beneath the surface conflict, the play creates a number of structural parallels between the two characters. To begin with, economic destitution is a source of mental anguish for both women. Just as Mother Sawyer's indigence is responsible for the trespass of her sow, poverty has led Anne Ratcliff to injure the animal. And although the two women are enemies, Anne's jabber about deprivation echoes the cynical perspective which Mother Sawyer has voiced in her claim that there is no justice for the dispossessed:

> RATC. Hoyda! a-pox of the Devil's false Hopper! all the golden Meal
> runs into the rich Knaves purses, and the poor have nothing but
> Bran. Hey derry down! Are not you Mother *Sawyer*?
> SAWY. No, I am a Lawyer.
> RATC. Art thou? I prithee let me scratch thy Face; for thy Pen has
> flea'd off a great many mens skins ... I'll sue Mother *Sawyer*, and her
> own Sow shall give in evidence against her.
> SAWY. Touch her. [Dog *rubs her.*]   (IV.i.177–86)

Significantly, the Familiar 'rubs' Anne when, like Mother Sawyer, she is railing against the disparity between the rich and the poor.

The verbal exchange between the two women underscores their mutual estrangement. Although the Dog touches Anne during her delirium, Mother Sawyer believes that she has induced Anne's madness. The old woman delights in inverting the power structure of her world by fancifully assuming the role of 'Lawyer' to Anne's victimization. As she rails at Anne for being uncharitable – 'That Jade, that foul-tongu'd whore, *Nan Ratcliff*' (IV.i.168) – Mother Sawyer denounces her enemy with epithets identical to those which the community had formerly levelled at her, namely 'Jadish' and 'Whore' (IV.i.4, 24). Mother Sawyer in effect strips the married woman of her socially sanctioned identity, taking revenge upon the community that has been responsible for her own alienation.

That Anne's derangement has also stemmed from coercion is indicated by the interpolation of society's need to associate women with madness:

> O. BANK. Catch her [Anne] fast, and have her into some close Cham-
> ber: do, for she's as many Wives are, stark mad.   (IV.i.193–4)

Anne's nameless anxiety, which the community attributes to supernatural causes, is related to a type of 'madness' exhibited by 'many Wives' (l. 94) in the village. Calling for Anne's confinement and Mother Sawyer's execution, the community hopes to temper the unnatural behaviour of all the village women:

[COUNTRYMAN] 2. Rid the Town of her [Mother Sawyer], else all our Wives will do nothing else but dance about ...
Country May-poles.
[COUNTRYMAN] 3. Our Cattel fall, our Wives fall, our
Daughters fall, and Maid-servants fall ...   (IV.i.10–13)

Following Anne Ratcliff's suicide, Old Banks spearheads the move 'to burn' Mother Sawyer 'for a Witch' (IV.i.215). During her arraignment, however, she is momentarily spared by the intervention of a Justice. In a significant departure from Goodcole's treatment of this event, the dramatists initially stress the Justice's wisdom and compassion in reprehending the villagers for their violent actions, which he labels 'ridiculous' (IV.i.40) and 'against Law' (l. 51). 'Instead of turning [Mother Sawyer] into a witch,' he warns, 'you'll prove your selves starke Fools' (ll. 41–2). The villagers' fury subsides when the Justice insists on treating the old woman with mildness. Mother Sawyer, however, continues to vilify her detractors. When Sir Arthur, a libertine and a schemer, joins the interrogation, she exposes his false rectitude and denounces a concept of honour based on class and privilege: 'Men in gay clothes, whose Backs are laden with Titles and Honours, are within far more crooked then I am; and if I be a Witch, more Witch-like' (IV.i.86–8). Her boldest denunciation is reserved for 'Princes Courts,' where, she claims, are found 'painted things ... / Upon whose naked Paps, a Leachers thought / Acts Sin in fouler shapes then can be wrought' (ll. 103–7). Henceforth, the accusations against Mother Sawyer abruptly shift from conspiracy with the devil to insubordination towards the status hierarchy. It is not Mother Sawyer's alleged crimes that secure her execution but her spirited vituperation. In Sir Arthur's words, she has given 'her Tongue gallop' (IV.i.100), and according to the Justice she has exhibited 'sawcie[ness]' and 'bitter[ness]' (l. 81).

Although the community shares responsibility for Mother Sawyer's death, and although some of the most prominent citizens are themselves guilty of moral backsliding, none of the villagers is punished through any real or symbolic intervention of Divine Providence, as is expected in domestic tragedy. And while in the denouement Mother Sawyer utters the conventional public-repentance speech of the genre (V.iii.50–1), we infer that in the world of the play she has been condemned irrevocably.

In locating the social roots of the witchcraze, *The Witch of Edmonton* claims a unique position in early modern English drama, the playwrights going beyond not only the analogues but also the pious indictments of both continental and English sceptics. The play's rational perspective had been current in a number of discourses on demonology since the second half of the sixteenth century. This perspective was forcefully articulated by the physician Johann Wier, whose *De Praestigiis Daemonum* (1563) was published at the time when witch prosecutions in Germany were entering their most intense phase. While not rejecting the reality of witchcraft, Wier claimed that the confessions for which women were being executed were illusions incited either by devils or by melancholia. Wier's misogynist bias, however, is evident in his proposal that women are easier prey than men to the sleights of demons because women are inherently prone to delusion,[48] a supposition echoing the long-standing claim for women's credulity. Critiques similar to Wier's were later put forth by Neoplatonists, hermeticists, Paracelsians, and a few neo-Aristotelian commentators, all of whom argued that worship of the devil as practised by sorcery was founded upon illusion and was therefore harmless.[49]

In England, Reginald Scot cast doubt on the prevalent belief in *maleficia* by offering non-magical theories of their causes. Dekker, Ford, and Rowley's sympathetic portrayal of Mother Sawyer suggests their possible debt to Scot's *The Discoverie of Witchcraft* (1584), a widely influential treatise which provoked James I to write his *Daemonologie*.[50] Scot claimed that witchcraft was a myth created by the faithless:

The fables of Witchcraft have taken so fast hold and deepe root in
the heart of man, that fewe or none can (nowadaies) with patience
indure the hand and correction of God. For if any adversitie, greefe,
sicknesse, losse of children, corne, cattell, or libertie happen unto
them; by & by they exclaime uppon witches.[51]

For Scot, the persecutions of those believed to be witches conflicted with the Protestant idea of Providence, which held that neither good nor evil can occur without God's will: 'certeine old women heere on earth, called witches, must needs be the contrivers of all mens calamities, and as though they themselves were innocents, and had deserved no such punishments.'[52] Scot considered Wier's assertion that melancholia induced women to confess to impossible acts as only one naturalistic cause among others; many aged women, he pointed out, were physically ill and in urgent need of medical and financial assistance, their vulnerability making them easy targets for witchmongers.[53] *The Witch of Edmonton* directly echoes Scot's critique of the persecution of those believed to be witches on the basis that such measures contradict a providentially ordained universe. The play also upholds the scepticism of George Gifford, who in 1593 wrote that legal convictions were founded on doubtful evidence and conjecture, and that the more gruesome the punishments the more people were wont to persecute the innocent.[54] By 1621 scepticism had gained widespread acceptance, as is evident from the growing number of accusations both of imposture on the part of those claiming demonic possession and of judicial fraud.[55]

Whereas Reginald Scot and others had dismissed witchcraft primarily on theological and rational grounds, *The Witch of Edmonton* exposes the tyranny of the collective law that prohibits behaviour which threatens to destroy the codes that define an individual's social identity. The Mother Sawyer action creates one field of displacement of social and homiletic imperatives by interrogating popular notions of magical causation. The marriage plot or Frank Thorney action locates the witch-craze in the social need to punish those who transgress social boundaries. The two plots are loosely connected by the influence of the supernatural on the protagonists. The marriage plot combines individual tragedy and domestic dissolution with the supposed effects of black magic. Frank Thorney, who has secretly married another woman, yields to familial pressures to marry Susan, the daughter of a rich yeoman, consoling himself with the thought that a wise woman, 'Known and approv'd in Palmestry,' (II.ii.116) has foretold that he would have two wives. In a sudden demonic impulse, attributed by society to the evil influences of the 'Witch' Sawyer (V.iii.21–7), Frank kills Susan. The supernatural link between the two plots has been consistently viewed as a melodramatic device which undermines the tragic potential of the events dramatized. George Rao writes that 'the popular belief in witchcraft is made one of the chief reasons for the domestic crime,' Mother Sawyer being 'shown as the source of mischief'; and George Herndl complains that in the Frank Thorney plot 'the action is so presented that the motive of the "sin" is hardly felt to lie within the will of the sinner, which is paralyzed by the power of evil,' while in the Mother Sawyer plot 'tragic emotions dwindle into sentimentality.'[56] A close analysis of the action, however, reveals considerable complexity in the portrayal of the association between witchcraft and domestic crime. The popular explanation for Susan's demise, namely Frank's bewitchment, is undermined by a number of complications, foremost of which is Frank's admission that he is defeated primarily from within. Moreover, we shall see that Susan, the paragon of wifely patience and humility, dies, like Mother Sawyer, at the moment when she is most talkative and assertive. That Mother Sawyer and Susan meet similar ends underscores the general fear of unauthorized female speech, a fear which, we have seen, underlies early modern witchcraft beliefs.

The marriage plot explores the relationship between power and gender as it bears upon the witch phenomenon and on notions of ideal domestic conduct. Under profound emotional strain, Frank Thorney commits bigamy rather than disobey the wishes of his father and the community that he marry Susan, whose wealthy family makes her a respectable catch. Rather than confess his clandestine marriage to Winnifride, Sir Arthur's maid, Frank submits to a series of inescapable compromises, indulging in a painful web of lies in order to retain his father's and the world's approval. Frank's inability to reconcile personal and social claims underwrites his murder of Susan, which thematically unifies the two plots. The brutality to which Susan is subjected parallels the violence experienced by Mother Sawyer and, by extension, Anne Ratcliff. Like the conventional patient wife, Susan enters marriage believing a wife's duty is to be passive and solicitous, and above all to yield to her husband's will (II.ii.79–88). Susan's notions of wifely perfection lead her to blame herself for Frank's discontent, a reaction based on a set of conventional moral prescriptions governing conjugal behaviour. When Susan finally thwarts convention by passionately voicing her sexual desire, Frank reproaches her for undermining her role as a 'perfect Embleme of ... modesty' (II.ii.104). Her ardent speech on Frank's 'power / To make me passionate as an *April*-day' (II.ii.89) elicits a startling reply:

FRANK. Change thy conceit, I prithee:
Thou art all perfection: *Diana* her self
Swells in thy thoughts, and moderates thy beauty. ...
... still as wanton *Cupid* blows Love-fires,
Adonis quenches out unchaste desires.   (II.ii.94–6, 101–2)

Susan's passion and garrulousness shock and confuse Frank, whose response affirms two quintessential distinctions between female and male virtue: he denies Susan's sexuality by expecting her to be an emblem of chastity, and he upholds the husband's duty to command by instructing his wife in female decorum. Before Susan reveals her passion, Frank cannot even contemplate her death:

> ... thou art so rare a goodness,
> As Death would rather put it self to death,
> Then murther thee. But we, as all things else,
> Are mutable and changing. (II.ii.138–41)

As a paragon of modesty, Susan is exempt from mutability; as a flesh-and-blood woman, Susan, like Mother Sawyer and Anne Ratcliff, pays dearly for her humanity.

Ignoring her husband's command to be silent, Susan importunes him (II.ii.107–9) to the point that her prattle makes her an easy victim: 'till this minute,' Frank charges, 'You might have safe returned; now you cannot: / You have dogg'd your own death' (III.iii.37–8). In Frank's claim that Susan has 'dogg'd' her own death, there is a direct association between Susan and carnality as represented by the Dog who courts Mother Sawyer and who independently paws Frank prior to Susan's murder (III.iii.15). Frank instinctively articulates the widespread suspicion that women are inherently disposed towards lust. Woman 'is more carnal than a man,' write the authors of the Malleus Maleficarum, 'as is clear from her many carnal abominations' for which 'there are more women than men found infected with the heresy of witchcraft.'[57] Susan dies because she cannot meet Frank's expectations of female virtue, whose cultural construction the play has emphasized.

The conclusion of the marriage plot is notable for its resistance to homiletic closure. Lying seriously ill as a result of a self-inflicted wound designed to make others believe he was attacked by Susan's murderers, Frank is overcome with remorse and guilt. He sleeps badly, eats little, and hallucinates about death, for which he longs. Unable to envision a better life, he muses on the possibility of suicide (IV.ii.19–27). In prison, he is forced to realize that he cannot escape divine justice. His repentance speech (V.iii.134–42), which includes the conventional didactic address to the audience, and which brings about society's forgiveness, conforms to the stock scaffold speeches of domestic tragedy, sharing with them the recognition of 'the justice of earthly punishment.'[58] However, Frank's didactic message to the world, namely that individuals should marry for love and not for material gain (V.iii.107–10), has a hollow ring when juxtaposed with the deep-seated impulses that have provoked Susan's murder. Unlike the heroine of A Woman Killed with Kindness, who 'dies repentant and in hope of heaven,'[59] Frank experiences an enduring spiritual malaise which further qualifies his repentance, for only the certainty of death gives him the inner strength to face his punishment.[60]

The final scenes, moreover, do not bring about a providential cleansing; instead, they highlight society's role in the tragic events we have been witnessing. On his way to Frank's hanging, Susan's grief-stricken father meets Mother Sawyer, who is being executed simultaneously for witchcraft. Without cause, Old Carter blindly accuses her of having been the 'instrument' (V.iii.21) of Frank's murder of Susan. A few moments later, however, when face to face with Frank, Old Carter acknowledges that social claims have been responsible for his daughter's demise: 'if thou had'st not had ill counsel, thou would'st not have done as thou didst' (ll. 116–18). Ironically, the 'ill counsel' to which Old Carter refers is neither palmistry nor witchcraft but his and Old Thorney's enforcement of Frank's marriage to Susan.

The marriage plot's complex structures are further clarified if we compare the Frank Thorney action with its analogue, George Wilkins's The Miseries of Enforced Marriage. Both plays open upon a pair of lovers promising to honour the contract per verba praesenti, by means of which they have secretly agreed to be husband and wife in the eyes of God;[61] and both trace the husband's fall from bridegroom to bigamist to repentant sinner. Wilkins, however, is chiefly concerned with the evil effects of forced marriage, not with the problematic relationship between character and social law. The two young lovers in The Miseries of Enforced Marriage, William Scarborow and Clare Harcop, are largely mouthpieces for companionate marriage, the betrothal scene celebrating the married couple as having been 'knit by heaven' (I, p. 480). William's subsequent bigamy and Clare's suicide are the tragic consequences of evil guardianship. Clare's suicide precipitates William's desertion of his other wife, Katherine, and his abandonment to a profligate life. William reaches the point where he contemplates murdering Katherine and his children, but his recognition of Katherine's virtue and the news of his evil guardian's death help to bring about his repentance. Before dying, the guardian had realized his cruelty and made appropriate amends by doubling William's inheritance. In the hastily contrived conclusion,

William and Katherine are reunited, and the play ends in praise of the workings of Providence:

> BUT[LER]. Heaven ... has his gracious eyes,
> To give men life, not life-entrapping spies. (V, p. 575)

In contrast, the deaths of Frank, Susan, Anne Ratcliff, and Mother Sawyer in *The Witch of Edmonton* stem from the characters' fragmentation, which is portrayed as inextricably linked to social barriers created by class, poverty, and misogyny. Interpreting the marriage code and the witchcraze as manifestations of a pervasive social anxiety, the play exposes the inadequacy of homiletic conclusions in mitigating tragic events.

5

Developments in Comedy

Prodigal Husbands and Patient Wives

Between 1600 and 1608 five comedies performed in the public theatres
reconstruct the Tudor Prodigal Son plots by focusing on the fall and
redemption of profligate husbands and the trials of the patient wife.
These comedies also retain the superstructure of domestic tragedy.
Alfred Harbage has observed that 'the "homiletic tragedies" in which
adultery leads to disaster are overwhelmed ... by what might be called,
with equal justice, the "homiletic comedies" where a woman's constancy
saves the day.'[1] *How a Man May Choose a Good Wife from a Bad* (generally
attributed to Thomas Heywood),[2] *The Fair Maid of Bristow*, *The London
Prodigal*, and the two parts of *The Honest Whore* have as a central character a heroine whose trials counterpose her husband's backsliding. The
Griselda archetype is modified in that the wife is now the husband's
social equal, and the emphasis is on her sexual fidelity. In addition to
the patient wife and prodigal husband (whose gambling and whoring
lead to insurmountable bad fortune) two of the plays include a lusty
admirer who pursues the patient wife. The virtue of all three characters
is tested but only the wife endures the trials, and at the end she humbly
receives her just rewards.[3] A peripheral figure is one who wields considerable authority (usually a father or a magistrate) and who functions
as the wife's protector. In *How a Man May Choose a Good Wife From a
Bad*, the prototype of these plays, the long-suffering Mistress Arthur is
subjected to the cruelty of her husband who poisons her in order to
please his mistress. The wife is rescued by a suitor who offers to marry
her and alleviate her misery, but she remains loyal to her marriage vow
of constancy. Her exemplary behaviour, which is assisted by Justice

Reason's protective influence, is commended by the community, and the play ends with the reformed prodigal's advice to would-be husbands concerning the merits of patient and self-effacing wives.

The prodigal's reformation and the wife's steadfastness are sanctioned by an extensive body of contemporary discourses, which provides instruction to those who would bring dishonour to their families. 'The prodigal,' writes Andrew Clark, 'compared with his original in the morality plays, is examined less as a general "moral" type than a contemporary *social* figure ... a transition symptomatic of the change overtaking both society and drama in the period, and already evident in [Wilkins's] *The Miseries.*'[4] An important consequence of the prodigal's eventual conformity to social norms is a considerable monetary reward made possible by the generosity of a rich relative.

As in domestic tragedy, however, the comedies treat contemporary social codes neither uniformly nor unequivocally. In some of these plays the tension between drama and the ideology of manners remains largely unalloyed, as it does in *How a Man May Choose* and to a great extent in *The Fair Maid of Bristow.* In the latter, the wild prodigal Edward Vallenger is disinherited by his father in order 'To make him see his sin' (IV.i.601),[5] and Edward's loyal wife Anabell never wavers in her conjugal fidelity or in her belief that she 'shall have a husband of new birth' (l. 603). Other plays anticipate the impulses of satirical comedy, in particular its overriding interest in sexual transgression within a money economy and in the exposure of folly and hypocrisy, usually of characters from the merchant class. *The London Prodigal* approaches the cynicism of Jacobean satire in its ambiguous treatment of marriage and the effects of wealth and social climbing. The father, Flowerdale Senior, is a wealthy London merchant who lacks both wisdom and propriety. Assisting his profligate son in scheming to retrieve the son's lost wealth, Flowerdale Senior deceives Sir Lancelot Spurcock (another rich merchant) into believing that a substantial will has been made out to his daughter Luce. Although Luce is promised in marriage to Sir Arthur Greenshield, whom she has vowed to 'affect / ... aboue any shuter' (i.e., 'suitor') (II.iii.1–2),[6] the mercenary Lancelot falls into the trap and forces Luce to marry young Flowerdale. The marriage to which the enforcement gives rise critiques the (social) need for the wife's submission at any cost.[7] While Luce, for example, resigns herself to having been 'inforced' and 'compelled' to marry by her father (III.iii.129), she also admits that 'hie heauen doth know, / With what vnwillingnesse I went to Church' (III.iii.127–8). Moreover, her decision to work towards con-

verting her libertine husband rather than annul the marriage is juxtaposed with her sister Delia's equally unremitting preference to remain
unmarried. Echoing Julia's misogamy in the 1599 *Patient Grissil*, Delia
boldly refuses to marry, pointing out that 'married life' is far harsher
for women than the ideal would suggest:

> Not that I doe condemne a married life,
> For tis no doubt a sanctimonious thing:
> But for the care and crosses of a wife,
> The trouble in this world that children bring;
> My vow is in heauen in earth to liue alone,
> Husbands, howsoeuer good, I will haue none. (V.i.463–8)

That Delia has been portrayed as neither lazy nor willful gives credence
to her misogamy. And while her scepticism is deflected by the comic
ending – the company is called to 'M(aister) *Ciuites* house' (V.i.473) for
a celebratory 'dinner' (l. 471) – her speech against marriage is never
contradicted, her would-be-suitor merely resigning himself to the fact
that, like many others, Delia 'will liue a Batcheller too' (l. 469).

The two parts of *The Honest Whore* reveal a more sustained resistance
to tidy play-making. Part I, by Dekker and Middleton, is a hybrid
domestic play which combines a loose blend of genres within three
separate plots, each of which reverses a central motif of domestic comedy. The romance plot, in which a hostile Duke tries to prevent the
marriage of his daughter and her suitor, alters the stock situation in
which a benign authority figure helps to bring about marital harmony.
In the domestic plot the heroine is not the conventional patient wife but
the prostitute Bellafront, whose conversion is followed by her marriage
to Matheo, the wastrel who originally seduced her. The subject of marriage, however, is relegated almost entirely to the Candido action, or the
merchant plot, which also has its separate conflicts and resolutions.[8]
Taken together, these disparate elements create a drama marked by
tentative narrative connections. Hippolito's suit in the romance plot, for
example, is only minimally tied to the Bellafront action through his
function as the courtesan's instructor in virtue, a role undermined by
his role as mad lover of the Duke's daughter Infelice.

The Bellafront action's debt to morality drama is often noted. Sylvia
Feldman argues that although 'a courtesan is a major character ... she
becomes the mankind figure, and the play deals with her regeneration';
and for Harry Keyishian, Bellafront's conversion represents the 'victory'

of 'traditional morality.'[9] The play, however, surpasses its morality-patterned analogues through two important modifications: (1) the homiletic
significance of Bellafront's progression from sin to reformation is undercut by her sustained passion for Hippolito and by her financially
opportunistic marriage to the gamester Matheo;[10] (2) in the Candido
plot, described in the quarto as being about 'The Humours of the
Patient Man,' homiletics are displaced by humour comedy.[11] The Candido action further transforms the patient wife into a patient 'mad-man'
(IV.iii.29–30)[12] ridiculed by a shrewish wife who commissions a guller
in order to thwart her husband's patience. Elsewhere, I have argued that
the Candido action demonstrates a strong debt to Italian popular comedy, in particular the *Commedia dell'arte*'s critique of an unbridled mercantile ethic as embodied by the senile Pantaloon, on whom Candido is
modelled. Candido's trials are remarkable for their absurdity; rather
than imitating the trials of the patient wife, they expose the merchant
as a Pantaloon or comic butt.[13]

Homiletic, melodramatic, and satirical structures clash in 1 *Honest
Whore* in such a way that characters who serve as models of ethical
conduct are at once venerated and exposed as foolish or mad. The
sequel demonstrates a more controlled dramatic interest in the myths
surrounding companionate marriage.[14] The Bellafront-Matheo action
rescues the patient wife and her prodigal husband from a reductive
literary and philosophical tradition, the tests of the patient wife becoming the trials of a converted prostitute struggling against both
economic deprivation and society's scepticism.[15] In the Infelice-Hip-
polito action, marital conflict is only tentatively resolved, with harmony being gained not through the wife's patience but through her
denial of it.

> INFE[LICE]. Were there no Men, Women might liue like gods.
> Guilty my Lord?
> HIP[POLITO]. Yes, guilty my good Lady.
> INF. Nay, you may laugh, but henceforth shun my bed,
> With no whores leauings Ile be poysoned.   (III.i.190–3)[16]

The pattern of sin, punishment, and redemption dramatized in the
prodigal husband action of the analogues is heavily qualified in that
Hippolito's adultery is never punished, and neither he nor Matheo is
given the prodigal's stock public-apology speech for reprobate behaviour. Hippolito comes close to an apology in his aphorism – "'Tis a good

signe when our cheekes blush at ill' (V.ii.192) – but it is a muted echo of young Flowerdale's confession to his wife in *The London Prodigal*:

> ... wonder among wiues!
> Thy chastitie and vertue hath infused
> Another soule in mee, red with defame,
> For in my blushing cheekes is seene my shame ...   (V.i.320–3)

and of Edward Vallenger's equally rhapsodic 'contryssion' (V.iii.1205) in *The Fair Maid of Bristow*:

> Sweet beautious lettes, the rauser of my smart,
> Forget in me what I haue done amisse,
> And seale my pardon with one balmy kisse
> My soule repents her lewd impyetie ...   (V.iii.1193–6)

Although Matheo's transgressions are redeemed in the end by his wife's patience and by the generosity of her father, Dekker alters the homiletic formula by having the prodigal remain silent during the remainder of the play. And while Matheo and Hippolito are pardoned, something of the ruthless remains in both characters.

The Household, the Brothel, and the House of Correction

Underlying the comic admixtures of the *Honest Whore* plays is an impulse which Northrop Frye ascribes to 'ironic comedy,' both classical and Renaissance, namely a 'tendency ... to ridicule and scold an audience assumed to be hankering after sentiment, solemnity, and ... approved moral standards.'[17] In addition to modifying the themes of patience and prodigality, the plays' textual strategies involve the scrutiny of another fundamental *topos* of domestic drama, namely the cult of hospitality as practised within sumptuous domestic spaces. We have seen how domestic tragedies exploit what Henry Wotton describes as 'the *Theater* of ... *Hospitality*, the *Seate* of *Selfe-fruition*,' which governs 'every Mans proper *Mansion* House and *Home*.'[18] In domestic comedy, hospitality becomes the *sine qua non* of the ideal householder's active virtue. The genre echoes a vast body of literature depicting hospitality as a duty sanctioned both by classical authorities and the biblical injunction, 'Be not forgetful to entertain strangers: for thereby some have entertained angels unawares' (AV, Hebrews 13:2).[19] In *How a Man May*

Choose hospitality deflects the adversity which the virtuous wife experiences at the hands of her cruel husband. Mistress Arthur maintains a decorous household despite her spouse's infidelities, her neighbourliness attenuating her suffering. The wife's hospitality also upholds the Christian household's obligation of neighbourliness to the poor: 'men,' she exclaims, 'though they be poor, / Should not be scorn'd' (ii, p. 85), her charity preserving the family's honour through the expression of good will towards others.[20]

Through hospitality the patient wife can transform the household into a private sanctuary. But as we saw in *A Woman Killed with Kindness* open-handed hospitality, offered to friends and family or to passers-by, is not only a Christian but also a social obligation. In the early modern period, notes Felicity Heal, hospitality becomes 'a household activity, emanating from the *domus* and concerned with the dispensing of those goods best afforded by it – food, drink and accommodation.'[21] John Taylor, the water-poet, defines the hospitable household as the supreme sign of the 'worthy' British gentleman and wife, whose noblesse oblige is determined by the number of guests they can accommodate, as well as by the variety of the entertainment and the quantity of the provisions they dispense free of charge.

Suppose ten, fifteene, or twenty men and horses come to lodge at their house, the men shall have flesh, tame and wild-fowle, fish, with all varietie of good cheere, good lodging, and welcome; and the horses shall want neither hay or provender; and at the morning at their departure, the reckoning is just nothing. This is the worthy gentlemans use, his chiefe delight being only to give strangers entertainement *gratis*.[22]

Hervet's translation (1534) of Xenophon's description of the householder's duties underscores in similar terms the social obligation to be generous to many:

... ye must nedes make many feastes and many great bankettes, or the people will scante abyde the syght of you. More ouer ye must receive into your houses many strangers, and intreate them honorably, keping good hospitalitee. Furthermore, ye must byd many men to dyner, and do them some pleasure, or elles at your nede, ye shall haue no manne to helpe you.[23]

Although ideally hospitality is to be exercised by individuals from all social classes, it is also an important indicator of social status. In *The*

Gentile Sinner Clement Ellis defines the model host who keeps 'Hospitality his Housekeeper, Providence his Steward, Charity his Treasurer' as a nobleman or gentleman.[24]

By the sixteenth century hospitality becomes identified with the gentry's and citizens' imitation of courtliness. As a social obligation, hospitality is an expression of courtesy and civility. Early modern definitions of hospitality frequently conflate it with courtesy, so that hospitality signifies not only 'generosity, benevolence, goodness' but also 'courtly elegance and politeness of manners' (*OED*). Anxious to sustain her role as model housewife and neighbour, Mistress Arthur in *How a Man May Choose* instructs her servants in deference as she awaits her distinguished guests: 'There was a curtsy! let me see't again; / Ay, that was well' (III.iii, p. 54). Completely lacking in irony, these scenes show the wife trusting the security of her marriage entirely to heaven, her chief concern being propriety and good manners: she worries, for example, that her 'guests will come / Ere we be ready' and that a servant 'cannot keep his fingers from the roast' (III.iii, pp. 54–5).

'Hospitality,' Wotton reminds his readers, is also 'a kinde of priuate *Princedome*' which 'may well deserve ... according to the degree of the *Master*, to be ... *delightfully* adorned.'[25] Wotton's definition of hospitality as an expression of the sumptuous household's adornment further associates hospitality with prosperity. John Gore, the rector of Wendenlofts in Essex, explained in a sermon preached at Paul's Cross that inward and outward prosperity are entirely compatible: while 'it is a blessing to have the grace of the Spirit and to prosper inwardly,' it is also 'a great blessing to have the wealth of the world and to prosper outwardly.'[26] *How a Man May Choose*, like *A Woman Killed with Kindness*, constructs the prosperous English household according to the measure of 'extent and variety'of hospitality[27] Mistress Arthur's neighbourliness is facilitated by the expensive provisions and furnishings that attest to her elevated social status.

MRS ART. Come, spread the table; is the hall well-rubb'd?
The cushions in the windows neatly laid?
The cupboard of plate set out? the casements stuck
With rosemary and flowers? the carpets brush'd?
MAID. Ay, forsooth, mistress.
MRS ART. Look to the kitchen-maid, and bid the cook take down the
oven-stone, [lest] the pies be burned ...
MAID. Yes, forsooth, mistress.

MRS ART. Where's that knave Pipkin? bid him spread the cloth.
Fetch the clean diaper napkins from my chest,
Set out the gilded salt, and bid the fellow
Make himself handsome, get him a clean band.   (III.iii, p. 54)

In Tilney's *Flower of Friendship* (1573) the Lady Julia warns that the married woman 'must be ... verye carefull, and circumspect of hir good name'; the 'chiefest way ... to preserve and maintaine this good fame, is to be resident in hir owne house. For an honest woman in sobernes, keping well hir house, gayneth thereby great reputation ...' With respect to her 'huswifery,' it must 'be well done ... even in thinges of least importaunce.'[28]

A great deal of the action of *How a Man May Choose* revolves around the preparation of meals. Cooking, writes Lu Emily Pearson, 'like ornate architecture or elaborate dress or anything else that might impress one's acquaintances with a display of wealth,' became in the early modern period an important sign of social rank.[29] In *The English Hus-Wife* (1615) Gervase Markham advises the female reader to develop and refine 'her skill in Physicke, Cookery, Banqueting-stuffe, Distillation ... Baking, and all other things belonging to an Household,' skills which attest to the 'inward and outward vertues which ought to be in a compleat woman.'[30] As early as the fifteenth and as late as the seventeenth century, class differences in what people consumed, and especially in what they ate, became more important than geographical differences. Meat, for example, such as that being prepared by Mistress Arthur's servants for Justice Reason and other wealthy guests (III.iii, pp. 54–5), was costly and not readily available, its consumption linked with the households of the privileged classes.[31]

The relation between prosperity, neighbourly reciprocity, and social status is explored in an earlier, 'peripherally domestic'[32] comedy, *The Two Angry Women of Abington* (c. 1598). From the outset the married couples try to outdo one another in courtesy. The dialogue emphasizes the preoccupation with 'quittance,' 'debt,' and 'disburse[ment],' throwing into relief the burdens and anxieties underlying 'familiar neighbourhood':

GOURSEY. Good Master Barnes, this entertain of yours,
So full of courtesy and rich delight,
Makes me misdoubt my poor ability
In quittance of this friendly courtesy.
BARNES. O Master Goursey, neighbour amity

Is such a jewel of high-reckoned worth,
As for the attain of it, what would not I
Disburse: it is so precious in my thoughts. ...
... truly I esteem
Mere amity, familiar neighbourhood,
The cousin-german unto wedded love. ...
MRS GOURSEY. O, Master Barnes ...
... 'tis we that are
Indebted to your kindness for this cheer,
Which debt, that we may repay, I pray let's have
Sometimes your company at our homely house.   (I.i. 1–8, 16–18, 32–6)[33]

In the denouement, the conflicts provoked by the anxieties attending debt are displaced by the trope of 'good will' (V.v.2898), the characters heeding Sir Ralph's 'courte[ous]' invitation (l. 2861) to 'rejoice' at 'dinner time' as his 'promised guests' and at his expense (ll. 2854–60). The trope also informs the final scenes of *How a Man May Choose, The Fair Maid of Bristow,* and *The London Prodigal,* in which the reconciliations between husbands and wives include the reaffirmation of their goodwill towards their communities.

The *Honest Whore* plays configure a more problematic link between the various tropes of civility and domesticity. In Part I, the Candido action builds on the parallel between the merchant's home and Bellafront's (bawdy) house, a parallel that has been ignored in critical assessments of the play. Peter Ure suggests that Part I achieves dramatic unity in that 'the converted shrew of the Candido scenes matches the converted courtesan of the Bellafront scenes'; and R.J. Palumbo argues for a 'thematic contrast between Candido and Bellafront' on the basis that Candido's role as an ideal tradesman and husband enhances the social order, while Bellafront's 'function – prostitute – is part of a custom that brings social disorder.'[34] The contrast along moral lines between the Candido and Bellafront actions is dramatically tidy, and obfuscates the more unsettling correspondences which link the sale of flesh with the sale of cloth. Both Candido and Bellafront ply a trade, and both consider human interaction in terms of how it furthers their economic ends. The scene immediately following Candido's sale of a penny's worth of cloth to the gullers introduces Bellafront who is described by a courtier in terms of linen: 'A skin, your satten is not more soft, nor lawne whiter' (II.i.172). The prostitute's trade is similar to the merchant's in that Bellafront must also comply with the demands of her customers.

In order to prosper Bellafront would please the devil himself 'Could the diuel put on a humane shape' (II.i.341); and Candido, who declares that he 'meanes to thriue,' avows that he would 'please the diuell, if he come to buy' (I.v.127–8).

'Hospitality,' writes Daryl Palmer, 'encourages a benign description of the world, even as it supports strategies of exploitation.'[35] In both Candido's and Bellafront's houses the bond between host and guest fosters economic prosperity through exploitation. Like the courtesan, Candido extends hospitality to those who can advance his wealth and prestige. We learn, for example, that Candido has 'vppon a time inuited home to his house certaine Neapolitane lordes of curious taste, and no meane pallats, coniuring his wife ... to prepare cheere fitting for such honourable trencher-men' (I.iv.25–8); while they waited, he 'entertained the lordes, and with courtly discourse beguiled the time' (l. 33). Although we never see Candido turning anyone away, his courtesy is never extended to the less fortunate, even though his trade is among the most prosperous.[36] Candido's selective hospitality accords with the anxiety surrounding friendship and courtesy in the early modern age as not entirely guaranteed by affective feelings but by external influences such as wealth, social position, and family objectives.[37]

In a striking juxtaposition, the scene in which Candido invites his wealthy customers to dinner (Part I, I.v.230–1) is immediately followed by Bellafront seated at her toilet preparing to receive her 'guests' (II.i.46). On one hand, the bawdy exchange between pimp and whore parodies the motif of the 'lady at her toilette' commonly found in Renaissance iconography and lyric poetry, in which an eroticized female figure is seated in her closet at her dressing table, gazing at her beauty and grace.[38] Formerly places of devotion, small rooms divided by a 'doore' (II.i.44), as is Bellafront's closet, were beginning to assume a distinctly secular value.[39] While witnessing the prostitute at her toilette, the audience is treated to an elaborate tableau of her private chambers, the brusque, energetic dialogue between whore and pimp further parodying the activities and rituals that attend private space.

> *Enter Roger with a stoole, cushin, looking-glasse, and chafing-dish. Those being set downe, he pulls out of his pocket, a violl with white cullor in it, and two boxes, one with white, another red painting ...*
> *Enter Bellafront not full ready, without a gowne, shee sits downe, with her bodkin curles her haire, cullers her lips.*
> BELL. Wheres my ruffe and poker you block-head?

ROG. Your ruffe, and your poker, are ingendring together vpon the
cup-bord of the Court, or the Court-cup-bord.
BELL. Fetch'em: Is the poxe in your hammes, you can goe no faster? ...
ROG. Thers your ruffe, shall I poke it?
BELL. Yes honest *Roger*, no stay: pry thee good boy, hold here ...
Pox on you, how doest thou hold my glasse?
ROG. Why, as I hold your doore: with my fingers. ...
BELL. Gods my pittikins, some foole or other knocks.
ROG. Shall I open to the foole mistresse? ...
BELL. ... hee shall serue for my breakefast, tho he goe against my
   stomack. (II.i.15–56)

The popular typology of camaraderie and hospitality between householders, servants, and guests is invested with grotesque overtones in
the racy dialogue, grounding Bellafront's trade in a world of exchange
and barter in which the prostitute and her 'guests' cannibalize one
another – 'hee shall serue for my breakefast, tho he goe against my
stomack' (l. 56).

Like the linendraper, the courtesan is 'hospitable' in order to meet her
material needs. The *domus* is not a fixed point of virtue and stability –
it has become a site of economic exchange and reciprocity.

The link between merchant and whore is common in sixteenth- and
seventeenth-century satirical and courtly literature; one of the earliest
examples is found in Giovanni della Casa's *Galateo Ovvero de' Costumi*
(1558), in which the harlot is anxious to hawk her wares and sell them
at a good price.[40] The alliance between household and brothel is also
found in the comedy of the Italian Cinquecento, when perspective
scenery was introduced. The Venetian architect and designer Sebastiano
Serlio (1475–1554) writes that the domestic dwellings in comedies
should be those of 'personaggi privati, come saria di cittadini, avocati,
mercanti, parasiti, & altre simili persone' (private persons, such as
citizens, lawyers, merchants, parasites, and other similar people); street
scenes are also suitable for comedy, and a brothel clearly demarcated
must be located immediately adjacent to the door of the smallest and
nearest citizen's house, together with a church, an inn, and shops.
Further specifications indicate practical windows and balconies, facilitat-
ing numerous sexual encounters.[41]

In *1 Honest Whore* the link between household and shop, and between
household and brothel, posits a similar assault on notions of civility and
the ideal marriage. Moving rapidly from household to household, the

plots converge in Bedlam which is described as a 'house' (V.ii.108) and in which Bellafront is referred to as a 'huswife' (l. 300). All of the couples are reunited in marriage, a dramatic convention severely undercut by the setting.[42] The couples solidify their marriage vows in Bedlam because, according to Matheo, 'none goes to be married till he be starke mad' (V.ii.35). The spoof on married love is sustained in Candido's panegyric in praise of Patience as 'the sap' of spiritual 'blisse' (V.ii.512), an utterance whose homiletic import is undermined by its *reductio ad absurdum* to 'the hunny gainst a waspish wife' (l. 514). Finally, as a portrait of a world 'vpside downe' (IV.iii.63) the asylum scene casts doubt upon the Duke's cheerful pronouncement that 'henceforth' everyone will find 'happinesse' and 'be blest' because 'Our families shall ... breath[e] in rest' (V.ii.391–2).

Paralleling the retreat to Bedlam at the end of 1 *Honest Whore*, the denouement of Part II subjects the spectator to a tour of yet another 'house,' this time Bridewell, the notorious House of Correction. On the surface, the Bridewell scene appears to lack proportion in that it ends the play without appropriate attention to the central characters, who are almost forgotten amid the Duke's arraignment of all the prostitutes in the city.[43] Yet the obtrusion of the irrepressible 'whores' and their pimp, who are pursued by constables and 'Beadles, one with Hempe, the other with a Beetle' (a 'pestle or mallet for pounding, mashing' [*OED*]) (*s.d.*, V.ii.214), serves both to blur the melodramatic effect of the final act and to highlight class tensions at the very moment when the patient wife is garnering her rewards for virtue. 'Domestic comedy,' writes Northrop Frye, 'is usually based on the Cinderella archetype ... the incorporation of an individual very like the reader into the society aspired to by both, a society ushered in with a happy rustle of bridal gowns and banknotes.'[44] Bridewell, with its emphasis on unruliness, repression, and toil, is an inversion of the idealized society towards which domestic comedy typically leads.

A professional writer who was imprisoned for debt in the Poultry Counter in 1598, and in the King's Bench Prison from 1613 to 1620, Dekker goes beyond the conventional stage practice of depicting Bridewell as merely of topographical interest.[45] 2 *Honest Whore* atypically portrays the House of Correction as a jail for the punishment of those who transgress social codes. In *A Survey of London* (1603) John Stow had stressed the cooperation between the aristocracy and the citizens in the creation of Bridewell, the 'sundrie well disposed' citizens' 'good and charitable prouisions ... for the poore' contributing to a well-run operation.[46] Dekker's guard praises in similar terms the orderliness and sense of purpose with which the inmates set about their daily tasks: 'All here are but one swarme of Bees,' he boasts, 'and striue / To bring with wearied thighs honey to the Hiue' (V.ii.35–6). But at the same time as the guard articulates the popular view of Bridewell's inception, he makes an unexpected disclosure: 'Fortune can tosse the World, a Princes Court / Is thus a prison now' (V.ii.16–17). The equation of Bridewell with prison is a notable departure from Stow, as is the extensive description of the types of punishment to which all inmates are subjected regardless of their offence:

> The sturdy Begger, and the lazy Lowne,
> Gets here hard hands, or lac'd Correction.
> The Vagabond growes stay'd, and learnes to 'bey,
> The Drone is beaten well, and sent away.
> As other prisons are, (some for the Thiefe,
> Some, by which vndone Credit gets reliefe
> From bridled Debtors; others for the poore)
> So this is for the Bawd, the Rogue, and Whore.   (V.ii.37–44)

Unlike the wholesome picture of the workhouse drawn by Stow, 'wherein a great number of vagrant persons be now set a worke, and relieued at the charges of the cittizens,'[47] Dekker's tour of Bridewell exposes not only the prison atmosphere but also the ineffectualness of the 'work' ethic practised there.

The problem is foregrounded in the exchange between the aristocrats and the rebellious prostitute Dorathea Target:

> DUKE. Why is this wheele borne after her?
> I. MASTER. She must spinne.
> DOR. A coorse thred it shall be, as all threds are.
> ASTO[LFO]. If you spin, then you'll earne money here too?
> DOR. I had rather get halfe a Crowne abroad, then ten Crownes here. ...
> INFAE[LICE]. Doest thou not weepe now thou art here?
> DOR. Say yee? weepe? yes forsooth ... doe you not heare how I weep?
> *Sings.*
>   (V.ii.289–94, 296–8)

Dorathea's spirited insubordination demonstrates the failure of one of the chief aims of the early modern House of Correction, namely to render the labour of idle individuals socially beneficial.[48] The new use of the workhouse as a prison was a radical departure from existing practices which derived from the belief that rehabilitation was achievable simply by the deterrent loss of individual liberty. Bridewell, writes Michel Foucault, came to possess 'not only the aspect of a forced labor camp, but also that of a moral institution responsible for punishing, for correcting a certain moral "abeyance" which ... cannot be corrected by the severity of penance alone.'[49]

Instead of witnessing the reformation of the Bridewell inmates which ideally should result from the 'Charitable vse' (V.ii.53) to which they are put, the audience is forced to take stock of the various punitive mechanisms regularly used by beadles: 'the whip' (V.ii.47); 'the Anuill' (l. 51); 'blowes' (l. 52); the 'Bason' (a piece of cast-iron) (s.d., V.ii.367); the 'blue Gowne' ('the dress of ignominy for a harlot' [OED]); 'Chalke and ... Mallet' (s.d., V.ii.312). Carolo's quip – 'An excellent Teeme of Horse' (V.ii.45) – underscores the dehumanizing punishments that prevail here. Demonstrating a willingness to obey only after they have submitted to 'beat[ings]' and 'lac'd Correction' (i.e., whipping, usually at the tail of a cart) and having acquired 'hard hands,' the inmates are thereupon released.[50] The discrepancy between the official view of Bridewell and the coercive place which Dekker reveals it to be, is reinforced in the guard's sceptical reply to Infelice's claim that Bridewell 'should make euen Lais honest' (V.ii.254). Suddenly confessing doubt about the universal value of prison, the guard admits to the general failure of its practices:

> Some it turnes good,
> But (as some men whose hands are once in blood,
> Doe in a pride spill more) so, some going hence,
> Are (by being here) lost in more impudence ... (V.ii.254–7; emphasis added)

The guard's misgivings belie his former maxim that 'Here Prouidence and Charity play such parts, / The House is like a very Schoole of Arts' (V.ii.28–9).[51]

Dekker's critique of the ethical imperative of punishment forestalls the conventional melodramatic ending of the marriage plot. As early as Act II, Bellafront had attributed her prodigal husband's 'wilde ... behauiour' (II.i.49) not only to a predisposition to vice, as is customary in domestic comedy, but also to his having been 'spoyld (i.e., "ruined" [OED]) by prison,' where 'he's halfe damned comes there' (l. 50). The prototypes of the prodigal husband – Young Arthur in *How a Man May Choose*, Mat Flowerdale in *The London Prodigal*, and Edward Vallenger in *The Fair Maid of Bristow* – are wastrels and profligates who reject their families, and whom Providence punishes with insurmountable ill fortune, but their reformation prevents any actual experience in prison.

Amid the Bridewell setting, Bellafront reaps her rewards for patience: like her counterparts in the play's analogues she is reunited with her husband, beginning life anew with the blessing of the Duke and with a handsome financial reward from her father. The social elevation of the couple contrasts sharply with the poverty and petty crimes for which the other Bridewell inmates have been incarcerated, underscoring the contradictions in Bellafront's 'new' world. The Duke's pronouncement, in the concluding lines of the play, that the city of London shall be a 'Spheare' of 'patience' and virtue (V.ii.495, 494) is a standard comic vehicle through which the old society is replaced with a renewed and healthier one. In counterpoint to the Duke's festive tone, the events in Bridewell have revealed a world of repression and chance – a world in which justice is arbitrarily dispensed, and in which those whose crime is to be poor and idle are punished and forced to perform dehumanizing tasks for their livelihood.

Whereas the final scenes of domestic comedy typically end in celebration of the reunited couples amid 'ioyfull mirth,' 'sportfull houres' (*Faire Maide of Bristow*, V.iii.1214, 1224) and 'feast[ing]' (*The London Prodigal*, V.i.443), the tragic tone of the Bridewell and Bedlam episodes in *The Honest Whore* plays casts doubt upon the widespread social regeneration promised by the Duke.

Epilogue

When *The Late Lancashire Witches* was published in 1634 domestic drama was already in decline. The waning of the genre's popularity coincides with widespread changes in dramatic fashion and taste, and with increasing social stratification.[1] Towards the middle of the seventeenth century, those plays specifically concerned with domestic conflict increasingly conform to the popular drama of manners with its emphasis on the illicit love duel. In the drama of the Restoration, domestic themes are subsumed within the satirical game of love. The satire revolves around marriage as the catalyst of disorder, although in the end characters usually forgo intrigue in favour of the status quo. The principal character is the rake (a distant relative of the prodigal husbands of early domestic drama) who scorns the constraints of marriage, but usually has the good sense to know when the game must be abandoned.

A different type of 'domestic play' appears with English Sentimental Comedy. In reaction against the code of illicit love reflected in the drama of manners, which, in the words of Jeremy Collier in his celebrated attack on the English stage, 'rewarded debauchery,' 'ridiculed virtue and learning,' and was 'disserviceable to probity and religion,'[2] English Sentimental Comedy revolves around didactic, sentimental vignettes of family life. In Richard Steele's *The Conscious Lovers* (1722), a prototype of the new domestic comedy, the hero is conscientious and morally faultless; he scorns cupidity and is kind to his servants. He is guided by an unfailing sense of honour and is above earthly passions, as evidenced by the personal sacrifice that he endures for the sake of his family's reputation. Although he loves the heroine, Indiana, he resolves to please his parents by marrying Lucinda, a decision agreed to by the equally noble Indiana.

Sentimental Comedy, which is closely related to the French *comédie larmoyante*, consistently sacrifices dramatic complexity for didacticism. The genre develops alongside the new domestic tragedies of Edward Moore, George Lillo, and Nicholas Rowe, who, like their early modern counterparts, alter the basic paradigm of heroic tragedy by making commoners – in this case middle-class characters – the protagonists of their plays. Lillo's *The London Merchant* (1731) inspired G.E. Lessing in Germany to write *Miss Sara Sampson* (1755) in his attempt to liberate German theatre from neoclassicism and to inspire middle-class tragedy. Although unequivocally didactic, *The London Merchant* contains the dramatically rich portrait of Millwood, the scornful but generous and witty prostitute who recalls the spirited heroines of the earlier English domestic plays. Millwood's bold pronouncements on the determining force of necessity upon personal desire echo the recalcitrance of Alice Arden, Bellafront, and Elizabeth Sawyer.

During the French Enlightenment domestic tragedy is reformulated in the plays and dramatic theories of Denis Diderot. Applying the term 'tragédie domestique et bourgeoise'[3] to his plays and to those of his predecessors, Moore and Lillo, whom he praises for heralding the new drama, Diderot distinguishes three characteristics of eighteenth-century domestic drama: (1) it must be serious, its subject morally significant, and the intrigue simple, domestic, and close to real life; (2) character must always be subordinate to plot; (3) the action must express pathos and inspire sentiment.[4] Diderot praises Moore's *Gamester*, which he translated, and Lillo's *London Merchant* in particular for incorporating these important dramatic principles, and applauds the manner in which the authors treat domestic and social problems in didactic, sentimental scenes leading to happy resolutions.

For Diderot, the basic function of the 'domestic theatre' is to perpetrate bourgeois values, the measure of a dramatist's success being the ability to flatter the audience. In an essay on dramatic language Diderot writes that the playwright's duty is to instruct the spectator, who must never be led to question the bourgeois order:

Tout doit être clair pour le spectateur. Confident de chaque personnage, instruit de ce qui s'est passé et de ce qui ce passe; il y a cent moment où l'on n'a rien de mieux à faire que de lui déclarer nettement ce qui se passera.

[All must be clear to the spectator, who must anticipate the fate of each character and be instructed in all that has passed and all that shall come to pass on stage. There must be many instances in which the spectator has nothing better to do than to anticipate what shall transpire.][5]

Diderot's is not a theatre interested in challenging the audience's expectations: 'que les spectateurs s'avancent au dénouement sans s'en douter' (the spectators must proceed to the resolution without ever doubting their own judgments).[6] At the same time that Diderot does not wish to disturb the spectator's complacency, we detect a note of condescension towards the audience that must be protected from complexity and ambiguity.

In Diderot's enthusiasm for the domestic plays of his English predecessors, he is conspicuously silent about the early modern drama. One possible reason for the neglect is that Diderot's theatre, as Michel Grivelet suggests, is much less domestic than it is bourgeois.[7] Diderot is interested neither in portraying character dialectically nor in scrutinizing the ideology of bourgeois domesticity, but in attaching importance to characters and sentiments which have been absent from the French stage. The domestic situation, notes Grivelet, has less intrinsic value for Diderot than does the social status of the characters (merchant, judge, lawyer, politician, citizen, magistrate, and so on).[8] By populating the stage with 'fathers, husbands, sisters, brothers,'[9] Diderot hopes to instruct in social conduct the class that now exerts power and influence. What Diderot's 'domestic and bourgeois theatre' does challenge, however, is the legitimacy of the aristocratic order which his audience is engaged in displacing.

The complex dramaturgy that informs early modern domestic drama more closely approximates the theatre of Ibsen and Arthur Miller than it does English Sentimental Comedy or the derivative theatre of Diderot. In *A Doll's House* Torvald Helmer recalls the self-satisfied husbands of domestic tragedy whose marriages, like those of George Sanders and Master Arden, break down when their wives realize that marriage has forfeited their agency. Nora rejects her life as a 'doll-child,'[10] denying the concept of the *mulier economica*. During her struggle to sustain the secret payments to Krögstad, Nora realizes that she must reject the notion of female self-denial:

NORA. ... It has been by no means easy for me to meet my commitments punctually ... there is something that is called, in business, quarterly interest, and another thing called payment in instalments, and it is always so dreadfully difficult to manage them. I have had to save a little here and there, where I could ... I haven't been able to put aside much from my housekeeping money, for Torvald likes good food ... Last winter I was lucky enough to get a lot of copying to do; so I locked myself up and sat writing every evening until quite late at night. Often I was desperately

> tired; but all the same it was a tremendous pleasure to sit there working
> and earning money. It was like being a man. (I, pp. 14–15)

Nora's struggle teaches her to value not patience but activity and independence, values traditionally associated with men. When Nora finally reproaches her husband, her words attest to her realization: 'I have waited so patiently for eight years; for goodness knows, I knew very well that wonderful things don't happen every day ... As I am now, I am no wife for you' (III, pp. 70–1). Nora rejects Torvald's definition of her as 'Before all else ... a wife and a mother' (III, p. 68); and in her claim 'that before all else I am a reasonable human being' (III, p. 70) she echoes an earlier defiance of a misogynist tradition that denies to woman the capability of reason and requires her to submit to the will of men.

The construction of the patient wife is also exploited in Miller's *Death of a Salesman*. Most of the action takes place in Willy and Linda Loman's tiny frame house. Willy Loman, a distant counterpart of the erring husband in early English domestic drama, is married to a dutiful and solicitous wife whom he has betrayed. Linda's patience, however, is shown to be as destructive as Willy's dream of success; and Linda's importunities, like Susan's in *The Witch of Edmonton*, cannot in the end redeem her husband from himself. A similar pattern informs Ibsen's *The Wild Duck*, whereby Hjalmar Ekdal's struggle derives from the tension between a comfortable life of illusion, represented by his elegant house, and his dream of art and freedom, represented by the wild duck. Smug, well fed, and complacent in his domestic comfort, Hjalmar fills his ennui with the vague and unsubstantial dream of being a great inventor, from which he awakens into despair. The affirmation of one's self-worth, which Miller sees as 'the underlying struggle ... of the individual' seeking to acquire a '"rightful" position' in the world, is, he argues, at the heart of tragedy, including those plays whose protagonists are from the common ranks: 'No tragedy can ... come about when its author fears to question absolutely everything, when he regards any institution, habit or custom as being either everlasting, immutable or inevitable.'[11] In domestic tragedy, the site of that struggle is the family, the institution from which the struggle 'extends itself ... into society ... broach[ing] those questions of social status, social honor and recognition, which expand its vision and lift it out of the merely particular toward the fate' of an entire culture.[12]

Ibsen and Miller, of course, are not the only modern dramatists who have exploited the themes and structures of early modern domestic drama. Other playwrights, among them Caryl Churchill, Tennessee Williams, and Eugene O'Neill, have also contributed to the genre's reconstitution in the twentieth century. *Long Day's Journey Into Night* especially warrants mention here because the power of the tragedy derives largely from O'Neill's intense focus on the *domus*. The latter is persistently threatened by fog, which throughout the play presses thickly against the window-panes. A foghorn is heard at intervals, alerting us to the family's fate. The haunting sound of the foghorn underscores the emptiness of the interior set. The play opens on the 'living room of the Tyrones' summer home / 8:30 A.M. of a day in August, 1912'; at the rear of the set

> are two double doorways with portières. The one at right leads into a front parlor with the formally arranged, set appearance of a room rarely occupied. The other opens on a dark, windowless back parlor, never used except as a passage from living room to dining room.[13]

The action unfolds before the doorways, in the shabby living room which holds a 'small bookcase' (s.d., I, p. 11) filled with important books. The Tyrone family acts out their despair in the mid-region between the bright and formal exterior which is the front parlour, and the darkness of the inner room. The characters confront themselves and one another, gradually wearing away at the protective veneer of their lives until each faces her or his own tragic destiny and that of the others with a measure of tolerance and pity. Mary Cavan Tyrone describes the tragic consequences awaiting those who cling to idealism and illusion: 'None of us can help the things life has done to us. They're done before you realize it, and once they're done they make you do other things until at last everything comes between you and what you'd like to be' (II.i, p. 61).

The facility with which we may locate the literary roots of a modern dramatic tradition suggests that there is much to recommend the earlier domestic play to the age in which we live.

Notes

Introduction

1 Thomas Heywood, *A Woman Killed with Kindness*, ed. R.W. Van Fossen. Further references to the play will be to this edition.

2 *A Warning for Fair Women*, ed. Charles Dale Cannon. Further references to the play will be to this edition.

3 Thomas Heywood, *An Apology for Actors*, 1612, sigs. B3r, G1r. Heywood elsewhere plays on the double meaning: in *The Rape of Lucrece*, p. 175, and in *The Captives* (see epigraph, above), p. 53.

4 Heywood, *Apology*, sig. G1r.

5 Heywood, *Apology*, sig. B5v, G1r.

6 Collier, *The History of English Dramatic Poetry to the time of Shakespeare: and Annals of the Stage to the Restoration*, vol 3, p. 49.

7 In *A Warning for Fair Women*, for example, we are told that the tragedy is both 'well knowne' (Prologue, l. 96) and 'true' (Epilogue, l. 2729). On the documentary texture of the murder plays see Doran, *Endeavors of Art*, p. 143; Sturgess, Introduction, *Three Elizabethan Domestic Tragedies*, pp. 8–9; and Gurr, *Playgoing in Shakespeare's London*, pp. 112 and 143–4. All extant and lost domestic plays are surveyed in Andrew Clark, *Domestic Drama*, vol 2, pp. 382ff.

8 Ward, Preface, *A Woman Killed with Kindness*, p. xiii.

9 Powell, *English Domestic Relations, 1487–1653*, p. 192, n. 1. Velte observed that 'simple direct accounts of tragic occurrences' are situated 'in the homes of ordinary citizens' (*The Bourgeois Elements in the Dramas of Thomas Heywood*, p. 101); Cromwell considered 'the common relations of family life' essential to the action (*Thomas Heywood: A Study in the Elizabethan Drama of Everyday Life*, p. 73); and Arthur M. Clark characterized the

genre as 'that body of plays which centres in the home and the institution of the family' (*Thomas Heywood: Playwright and Miscellanist*, p. 228).

10 Adams, *English Domestic or, Homiletic Tragedy 1575–1642*, p. viii.

11 Adams, *English Domestic or, Homiletic Tragedy 1575–1642*, p. 185.

12 Harbage, *Shakespeare and the Rival Traditions*, p. 235.

13 Wright, *Middle-Class Culture in Elizabethan England*, p. 638. Wright's whole-sale definition of 'middle-class' spectators has more recently been adopted by Susan P. Cerasano in her study of the writers, players, and audiences of the First Fortune Playhouse (1600–21), the most important public theatre of its day. Heywood, Dekker, and Middleton, the chief Fortune playwrights, are depicted as shrewd and perceptive of their audience's lack of 'cultural sophistication: naive, conservative, often complacent in its own ignorance'; and the plays are deemed more likely 'to [have] created a secure position from which the middle-class viewer could be coaxed to consider alternatives to his own conduct and morality than to openly challenge bourgeois values' ('Alleyn's Fortune: The Biography of a Playhouse,' p. 144). In *Dekker and Heywood: Professional Dramatists* Kathleen McLuskie corrects the longstanding view of Dekker and Heywood as playwrights who merely catered to the unsophisticated tastes and expectations of popular audiences. Like Shakespeare, she points out, Dekker and Heywood 'were professionals, and it is as professionals that their work offers a useful vantage point from which to understand the conditions of theatre as it became firmly established in the artistic and commercial world of London at the turn of the seventeenth century' (p. 1). Yet in her analysis of the two dramatists' works McLuskie sometimes falls back on conventional assessments, citing their 'commitment to old-fashioned values and styles of popular entertainment' (p. 75).

14 Harrison, *The Description of England* (1577, 1587), pp. 94–118. Cf. Smith, *De Republica Anglorum: A Discourse on the Commonwealth of England*, chs. 16–24.

15 Gurr, *Playgoing in Shakespeare's London*, p. 49.

16 Anne Jennalie Cook argues that Elizabethan audiences consisted almost exclusively of those privileged few who 'ruled the political world, the mercantile world, and the rest of the cultural world,' and who 'stood firmly apart from the mass of society' (*The Privileged Playgoers of Shakespeare's London, 1576–1642*, p. 272); Hattaway generally concurs, suggesting that 'the number of poorer people in the audience must have been comparatively small' (*Elizabethan Popular Theatre: Plays in Performance*, p. 48). Butler, on the other hand, points out that the privileged 'could best afford' to attend the theatre, and 'left most written records of ... attend-

ance; but their 'presence ... does not logically entail the absence of the unprivileged' (*Theatre and Crisis 1632–1642*, p. 298). Gurr also contends that spectatorship spanned a wider range of social groups than Cook suggests (*Playgoing in Shakespeare's London*, p. 49).

17 See Howard, *The Stage and Social Struggle in Early Modern England*, p. 13; and Cohen, *Drama of a Nation*, pp. 17–20. Cohen notes that in England the synthesis of 'native popular and neoclassical learned traditions' is evident chiefly in the plays 'composed for the permanent, public, commercial theaters that opened in the late 1570s and only closed, under government order, seventy years later' (p. 17).

18 Trainor, '"Guilty Creatures at a Play,"' p. 40. For Cawley, on the other hand, Elizabethan domestic tragedies 'such as *Arden of Feversham* and *A Woman Killed with Kindness*' may be classified as 'salvation plays which carry on the tradition of the Catholic moral plays,' and *A Yorkshire Tragedy* as 'first cousin to Protestant homiletic tragedies,' although the play 'may also be related to damnation plays in the biblical cycles' ('*A Yorkshire Tragedy* Considered in Relation to Biblical and Moral Plays,' p. 165).

19 Rao, *The Domestic Drama*, p. 50; Carson and Carson, *Domestic Tragedy in English*, vol 1, pp. 6, 12; Grivelet, *Thomas Heywood et le Drama Domestique Elizabéthain*, p. 353; Clark, *Domestic Drama*, vol 1, pp. 20–1; McLuskie, '"Tis but a Woman's Jar": Family and Kinship in Elizabethan Domestic Drama,' p. 229. Recently, the homiletic reading has been revived by Harry Levin, who suggests that the 'admonitory and moralistic tone' of the murder plays 'recalls the occasional urban echoes in the moralities and interludes' ('Notes toward a Definition of City Comedy,' p. 140).

20 Leggatt, *Citizen Comedy in the Age of Shakespeare*, pp. 4, 11. Arthur Brown has taken the unique view that there is virtually no distinction between citizen and domestic drama. Dealing almost entirely with comedies by Dekker, Heywood, and Jonson, 'the most consistent workers in the field,' Brown notes these playwrights' common interests: the London settings, the didactic patterns, national loyalty and patriotism, morality-play elements, and the psychology of humours ('Citizen Comedy and Domestic Drama,' pp. 63–83). Nevertheless, he differentiates between those plays which include but do not stress family relations, and those which deal extensively with domestic problems, acknowledging that differences in plot structure and characterization ultimately distinguish the two dramatic forms (pp. 66–9).

21 Heywood, *Apology*, sig. F4r.

22 Heywood, *Apology*, sig. F3v. 'A Tragedy,' for example, 'include[s] the fatall and abortiue ends of such as commit notorious murders, which is

aggrauated and acted with all the Art that may be, to terrifie men from the like abhorred practises' (sig. F3v); comedy is 'a discourse consisting of diuers institutions, comprehending ciuill and domesticke things, in which is taught, what in our liues and manners is to be followed, what to bee auoyded' (sig. F1v); 'a morall' succeeds by 'perswad[ing] men to human-ity and good life, to instruct them in ciuility and good manners'; in 'a forreigne History, the subiect is so intended, that ... either the vertues of our Country-men are extolled, or their vices reproued' (sig. F3v); and a domestic history treats 'domestike, and home-borne truth[s]' in such a way that the 'vnchaste are by vs [i.e., playwrights] shewed their errors' (sig. G1v).

23 Baldwin, Preface, *A Mirroure for Magistrates*, in *The Mirror for Magistrates*, ed. Lily B. Campbell, pp. 65–6.

24 Howard, *The Stage and Social Struggle in Early Modern England*, p. 4.

25 Heywood, *Apology*, sigs. C3r, F3v.

26 I.G. [John Greene?], *A Refutation of the Apology for Actors*, sig. F1r.

27 Heywood, *Apology*, sig. F1v.

28 Greene, *A Refutation*, sig. F1r.

29 Richard Whitford, *The Pype or Tonne of the Lyfe of Perfection* (Redman, 1532); cited in Marie Denley, 'Strictures on Interludes and Plays to Relig-ious and Lay People in the Earlier Sixteenth Century,' pp. 444–5.

30 Luxton, 'The Reformation and Popular Culture,' p. 57. See also Thomas, *Religion and the Decline of Magic*, and Amussen, *An Ordered Society*, p. 3. On the limitations of reading early modern texts according to our as-sumptions about audiences' orthodox beliefs see Hodge, 'Marlowe, Marx and Machiavelli: Reading into the Past,' pp. 1–22; and Gurr, who cautions that 'a great deal of room is left for memorable poetry and Jonsonian "application" in the hinterland of audience responses. But there is sadly little tangible evidence there' (*Playgoing in Shakespeare's London*, p. 112).

31 Zagorin, *Ways of Lying: Dissimulation, Persecution, and Conformity in Early Modern Europe*, p. 222.

32 Febvre, *The Problem of Unbelief in the Sixteenth Century*, see esp. pp. 253, 326, 412–14, and 455–7; Kahn, *Rhetoric, Prudence, and Skepticism in the Renaissance*, pp. 35–6.

33 See Beier, *The Problem of the Poor in Tudor and Early Stuart England*, p. 10; Amussen, 'Gender, Family and the Social Order, 1560–1725,' p. 216; and Underdown, 'The Taming of the Scold,' p. 116.

34 See Wrightson, 'The Social Order of Early Modern England,' p. 187.

35 Cited in Neale, *Elizabeth I and Her Parliaments 1584–1601*, p. 70.

36 'An Exhortacion concernyng Good Ordre and Obedience to Rulers and Magistrates,' in Bond, ed., *Certain Sermons or Homilies [1547]*, p. 167. Puritans, notes Bond, challenged the homilies on the basis that they 'stood in the way of a "free pulpit"' (Preface, p. x). On the propagandistic nature of homiletic tracts see Bond, pp. ix–x; Siegel, 'English Humanism and the New Tudor Aristocracy,' pp. 450–68; Stone, *The Crisis of the Aristocracy 1558–1641*, p. 36; and Dollimore, *Radical Tragedy*, p. 84.

37 Wrightson, 'The Social Order of Early Modern England,' pp. 193–4.

38 Dubrow, *A Happier Eden*, p. 27.

39 See especially Dollimore, *Radical Tragedy*; Belsey, *The Subject of Tragedy*; Kastan and Stallybrass, Introduction, *Staging the Renaissance*, pp. 6–7; and Howard, *The Stage and Social Struggle*.

40 Harrison, *Description of England*, p. 118.

41 Michael Jardine and John Simons observe that in many of these plays the characters are 'comparatively wealthy: they are landed, have fiscal/mercantile interests, and employ more than token retinues' (Introduction, *The Two Angry Women of Abington* [Nottingham: Nottingham Drama Texts, 1987], p. iii). Holbrook notes that many characters in domestic tragedy belong to the 'minor gentry' (*Literature and Degree in Renaissance England*, p. 87) and suggests that the genre be called 'bourgeois tragedy' (p. 86) in order 'to express the middling station of the heroes of these plays, occupying a rank different from both the lowest and the highest in society' (p. 175, n. 7). The term 'bourgeois tragedy,' however, effaces two fundamental aspects of the genre: (1) it includes comedies and tragicomedies as well as tragedies; (2) a number of the plays (for example, *Two Lamentable Tragedies*, *The Witch of Edmonton*, and the *Honest Whore* plays) include protagonists who are extremely poor.

42 Farley-Hills, *Shakespeare and the Rival Playwrights 1600–1606*, p. 122.

43 Guillén, *Literature as System*, p. 126.

44 Cohen, *Drama of a Nation*, p. 19.

45 *The Tragedy of Master Arden of Faversham*, ed. M.L. Wine. Further references to the play will be to this edition. Because the spelling of Faversham is 'the customary spelling of the town' (Wine, Introduction, p. xxxiv, n. 1), Wine has emended the title, which appears in the quarto as 'Feversham,' to 'Faversham.' In deference to the quarto, I will retain the traditional title.

46 Holbrook, *Literature and Degree in Renaissance England*, pp. 87–8.

47 Schaeffer, 'Literary Genres and Textual Genericity,' p. 182. Greene, in *The Light in Troy*, pp. 20–7 and 32–43, urges the consideration of genre in

terms of a text's *mundus significans* or the rhetorical/symbolic vocabulary shared by early modern writers and their audience.

48 Guillén, *Literature as System*, p. 61.

49 Fowler, *Kinds of Literature*, p. 41.

50 See Miner, 'Some Issues of Literary "Species, or Distinct Kind",' p. 24. Similarly, in *The Dialogic Imagination*, p. 374, Mikhail Bakhtin emphasizes the flexibility and inclusiveness of early modern genres. On the elasticity and complexity of genres in both Renaissance theory and practice, see Colie, *The Resources of Kind*, and Lewalski, 'Introduction: Issues and Approaches,' *Renaissance Genres*, pp. 1–12.

51 Althusser, 'Ideology and Ideological State Apparatuses (Notes towards an Investigation),' in *Lenin and Philosophy and Other Essays*, p. 164.

52 Todorov, *Genres in Discourse*, p. 19. On the historicity of literary genres, see also Jameson, *The Political Unconscious*, pp. 140–1; Jameson, *Marxism and Form*; Bakhtin, *Rabelais and His World*; and Hulse, *Metamorphic Verse*, p. 14.

53 Medvedev and Bakhtin, *The Formal Method in Literary Scholarship*, p. 19.

54 Bakhtin, *Problems of Dostoevsky's Poetics*. See also Williams, *The Long Revolution*, p. 47.

55 Bradley, *Shakespearean Tragedy*. Bradley's schematic is echoed in Hardison's assessment of dramatic 'greatness': although 'the belief that the aim of literature is moral instruction ... underlies a vast (and often rather tedious) body of homiletic writing,' we can be grateful that 'Marlowe, Shakespeare, Chapman, Webster, and Ford ... do not write tragedies like those described by Heywood [in *An Apology for Actors*], in which the protagonist exemplifies a neatly labeled moral flaw that the audience is taught to "abhor" by the catastrophe' ('Three Types of Renaissance Catharsis,' pp. 8–9). Levin differentiates in similar terms between domestic and heroic tragedy: 'Sordid crimes befalling commoners might have been considered unworthy of dramatization by classical-minded critics' ('Notes toward a Definition of City Comedy,' p. 140). Cf. Rick Bowers's application of the label 'small' to the artistry that underwrites domestic plays ('*A Woman Killed With Kindness*: Plausibility on a Smaller Scale,' p. 295). Although Holbrook, in *Literature and Degree in Renaissance England*, p. 86, argues that domestic tragedies reveal 'a complex investment in "the tradition" [of tragic form] as well as a distance from it,' he nevertheless classifies them as an 'Elizabethan minigenre.'

56 Neely, 'Remembering Shakespeare Always but Remembering him Differently,' p. 1.

57 For Farley-Hills, '*Othello*'s domesticity is a very different affair from [that

of *A Woman Killed with Kindness*] ... The deliberately low-key presentation
of character through a linguistic medium that is ... as unpretentious as it
is efficient, contrasts vividly with the tone of the *Othello* music'
(*Shakespeare and the Rival Playwrights 1600–1606*, p. 123). Nuttall, in *A New
Mimesis*, also argues for *Othello*'s superiority to other domestic plays: 'It is
fairly obvious that these plays catered for appetites which are served
today by the more sensational Sunday newspapers. The title pages of
these domestic tragedies repeatedly strike a note of prurient censorious-
ness which is immediately recognizable'; the only connection between
Shakespeare's play and 'these domestic tragedies' is seen to be 'the then
uncommon theme of marriage' (p. 133). And although Shaffer suggests
that *Othello* 'fits the general mold' of domestic tragedy, he singles out
Shakespeare for 'inevitably overthrowing the tradition' in order to 'move
toward a different vision' ('"To Manage Private and Domestic Quarrels",'
pp. 448, 450–1).

58 Doran, *Endeavors of Art*, p. 143.

59 Ure, 'Marriage and the Domestic Drama in *A Woman Killed with Kindness*,'
p. 197.

60 Ure, 'Marriage and the Domestic Drama in Heywood and Ford,' p. 201.

61 Ure, 'Marriage and the Domestic Drama in *A Woman Killed With Kindness*,'
p. 197; 'Marriage and the Domestic Drama in Heywood and Ford,' p. 203.
A similar conclusion is drawn by Lieblein, for whom the murder plays
'neither alter nor shirk the morality of their sources,' although in contrast
to the 'unequivocal moral judgments' of the 'chronicles, journalistic pamphlets, court testimony, underworld narratives, and ballads' on which
they are based, they 'elaborate the social context, examine motives, and
suggest the complicity of the victim in a way which changes the
audience's perception of events' ('The Context of Murder in English
Domestic Plays, 1590–1610,' p. 181).

62 The tendency to view the genre as largely determined by its social context
informs Orlin's otherwise illuminating study of the role of the household
in domestic tragedy ('Man's House as His Castle in *Arden of Feversham*,'
pp. 57–89. (The essay is derived from Orlin's 'Man's House as His Castle
in Elizabethan Domestic Tragedy.') Elsewhere, Orlin qualifies the extent of
the influence of the social context by suggesting that although 'domestic
tragedy had its formal genesis in domestic patriarchalism,' certain
'examples of the genre ... tested the ideational system' ('Familial Transgressions, Societal Transition on the Elizabethan Stage,' p. 30). In her fine
book, *Private Matters and Public Culture in Post-Reformation England*, Orlin
treats domestic tragedy as largely reflective of the structures that inform

'the history of the private' (p. 4). For McLuskie, plays such as *A Woman Killed with Kindness, A Yorkshire Tragedy, The Wise Woman of Hogsdon*, and *Two Angry Women of Abington* 'serve to authenticate ... the social relations ... [which they] present' ('"Tis but a Woman's Jar": Family and Kinship in Elizabethan Domestic Drama,' p. 232). Attwell, in his new historical reading of *Arden of Feversham*, provides a valuable analysis of early modern 'bourgeois' ideology, but he ignores the play's ironic impulses when he suggests that it ultimately upholds 'the cultural processes that accompanied the consolidation of middle-class hegemony' ('Property, Status, and the Subject in a Middle-class Tragedy: *Arden of Faversham*,' p. 348). Adams's argument in favour of a culturally homogeneous group of plays and audiences is thus dislodged by Attwell's 'culturally determinate' reading of the text as unambiguously involved in the 're-narrativization of events and the representation of social relations and values' (p. 329).

63 Stone, *The Family, Sex and Marriage in England 1500–1800*, p. 7.

64 On the emergence of distinct family units during the Middle Ages see Herlihy, *Medieval Households*, pp. v–vi; on the development of medieval 'individualism' see McKeon, *The Origins of the English Novel 1600–1740*, p. 3.

65 Schochet, *Patriarchalism in Political Thought*, p. 54.

66 Smith, *De Republica Anglorum*, pp. 23, 29. Cf. Bodin's refutation of Aristotle's distinction between political and domestic hierarchy on the grounds that the family 'is the true seminarie and beginning of euery Commonweale, as also a principall member thereof' (*The Six Bookes of a Commonweale* [1586], Book I, ii, p. 8).

67 *The Good Hows-holder*, pp. 2–9; *Certayne Sermons Appointed by the Queen's Majesty*, sigs. K1, I7.

68 Cleaver, *A Codly [Godly] Form of Householde Government*, sig. B5. Hooker also describes the close link between paternal and kingly authority: 'It is no improbable opinion ... that as the chiefest person in every household was always as it were a king, so when numbers of households joined themselves in civil society together, kings were the first kind of governors amongst them. Which is also ... the reason why the name of *Father* continued still in them, who of fathers were made rulers' (*The Laws of Ecclesiastical Polity*, in *Works*, vol. 1, pp. 242–3).

69 Thomas, 'Women and the Civil War Sects,' p. 317.

70 Todd, *Christian Humanism and the Puritan Social Order*, p. 99. Todd illustrates that the long-held assumption concerning the Puritan rearrangement of the definition of marriage in favour of the emphasis on companionship 'is wide of the mark' (p. 99). She cites Christian humanists such

as Erasmus, Vives, and Thomas More, as well as Anglican conformists, on the importance of companionate marriage, and points out that in the command given in the 1562 homily on matrimony (which 'remained unchanged down to 1662' [p. 99, n. 13]), marriage is defined as 'instituted of God, to the intent that man and woman should live lawfully in a perpetual friendship, to bring forth fruit, and to avoid fornication' (p. 99). In *The Renaissance Notion of Woman*, Maclean contends that with respect to matrimony 'it is difficult to see more than minor shifts of emphasis occurring during the Renaissance' (p. 66). On the continuities and differences between the conceptualization of marriage as conceived by Plutarch and by medieval and early modern commentators, see Wayne, Introduction, *The Flower of Friendship*, pp. 12–21.

71 Becon, *The Golden Boke of Christen Matrimony* (1542), pp. 1–2. On the status of matrimony in Puritan writings see Lucas, 'Puritan Preaching and the Politics of the Family,' pp. 224–40.

72 Erasmus, *A ryght frutefull Epystle ... in laude and prayse of matrymony*, sigs. Cvi–Cvii; on the dates of composition and translation, see Telle, *Erasme de Rotterdam et le Septième Sacrement*, p. 160.

73 Vives, *The Office and Duties of an Husband*, sig. A4v; *The Instruction of a Christen Woman*, sig. Diir–Diiv. Cf. Battus's description of wedlock as 'the most excellent state and condition of life ... which all the godly both by preaching and example have commended unto us, and placed the same in the top of all good works' (*The Christian Man's Closet*, sig. 4v).

74 Houlbrooke, *The English Family 1450–1700*, p. 14.

75 Ezell, *The Patriarch's Wife*, pp. 161, 163.

76 Coudert, 'The Myth of the Improved Status of Protestant Women,' p. 78 and passim; Hanley, 'Engendering the State,' p. 5. On the problem of female rebelliousness in France, see also Davis, *Society and Culture in Early Modern France*, chap. 5.

77 Dolan, *Dangerous Familiars*, p. 24.

78 *Certain Sermons or Homilies* [1547], p. 174. On the pervasiveness of adultery and other disruptions in the ideal of the orderly family, see Ingram, *Church Courts, Sex and Marriage in England, 1570–1640*; and Amussen, 'Gender, Family and the Social Order,' pp. 205–6. On the social and economic impact of the fragmentation of family life, see also Beier, *Masterless Men*, p. 56, and *The Problem of the Poor in Tudor and Early Stuart England*, pp. 8–9.

79 Nichols, *An Order of Household Instruction*, sigs. B3v–B4r; Perkins, *Christian Oeconomie*, sig. Qq5r; Robert Sanderson, Sermon, 6 May 1632, in MacLure, *Register of Sermons Preached at Paul's Cross 1534–1642*, p. 137.

80 Houlbrooke, *Church Courts and the People*, pp. 68–9.

81 Dolan, *Dangerous Familiars*, p. 2.

82 Amussen, *An Ordered Society*, p. 122.

83 Cited in Emmison, *Morals and the Church Courts*, pp. 163, 162.

84 See Houlbrooke, *Church Courts and the People*, p. 68. Although, as Houlbrooke notes, 'no one pretext for separation predominates among the surviving record of suits,' a number of petitioners sought 'separation on the ground of their inability to live together because of continual quarrels'; moreover, while 'separation cases sometimes ended peacefully ... there is no convincing evidence of vigorous efforts to reconcile estranged spouses' (p. 68).

85 Dubrow, *A Happier Eden*, p. 26. A similar suggestion is made by Lucas, in 'Puritan Preaching and the Politics of the Family,' p. 227.

86 *Xenophons Treatise of Hovseholde*, trans. Gentian Hervet, p. 11.

87 *Certain Sermons or Homilies Appointed to be Read in Churches in the Time of Queen Elizabeth*, p. 535.

88 Griffith, *Bethel: or a Forme for Families*, pp. 292–3; Gouge, *Of Domesticall Duties*, p. 275; Whately, *A Bride-Bush Or, A Wedding Sermon*, sig. A2r and title page.

89 Hull, in *Chaste, Silent & Obedient*, notes that 'few marriage guides addressed women readers directly in either titles or dedications' (p. 48).

90 Smith, *De Republica Anglorum*, p. 23.

91 On the political function of the marriage manuals see Klein, Preface, *Daughters, Wives, and Widows*, p. x.

92 Cases in point include Edward Gosynhyll's *The Vertuous Scholehous of Vngracious Women* (c. 1550); *The Good Huswives Handmayde; contayning many principall poyntes of Cookery* (anonymous, 1591); and *The Good Houswives Treasurie. Being a ... booke instructing to the dressing of meates* (anonymous, 1588).

93 Jeanneret, *A Feast of Words: Banquets and Table Talk in the Renaissance*, p. 3. See also Elias, *The Civilizing Process*, pp. 84–129.

94 Ferry, *The 'Inward' Language*, p. 53.

95 Gouge, *Of Domesticall Duties*, p. 76.

96 Althusser, 'Ideology and Ideological State Apparatuses,' p. 144. On the emergence of the ideology of privacy in early modern Europe in general, see also Chartier (ed), *Passions of the Renaissance*; on its development in England see Belsey, *The Subject of Tragedy*, p. 130; Rose, *The Expense of Spirit*; and Orlin, *Private Matters and Public Culture in Post-Reformation England*.

97 Hooker, *The Laws of Ecclesiastical Polity*, in *Works*, vol. 1, p. 242.

98 Dubrow, *A Happier Eden*, p. 27.

99 Gouge, *Of Domesticall Duties*, p. 272. On the 'ironies and paradoxes that are continually inscribed but inconsistently acknowledged' in Puritan discussions of companionate marriage and in 'the conceptualization of women,' see Rose, *The Expense of Spirit*, p. 126 and pp. 124–31.

100 See Wayne, Introduction, *The Flower of Friendship*, pp. 42–5. Wayne notes that 'the history of ideologies of marriage in Renaissance England does not readily make a coherent narrative'; the conduct books, for example, when 'address[ing] such tangled issues as love and power, public and private duty,' lack 'convincing clarity and a single line of argument' (pp. 1, 2). Cf. Jordan's suggestion that humanist treatises on the religious value of marriage as a vehicle of 'personal salvation' are not always consistent in subordinating political concerns (*Renaissance Feminism*, p. 56).

101 Woodbridge, *Women and the English Renaissance*, p. 172.

102 Belsey, *The Subject of Tragedy*, p. 9.

103 Lewalski, *Writing Women in Jacobean England*, p. 3.

104 On the critical tendency to ignore feminine transgression in early modern England, see Newman, *Fashioning Femininity and English Renaissance Drama*, pp. xviii–xix.

105 For a valuable discussion of the prevalence of 'symbolic inversion' in western culture, see Babcock, *The Reversible World*, p. 14.

1: Medieval and Tudor Contexts

1 On the longevity of the cycles see Bradner, 'The Rise of Secular Drama in the Renaissance,' p. 7; Parente, *Religious Drama and the Humanist Tradition*; Johnston, 'Cycle Drama in the Sixteenth Century,' pp. 1–15; and 'The Inherited Tradition: The Legacy of Provincial Drama,' pp. 1–25.

2 Although the notion that the cyclical plays often bear closely on everyday life has, as Lumiansky notes, 'become axiomatic' ('Comedy and Theme in the Chester *Harrowing of Hell*,' p. 11), commentary on the links between domestic and biblical drama remains cursory and anecdotal. Cawley, in defining *A Yorkshire Tragedy* as an example of 'Protestant homiletic traged[y],' has suggested that the play's origins can be located 'in the biblical cycles and moral plays of the Middle Ages' ('*A Yorkshire Tragedy* Considered in Relation to Biblical and Moral Plays,' pp. 165, 155). Ada and Herbert Carson have noted that 'repentant sinners' in miracle plays sometimes 'came from the lower classes ... domestic realism [being] often used to explain biblical stories or moral behavior to the

peasantry' (*Domestic Tragedy in English*, vol. 1, p. 26). And Andrew Clark has more broadly proposed that 'the naturalistic representation' in some mystery plays 'of everyday scene and subject, as well as the popularity of the *relations* of husband and wife, proved an important evolutionary force in the development of domestic drama' (*Domestic Drama*, vol. 1, p. 103, n. 4). The observation is nevertheless incidental to Clark's project. For Adams, the only relation between the mystery cycles and domestic drama is their mutual festive role of providing 'serious entertainment for the general populace' (*English Domestic or, Homiletic Tragedy, 1575–1642*, p. 54).

3 See, for example, Bloch, *Feudal Society*, vol. 1, pp. 130–1.

4 Herlihy, *Medieval Households*, p. v; Hanawalt, *The Ties that Bound*; Macfarlane, *Marriage and Love in England*. On the development of the aristocratic nuclear family during the later Middle Ages, see James, *Family, Lineage, and Civil Society*, pp. 13–16; and Philippe Contamine, 'Peasant Hearth to Papal Palace: The Fourteenth and Fifteenth Centuries,' pp. 427–30.

5 See Barthélemy, 'Civilizing the Fortress: Eleventh to Thirteenth Century,' pp. 397–423.

6 The decrees are listed in Donahue, 'The Canon Law in the Formation of Marriage and Social Practice in the Later Middle Ages,' pp. 144–58.

7 The chief exponents of the now outdated view are Ariès, *Centuries of Childhood*, and Stone, *The Family, Sex, and Marriage in England*. Both contended that medieval families lacked affective ties (chiefly as a result of demographic conditions such as the high mortality rate for children), fostering the interests of the lineage at the expense of those of individual families.

8 Brooke, *The Medieval Idea of Marriage*, p. 129. Other recent revisionist treatments of the development of marriage and the family in the Middle Ages include Shahar, *Childhood in the Middle Ages*; Nicholas, *The Domestic Life of a Medieval City*, esp. p. 33; Klapisch-Zuber, *Women, Family, and Ritual in Renaissance Italy*; Howell, *Women, Production, and Patriarchy in Late Medieval Cities*; and Marshall, *The Dutch Gentry: 1500–1650*, esp. chap. 1, 'The Core Family Unit and the Lineage: Identity, Relations, and Realities.'

9 McKeon, *The Origins of the English Novel*, p. 142. See also Goody, *The Development of the Family and Marriage in Europe*, pp. 152–6 and chaps. 5 and 6.

10 Bernard of Anjou, *Miracles of Ste. Foi* (994); cited in Herlihy, *Medieval Households*, p. 112.

11 In her exhaustive investigation of parent-child relationships between 1330 and 1479, Shahar writes that 'the high rate of mortality of infants and children in the Middle Ages was the consequence of limited medical skills

and not of the absence of emotional involvement' (*Childhood in the Middle Ages*, p. 2). On the nurturing of and emotional attachment to children during the medieval period see also Macfarlane, *Marriage and Love in England*, pp. 56 and 328–36.

12 Herlihy, *Medieval Households*, pp. 125–6; Shahar, *Childhood in the Middle Ages*, p. 84.

13 *The Towneley Plays*, ed. Martin Stevens and A.C. Cawley, vol. 1. Further references to the Towneley cycle will be to this edition.

14 Cole, *Suffering and Evil in the Plays of Christopher Marlowe*, pp. 22–3.

15 On the dramatic function of Mary's role in the medieval lyric, see Sticca, *The Planctus Mariae in the Dramatic Tradition of the Middle Ages*, p. 175.

16 *The N-Town Play: Cotton MS Vespasian D.8*, ed. Stephen Spector, vol. 1. Further references to the N-town pageants will be to this edition. The manuscript on which the edition is based is from East Anglia and comprises 'a proclamation, or banns ..., describing a series of forty pageants, and a text of what appears to be forty-one pageants (wrongly numbered forty-two), almost entirely written in the hand of a single scribe.' The pageants, however, do not form 'a straightforward cycle'; the manuscript 'contains part of such a cycle ... but it also contains some quite different dramatic pieces' (Meredith, Introduction, *The Passion Play from the N. Town Manuscript*, pp. 1–2).

17 *The Chester Mystery Cycle*, ed. R.M. Lumiansky and David Mills, Vol. 1. Further references to the Chester cycle will be to this edition.

18 Stevens and Cawley, eds., *The Towneley Plays*, vol. 2, p. 580, n. 349.

19 Keiser, 'The Middle English *Planctus Mariae* and the Rhetoric of Pathos,' p. 172. On Mary's multiple signification in the liturgical drama, see also McNeir, 'Corpus Christi Passion Plays as Dramatic Art,' p. 624.

20 'The Brome Play of *Abraham and Isaac*,' in *Non-cycle Plays and Fragments*, ed. Norman Davis, Play 5.

21 Schell observes that Abraham undertakes the sacrifice only 'by an act of desperate ecstasy' ('The Distinctions of the Towneley Abraham,' p. 326).

22 'Abraham's will' in the Chester pageant, writes Mills, is 'to do God's will,' just as 'it becomes Isaac's will to do his father's will' ('The Chester Cycle,' p. 126). For a survey of medieval sermons on filial obedience, see Owst, *Literature and Pulpit in Medieval England*, p. 493.

23 White, *Theatre and Reformation*, pp. 112–13.

24 Cited in Simon, *Education and Society in Tudor England*, p. 80.

25 Although staging, plot development, and characterization in these plays bolster their homiletic superstructure, they inscribe an important tension

'between a basically Humanist-derived belief that a Christian education can ensure moral and spiritual regeneracy and the prevailing Calvinist conviction that salvation is a predestined consequence of irresistible grace' (White, *Theatre and Reformation*, p. 114).

26 The Northampton Play of *Abraham and Isaac*, in *Non-cycle Plays and Fragments*, ed. Norman Davis, Play 4. Further references to the play will be to this edition.

27 *Christ before Pilate I: The Dream of Pilate's Wife*, in *The York Plays*, ed. Richard Beadle. Further references to the York cycle will be to this edition.

28 Twycross, 'The Theatricality of Medieval English Plays,' p. 42.

29 Nicoll, *The Development of the Theatre*, p. 52.

30 Southern, *The Medieval Theatre in the Round*, p. 117; see also pp. 132 and 230–1.

31 Tydeman, *The Theatre in the Middle Ages*, p. 147.

32 Nicoll, *The Development of the Theatre*, p. 52.

33 *Adam: A Twelfth-Century Play*, trans. Lynette Muir, s.d., pp. 166, 183.

34 di Somi, *Dialogues and Stage Affairs*, trans. Allardyce Nicoll, in *The Development of the Theatre*, p. 273.

35 Beadle, 'The York Cycle,' p. 89.

36 See Robinson, 'The Art of the York Realist,' p. 237.

37 On the verisimilitude of York Play 30, Robinson comments: 'the reason why Caiaphas should be in bed when Jesus is brought to him is a very simple one: Jesus was arrested during the night. Taking this fact as his starting point, the playwright could have reasoned ... that a bedtime and waking scene for Caiaphas should naturally follow' ('The Art of the York Realist,' p. 237).

38 Twycross, 'The Theatricality of Medieval English Plays,' p. 42. See also Robinson, 'The Art of the York Realist,' p. 237.

39 Weimann, *Shakespeare and the Popular Tradition in the Theater*, p. 102.

40 *Saint Augustine: Confessions*, bk. 8, p. 215.

41 The 'great rebuilding' in England did not affect the homes of the peasantry until the late sixteenth or early seventeenth centuries, depending upon the region.

42 Montaigne, *The Essayes of Montaigne*, p. 746. On the semiotic function of retiring to a private space see below, chap. 3.

43 The raucous clashes between Noah and Uxor, observes Gash, echo the carnivalesque brawls between spouses that took place after Easter at Hocktide ('Carnival against Lent: The Ambivalence of Medieval Drama,' p. 79).

44 Sutherland, '"Not or I see more neede": The Wife of Noah in the Chester, York, and Towneley Cycles,' p. 184.

45 Gash, 'Carnival against Lent,' p. 79.

46 The plays are Dekker, Chettle, and Haughton's *Patient Grissil* (c. 1599); Heywood's *How a Man May Choose a Good Wife from a Bad* (1601–2); *The Fair Maid of Bristow* (anonymous, 1603–4); *The London Prodigal* (anonymous, 1603–5); and the two parts of Dekker's *Honest Whore* (1604–c. 1607), Part I of which is co-authored with Middleton. George Wilkins's *The Miseries of Enforced Marriage* (c. 1606), a tragicomedy, also has affinities with these plays. On the constitutional features of domestic comedy, see below, chap. 5.

47 Quinn, Introduction, *The Faire Maide of Bristow*, p. 27.

48 See the discussion above of the Reformation interludes dealing with the rearing and education of children. See also Wilson, *The English Drama 1485–1585*, pp. 96–101, and White, *Theatre and Reformation*, p. 112.

49 Ingelend, *The Disobedient Child*, p. 303.

50 Thomas Heywood, *How a Man May Choose a Good Wife from a Bad*, V.iii, p. 96. Further references to the play will be to this edition.

51 *Two Coventry Corpus Christi Plays*, ed. Hardin Craig. Further references to the two plays will be to this edition. On the classical roots of the actor's address to the spectator and its adaptation to the medieval stage, see Albert Cook, *The Dark Voyage and the Golden Mean*, p. 44; and Munson, 'Audience and Meaning in Two Medieval Dramatic Realisms,' pp. 183–206.

52 See Phythian-Adams, *Desolation of a City*, p. 89.

53 Bevington, *Medieval Drama*, p. 461.

54 Axton and Happé, Introduction, *The Plays of John Heywood*, p. 15.

55 Norland, 'Formalizing English Farce: *Johan Johan* and Its French Connection,' p. 145.

56 John Heywood, *Johan Johan*, in *The Plays of John Heywood*, ed. Richard Axton and Peter Happé. Further references to the play will be to this edition.

57 Spivack, *Shakespeare and the Allegory of Evil*, pp. 253–4. The more than twelve plays which survive, argues Spivack, 'represent a substantial body of dramatic literature most of which has not survived' (p. 253). Bevington, in his discussion of the English popular theatre, has also argued for an identifiable group of 'hybrid moralities' which do not belong 'to the canon of the orthodox morality because they deal with historical or romantic material and present as main characters specific personalities rather than types ...' (*From Mankind to Marlowe*, p. 10).

58 Spivack, *Shakespeare and the Allegory of Evil*, p. 255.

59 Belsey, *The Subject of Tragedy*, p. 33; Dolan, 'Gender, Moral Agency, and Dramatic Form in *A Warning for Fair Women*,' p. 202.
60 For a survey of the hybrid plays that incorporate the romantic *topos* see Spivack, *Shakespeare and the Allegory of Evil*, pp. 218–26.
61 Garter, *The Most Virtuous & Godly Susanna*, ed. W.W. Greg. Further references to the play will be to this edition.
62 Bevington, *From Mankind to Marlowe*, p. 63.

2: Fashioning the Marriage Codes

1 The tale of Patient Griselda was first recorded in European literature in 1353 in Boccaccio's *Decameron*. Whether the legend had an original folktale source is unknown. Bettridge and Utley, in 'New Light on the Origin of the Griselda Story,' note that a number of folk-tale versions have been identified as deriving from Northern Europe, but that 'the Mediterranean ... does not furnish one version which could be construed either as a possible modern derivative of Boccaccio's oral source or as a local derivative of the ... originals' (p. 154). After Boccaccio transcribed the tale it became immensely popular in European folklore and literature. Inspired by Boccaccio's tale, Petrarch expanded it in Latin in 1374 (*De Insigni Obedientia et Fide Uxoris*), while in the same year Giovanni Sercambi retold Boccaccio's novella in condensed form. A number of medieval French versions are based on Petrarch's rendition, including the first secular dramatization in the anonymous *L'Estoire de la Marquise de Saluce mix par personnages et rigmé* (1395). Chaucer's *Clerk's Tale*, which is based on Petrarch's and a French redaction, is the first of numerous English versions. In Europe the legend continued to be rendered in chapbooks, anonymous tales, and in operatic and dramatized versions down to the twentieth century, retaining its popularity among a variety of audiences. The medieval adaptations are noted in Bryan and Dempster, eds., *Sources and Analogues of Chaucer's Canterbury Tales*, pp. 288–331. All extant and lost analogues are cited in Hoy, *Introductions, Notes, and Commentaries to texts in 'The Dramatic Works of Thomas Dekker' Edited by Fredson Bowers*, vol. 1, pp. 131–43. See also Griffith, *The Origin of the Griselda Story*.

The earliest sixteenth-century version of the legend appears to be Ralph Radcliffe's lost text *De Patientia Griseldis* (1546–56?). The extant sixteenth-century adaptations are Phillip's hybrid morality *The Play of Patient Grissell* (c. 1558–66); the ballad 'Of Patient Grissel and a Noble Marquess,' two versions of which exist (one in manuscript form [c. 1600], the other as a short poem by Deloney in *The Garland of Good Will* [registered 1593]); and

the *Pleasant Comedy of Patient Grissil* (written 1599; printed 1603) by
Dekker, Chettle, and Haughton. In her survey of the sixteenth- and seventeenth-century texts, Anna Baldwin suggests that the anonymous chapbook *History of Patient Grisel*, the earliest edition of which is dated 1619,
could possibly have been written in the late sixteenth century, but the
evidence is inconclusive ('From the *Clerk's Tale* to *The Winter's Tale*,'
p. 201).

2 Although it has been customary to assign the authorship of the play to
Phillip, Roberts in his unpublished edition of the play has argued that it
was possibly written in collaboration with John Heywood (*An Edition of
John Phillip's Commodye of Pacient and Meeke Grissill*, p. 199). The observation, however, remains conjectural.

3 Until the 1980s the sixteenth-century adaptations of the Griselda legend
were largely ignored in criticism. In an early essay on the Elizabethan
dramatizations of the legend, Keyishian generally dismissed Phillip's
adaptation, and characterized the 1599 play as a tiresome morality written
for audiences who 'could deal with mighty truths' but who 'evidently
also needed the sickly reassurance of the Griselda story' ('Griselda on the
Elizabethan Stage,' p. 261). More recently, Champion, in *Thomas Dekker
and the Traditions of English Drama*, has argued that although the 1599 play
'fails to provide motivation that is either adequate or consistent' (p. 19),
its 'comic structure ... appears firm' (p. 18). Bliss characterizes Dekker and
his collaborators as 'experienced men of the theater who seek plot
material for saleable, stageworthy entertainments,' and who in securaliz-
ing the story of Griselda provide 'only token answers to the problems ...
[the play] stages' ('The Renaissance Griselda,' pp. 325–6). Belsey, while
claiming little originality for the 1599 play, concedes that Grissil's suffering 'leaves the audience to ... ponder the question whether there is any
proper limit to the silent endurance of patriarchal tyranny' (*The Subject of
Tragedy*, p. 171), but she does not pursue the insight. Bronfman suggests
that the 1599 play treats issues such as 'class prejudice' and 'sovereignty
in marriage ... with far more complexity than had its predecessors'
('Griselda, Renaissance Woman,' p. 217). Pechter, in '*Patient Grissil* and
the Trials of Marriage,' views the marquess-Grissil relationship as a story
of 'desire,' which 'implicate[s]' the audience 'as the subjects ... of a continuing history' (pp. 7, 24).

4 Petrarch's letter is included in Giovanni Boccaccio, *The Decameron*, pp.
184–7; the quotations are from p. 186.

5 Dinshaw, *Chaucer's Sexual Poetics*, p. 150.

6 Dinshaw, *Chaucer's Sexual Poetics*, p. 150.

7 Boccaccio, *The Decameron*, trans. and ed. Mark Musa and Peter E. Bondanella, p. 138. Further references to the text will be to this edition.

8 Hawkins remarks that Chaucer 'inserts' into the allegorical significance of the Griselda tale an interpretation 'which he inherited from Petrarch, and which supplies his audience with an alternative frame of reference, only after having criticized Walter far more powerfully ... than did his predecessor' ('The Victim's Side: Chaucer's *Clerk's Tale* and Webster's *Duchess of Malfi*,' p. 345). Ellis, noting Chaucer's concern with female powerlessness, argues that in the *Clerk's Tale* 'associations of the home with ambiguity, insecurity, and women's vulnerability merge most effectively' ('Domestic Treachery in the *Clerk's Tale*,' p. 101). Hansen, on the other hand, suggests that while *The Clerk's Tale* 'offers readers a ... rich and compelling ... confrontation with patriarchal power,' Chaucer, 'the male poet,' ultimately realizes the powers of silence and unintelligibility that he usurps from and must finally deny to his female heroines' ('The Powers of Silence: The Case of the Clerk's Griselda,' pp. 230, 247); and Dinshaw concludes that 'for all his sympathy with the trials of the female,' the Clerk's 'primary point is not sympathetic' ('Griselda Translated,' p. 152).

9 Geoffrey Chaucer, *The Clerk's Tale*, in *The Works of Geoffrey Chaucer*, ed. F.N. Robinson. Further references to the tale will be to this edition.

10 Both Hunt, in *Thomas Dekker: A Study*, p. 59, n. 35 and Jenkins, in *The Life and Work of Henry Chettle*, p. 161 disclaim the 1599 play's debt to Phillip. More recently, however, Hoy has suggested that 'Phillip's play represents a stage in the development of the Griselda story, specifically as concerns the Marquess' motivation, that ought not to be overlooked, for it points in the way that both ... [Deloney's] Ballad and the play of 1599 will take in their attempts to account for Griselda's treatment at the hands of her noble husband' (*Introductions, Notes, and Commentaries to Texts in 'The Dramatic Works of Thomas Dekker,'* vol. 1, p. 139). Although Hoy does not analyze the marquess's behaviour in the context of Phillip's presentation of the ideal marriage, I am indebted to his discussion of the evolution of the testing motif.

11 Pechter, '*Patient Grissil* and the Trials of Marriage,' p. 12, n. 32. Although Pechter's observation is useful in locating the protobourgeois structures of the play, I disagree with his contention that 'we see no evidence of his [Gwalter's] ruling' (p. 12, n. 32); on the contrary, the 1599 play goes beyond its analogues by problematizing the early modern analogy between sovereigns and husbands/fathers.

12 Erasmus, *A ryght fruteful Epystle ... in laude and prayse of matrymony*, sigs. Cvi–Cvii.

13 Jeremy Taylor, *A Course of Sermons for All the Sundays of the Year* (1653), Sermon XVII: 'The Marriage Ring,' Part I, pp. 209, 210; Perkins, *Christian Oeconomie*, pp. 669, 671.

14 Puttenham, 'The Maner of Reioysings at Mariages and Weddings,' p. 53; Spenser, *Amoretti*, in *Spenser: Poetical Works*, ed. J.C. Smith and E. De Selincourt, p. 573. Further references to the poem will be to this edition.

15 'From at least the 1520s,' observes Wrightson, 'there were forces active which served to accentuate inequalities and to enhance social and cultural differentiation, and which overlapped in such a way as to intensify the risk of conflict – between landlords and tenants, the "better sort" and the "meaner sort," the "godly" and the "ungodly," the "polite" and the "vulgar." Yet at the same time there were factors which worked against such an outcome: the active paternalism of the Tudor and Stuart state and of individuals responsive to traditional social obligations; the ubiquitous ideology of order and obedience; the ambivalent position of the growing "middling sort"'; and 'the growing complexity of the social order, which undermined some traditional group identities without yet creating new ones of a stable nature' ('The Social Order of Early Modern England,' pp. 200–1).

16 For a survey of the plays and treatises dealing with the subject of forced marriage, see Blayney, 'Enforcement of Marriage in English Drama (1600–1650),' pp. 459–72.

17 Wilkins, *The Miseries of Enforced Marriage*, Act I, p. 488. Further references to the play will be to this edition.

18 Heywood, *A Curtaine Lecture*, sigs. F2–3.

19 Taylor, Sermon XVII, 'The Marriage Ring,' Part I, p. 211.

20 Phillip, *The Play of Patient Grissell*, ed. R.B. McKerrow. Further references to the play will be to this edition.

21 Phillip's introduction of these details, notes Bliss, 'helps shift his play's emphasis to the domestic unit' ('The Renaissance Griselda: A Woman for all Seasons,' p. 307).

22 Hoy, *Introductions, Notes, and Commentaries to Texts in 'The Dramatic Works of Thomas Dekker,'* vol. 1, pp. 140–1.

23 Deloney, *The Garland of Good Will*, ed. J.H. Dixon, stanza 1. Further references to the ballad will be to this edition.

24 Dekker, *Patient Grissil*, in *Dramatic Works*, ed. Fredson Bowers, vol 1. Further references to the play will be to this edition.

25 In my assessment of the play's psychological overtones I take issue with those who disclaim any complex motivation for Gwalter's cruelty. For Keyishian, 'Gwalter's decision to test his wife is motivated by no external circumstances' ('Griselda on the Elizabethan Stage,' p. 255). Similarly, Hoy

contends that the urge to test Grissil 'seems to have sprung full blown from the head of the Marquess' and is 'not occasioned by any felt need to win for her the hearts of his people' (*Introduction, Notes, and Commentaries to Texts in 'The Dramatic Works of Thomas Dekker*,' vol. 1, p. 141).

26 Amussen, *An Ordered Society*, p. 123.

27 Taylor, Sermon XVIII: 'The Marriage Ring,' Part II, pp. 219–20.

28 Stallybrass, 'Patriarchal Territories: The Body Enclosed,' p. 127.

29 Tilney, *The Flower of Friendship*, p. 134; Wayne, Introduction, *The Flower of Friendship*, p. 47.

30 Tilney, *The Flower of Friendship*, pp. 110, 112.

31 Gouge, *Domesticall Duties*, p. 272. On the inconsistencies in the conduct literature concerning equality in marriage, see above, chap. 1.

32 Levin, *The Multiple Plot in English Renaissance Drama*, p. 50.

33 It is widely accepted that Dekker seems to have been responsible for those sections of the play involving Grissil's indigent family, the scenes depicting poverty and human suffering being characteristic of Dekker's pamphlets and later plays. See Hunt, *Thomas Dekker*, pp. 15–16; and Hoy, *Introductions, Notes and Commentaries to Texts in the 'The Dramatic Works of Thomas Dekker*,' vol. 1, pp. 143–6.

34 Dekker, *Foure Birds of Noahs Arke*, ed. F.P. Wilson, pp. 124–5.

35 'A Speach to the Lords and Commons of the Parliament at White-Hall,' in *The Political Works of King James I*, ed. Charles H. McIlwain, p. 307.

36 Perkins, *Christian Oeconomie*, sig. Qq5.

37 'A Speach to the Lords and Commons of the Parliament at White-Hall,' p. 307.

38 Cited in Hoy, *Introductions, Notes, and Commentaries to Texts in 'The Dramatic Works of Thomas Dekker*,' vol. 1, p. 133.

3: Domestic Tragedy and Private Life

1 Houlbrooke, *The English Family 1450–1700*, p. 114. Beier notes that 'the disintegration of families took many forms, but a classic one was desertion by the male partner ... Men departed for many reasons – poverty and debt, family disputes, impressment and adultery' (*Masterless Men*, p. 52). Belsey, in 'Alice Arden's Crime,' p. 83, writes that 'crimes of violence,' including domestic crimes, 'were by no means uncommon' in early modern England. See also Amussen, 'Gender, Family and the Social Order, 1560–1725,' pp. 205–10; Stone, *The Family, Sex and Marriage in England 1500–1800*, p. 137; and Macdonald, *Mystical Bedlam*, chap. 1.

2 Griffith, Preface, *Bethel: or a Forme for Families*, sigs. B2v–B3v.

3 Herrup, 'Law and Morality in Seventeenth-Century England,' p. 110.
4 Herrup, 'Law and Morality in Seventeenth-Century England,' p. 111.
5 Between c. 1590 and 1610 approximately twenty domestic tragedies, most of them murder plays, were written, only five of which survive in their entirety: *Arden of Feversham* (c. 1590–2), *A Warning for Fair Women* (c. 1593–9), *Two Lamentable Tragedies* (c. 1594–1601), *A Woman Killed with Kindness* (c. 1603), and *A Yorkshire Tragedy* (c. 1605–8).
6 Hobbes, *Philosophical Rudiments Concerning Government and Society,* pp. 130–1.
7 Hobbes, *Philosophical Rudiments Concerning Government and Society*, p. 129. Although in *Leviathan*, as Thomas notes, Hobbes 'refutes the simple patriarchal theory of government' ('The Social Origins of Hobbes's Political Thought,' in *Hobbes Studies*, ed. K.C. Brown, p. 189), Hobbes's treatise on the different kinds of government locates the origins of paternal, monarchical government in the eternal, divinely obtained universal order.
8 Hooker, *Laws of Ecclesiastical Polity*, in *Works*, vol. 1, p. 242; Smith, *De Republica Anglorum*, p. 23.
9 Smith, *De Republica Anglorum*, p. 23; T.E., *The Lawes Resolutions of Womens Rights*, p. 6. Belsey comments that women, upon marrying, 'surrendered ... to their husbands' their right to acquire and inherit property, 'exercis-[ing] no legal rights as members of the social body' (*The Subject of Tragedy*, pp. 152–3). See also Alice Clark, *Working Life of Women in the Seventeenth Century*.
10 Medvedev and Bakhtin, *The Formal Method in Literary Scholarship*, p. 8.
11 Erasmus, 'On Good Manners for Boys' / *De civilitate morum puerilium libellus*,' trans. Brian McGregor, in vol. 25 of *Collected Works of Erasmus*, p. 275.
12 Erasmus, 'On Good Manners for Boys,' pp. 273–4.
13 Montaigne, *Essayes*, p. 112. Noting the various social applications of early modern discourses on manners, Jacques Revel remarks that 'the sixteenth century was a time of intense effort to control social intercourse through the rules of civility. Society insisted that a person's gestures be intelligible to others. Behavior was judged by the group,' the codes of manners becoming 'increasingly effective as they were internalized by individuals' ('The Uses of Civility,' in *Passions of the Renaissance*, p. 167).
14 Heywood, *Apology*, sig. F3v.
15 I.G. [John Greene?], *A Refutation of the Apology for Actors*, sig. F1r.
16 More, *An Account of Virtue*, p. 139.
17 Williams, *The Long Revolution*, p. 48.

18 Williams, *The Long Revolution*, pp. 45, 48.

19 Williams, *The Long Revolution*, p. 48.

20 These and other household items have been verified as late sixteenth-
and early seventeenth-century stage properties by King in his valuable
study of plays staged between 1599 and 1642 (*Shakespeare and Staging,
1599–1642*). King has compiled 'a systematic survey of theatrical require-
ments for 276 plays' by seeking 'positive correlations between the external
evidence, as provided by contemporary architecture and pictures of early
English stages, and the internal evidence, as provided by the texts of
plays first performed in the years 1599–1642' (p. 1). King lists the following as frequently used domestic props: tables (sometimes 'set with meat,'
as in *Patient Grissil* [p. 19]); chairs and stools; beds; canopies; carpets;
chests; curtains; hangings; cushions; trunks and hampers; and tiring
rooms. For a condensed list of similar items included in a 1598 inventory
preserved in Henslowe's papers, see Brockett, *History of the Theatre*, p. 181.

21 On England's 'Great Rebuilding,' see Hoskins, *Provincial England*, p. 131,
and Orlin, '"The Causes and Reasons of all Artificial Things" in the Elizabethan Domestic Environment,' pp. 19–75. In design, notes Orlin, houses
in the early modern period were 'machine[s] for conspicuous self-expression, never more so than in the choices available through and exerted in
ornament' (p. 61). On the social and economic function of lavish private
space, see also Contamine, 'Peasant Hearth to Papal Palace,' pp. 425–505;
and Fisher, 'The Development of London as a Centre of Conspicuous
Consumption in the Sixteenth and Seventeenth Centuries,' pp. 199–220.
Fisher observes that the houses of the gentry were often multiple-story
mansions, 'double, triple, even quadrupled-fronted structures,' adorned
with elaborately engraved balconies and windows (p. 200).

22 Harrison, *Description of England*, pp. 200–1, 199.

23 Harrison, *Description of England*, p. 200.

24 Harrison, *Description of England*, p. 200.

25 Wotton, *The Elements of Architecture*, p. 82.

26 Harrison, *Description of England*, p. 140.

27 Goody, *Cooking, Cuisine and Class*, p. 152. Mennell, in *All Manners of Food*,
p. 83, points out that 'new cookery books were much more plentiful in
sixteenth-century England than in France, where it was medieval texts
which were frequently reprinted.'

28 See Burton, *The Early Tudors at Home*, pp. 103–9. Burton notes that in the
1560s silver and pewter 'rapidly displaced the thick pieces of bread or
wooden trenchers formerly used' (pp. 103–4). 'The exchange of vessel,'
writes Harrison, 'as of treen [wooden] platters into pewter, and wooden

spoons into silver or tin,' marked another major step toward domestic
decorum in the mid-sixteenth century (*Description of England*, p. 201).

29 Heal, *Hospitality in Early Modern England*, p. 6. A number of commentators
have observed the importance of Frankford's house. Bescou has noted its
symbolic value: 'en verité la maison est ici l'un des personnages princi-
paux' ('Thomas Heywood et le problème de l'adultère dans *Une femme
tuée par la bonté*,' p. 139), as has Rauchbaur, in 'Visual and Rhetorical
Imagery in Th. Heywood's *A Woman Killed with Kindness*,' p. 203, and
Levin, in *The Multiple Plot in English Renaissance Drama*, p. 94. Henderson,
in 'Many Mansions,' p. 291, has illustrated the Christian typology that
informs the architecture. Scobie has suggested that although the play
'differs from many if not all of the plays written within the domestic
tragedy type by not being a dramatisation of contemporary historical
events, as were *Arden* and most of the plays that followed it,' it nevertheless 'shares' with other domestic tragedies 'the domestic emphasis and the
middle-class setting' (Introduction, *A Woman Killed with Kindness*, p. xxi).
Orlin has argued that Frankford's house is prototypical of the early modern house in that 'it is a political association, an economic enterprise, a
social institution, and ... a moral system' (*Private Matters and Public Culture
in Post-Reformation England*, p. 151).

30 Wotton, *The Elements of Architecture*, p. 82.

31 Bruni, for example, urges women to study the liberal arts but warns that
'public' pursuits are 'absolutely outside the province of woman' (*De
Studiis et Literis* [1409], p. 126).

32 The play was performed by Worcester's Men in 1603. On the company's
expenditure for Anne Frankford's attire, see Gurr, *The Shakespearean Stage
1574–1642*, p. 82.

33 Woodbridge, *Women and the English Renaissance*, p. 27.

34 Woodbridge remarks that the 'connection between women and property
was so deeply engrained in Renaissance thought that such diction was
often used as an innocent compliment' (*Women and the English Renaissance*,
p. 268, n. 4); and Newman observes that in many sermons of the period
'woman is a series of prosthetic parts and the "*bodie* whereunto it is
fastned" is the husband. The larger metaphorical frame is the Pauline
letter to the Ephesians, the commonplace notion of marriage as the union
of man and woman into one flesh ... ' (*Fashioning Femininity and English
Renaissance Drama*, p. 9).

35 See Partridge, *Shakespeare's Bawdy*, p. 112.

36 Ranum, 'Refuges of Intimacy,' p. 218.

37 For Canuteson, Frankford is 'a refined revenger of his tainted honor ...

protest[ing] to be acting out of kindness' ('The Theme of Forgiveness in the Plot and Subplot of *A Woman Killed with Kindness*,' p. 139). Bromley, on the other hand, argues that Frankford is an 'ideal' Christian 'gentleman' who 'takes the moderate ... course' ('Domestic Conduct in *A Woman Killed with Kindness*,' p. 268); and David Cook, in '*A Woman Killed with Kindness*: An Unshakespearian Tragedy,' p. 363, suggests that Frankford's action upholds the principle of Christian charity.

38 Ferry, *The 'Inward' Language*, p. 46.
39 *The Good Hows-holder*, pp. 5–6.
40 Reynolds, *The Staging of Elizabethan Plays at the Red Bull Theater: 1605–1625*, p. 125.
41 Jourdain, *English Decoration and Furniture of the Early Renaissance (1500–1650)*, p. 158.
42 Ranum, 'Refuges of Intimacy,' pp. 207, 218.
43 Ranum, 'Refuges of Intimacy,' p. 217.
44 Montaigne, *Essayes*, p. 745.
45 D'Ewes, *The Diary of Sir Simonds D'Ewes (1622–1624)*, p. 103.
46 Guazzo, *The Civile Conversation of M. Steeven Guazzo*, vol. 1, p. 48.
47 Montainge, *Essayes*, p. 746 (emphasis added).
48 Roper, *The Lyfe of Sir Thomas Moore, Knighte*, pp. 30–1 (emphasis added).
49 D'Ewes, *The Diary of Sir Simonds D'Ewes*, p. 60.
50 Although I arrived at my analysis of the study in relation to Frankford's subjectivity before the publication of Orlin's *Private Matters and Public Culture in Post-Reformation England*, Orlin offers the similar suggestion that the study, in 'allow[ing] of private meditation and linguistic formulation,' also 'produced Frankford's judgment,' which 'valorized his agency ... author[ing] him as an apparently determinate male self' (p. 188).
51 McLuskie, in *Renaissance Dramatists*, p. 136, writes that 'in *A Woman Killed with Kindness* Anne Frankford's part fulfils both mimetic and symbolic functions within the narrative. She is, on the one hand a figure in a particular story of adultery and repentance and, on the other, a paradigm case of the adulteress and repentant wife.'
52 *Certain Sermons or Homilies Appointed to be Read in Churches in the Time of Queen Elizabeth*, p. 537; Gosynhyll, *The Scole House of Women* (c. 1541), sig. B iiv.
53 Comparing Heywood's play with Robert Greene's 'Conversion of an English Courtesan,' a story appended to *A Disputation Between a He Conny-catcher and a She Conny-catcher* (1592), McNeir argues that 'Greene's heroine ... falls not long after marriage in the same precipitate, unpre-

meditated, and apparently unmotivated manner' as does Anne Frankford ('Heywood's Sources for the Main Plot of *A Woman Killed with Kindness*,' p. 203). Hoffman speculates that 'the demands of the ballad plot [of "Little Musgrave and Lady Barnard"] also compromised Heywood's development of Anne's character and thus resulted in her unsatisfyingly rapid submission to a lover' ('"Both bodily deth and werdly shame": "Little Musgrave and Lady Barnard" as Source for *A Woman Killed With Kindness*,' p. 170). Other apologists for Heywood's dramaturgy include Bromley, who suggests that we consider the play according to its merits as a morality: 'the question of motivation, applied to Anne or other characters, is sometimes irrelevant ... because Heywood is not interested in individual psychology'; Anne 'responds to her trials courageously, and Heywood fashions her into an exemplary gentlewoman at the end of the play' ('Domestic Conduct in *A Woman Killed with Kindness*,' pp. 261, 260). Kiefer contends that Heywood deliberately refrains from providing motivation for Anne's fall because 'he recognized that to give Anne a credible motive – any motive – for adultery would compromise his intent. To have supplied a motive would have meant explaining and thus, implicitly, condoning Anne's transgression' ('Heywood as Moralist in *A Woman Killed with Kindness*,' p. 87). And Panek argues that 'by largely avoiding the question of motivation, Heywood presents the act of adultery ... unobscured by either mitigating or damning circumstances, so that we may focus ... on ... Anne's repentance and Frankford's "kindness"' ('Punishing Adultery in *A Woman Killed with Kindness*,' p. 367). For Spacks, on the other hand, dwelling on the issue of Anne's lack of motivation obfuscates the abandonment of morality shared by all of the principal characters: 'The world of *A Woman Killed with Kindness* is not a world of true and significant moral standards – it is rather a world of appearance ... The only major character who does conform to a true and rigid vision of honor, Master Frankford, is himself trapped in the world of appearances to the extent that he is unable to perceive and judge truly' ('Honour and Perception in *A Woman Killed with Kindness*,' p. 330). On Heywood's conscious didacticism in *A Woman Killed* see also Townsend, 'The Artistry of Thomas Heywood's Double Plots,' p. 102.

54 The view of Anne's motivation as dramatically unimportant was originally proposed by Cromwell, for whom Heywood's chief concern is 'the nature of Frankford's revenge,' and not Anne's infidelity (*Thomas Heywood: A Study in the Elizabethan Drama of Everyday Life*, p. 55). Day cautions modern readers that 'Heywood's contemporaries deemed women

frail creatures, quick to fall if not carefully supervised ... [so that] dwelling on the fall of Frankford's wife would lead the play too far from Heywood's purpose' (*History of English Literature to 1660*, p. 345). Wentworth suggests that Anne, who is 'initially victimized by her compassion for Wendoll and a corresponding' insufficiency of 'understanding ... lacks the intellectual resources and the moral insight to discern any solution to her predicament' ('Thomas Heywood's *A Woman Killed with Kindness* as Domestic Morality,' p. 155). Cook views Anne's fall as evidence of her naïvety: 'This patently is her first encounter with passion – of which she knows nothing after her secluded youth and calmly affectionate marriage' ('*A Woman Killed with Kindness*: An Unshakespearian Tragedy,' p. 357). Canuteson also contends that 'Anne's sudden fall ... should give us few problems ... the relationship of Wendoll and Frankford, with the betrayal of a friend, is the moral issue' ('The Theme of Forgiveness in the Plot and Subplot of *A Woman Killed with Kindness*,' pp. 130–1).

55 Heywood, *Apology*, sig. G1v; Preface, *Gunaikeion*, unnumbered page.
56 Townsend, 'The Artistry of Thomas Heywood's Double Plots,' p. 102. Canuteson points out 'the matter of the expensive "black veluett" gown which Anne would have worn from scene xvi to the end of the play in contrast with Susan's white wedding dress – probably the same white dress that Anne wore in the first scene' ('The Theme of Forgiveness,' p. 125).
57 *Certain Sermons or Homilies Appointed to be Read in Churches in the Time of Queen Elizabeth*, p. 537.
58 The play's debt to the homily contradicts the widely held view that during a time when it was customary practice for adulterous wives to be publicly exposed and humiliated by their husbands, Heywood transformed the revenge ethic by portraying a husband who forgives his wife's transgression. The exponents of this view include Adams, *English Domestic or, Homiletic Tragedy 1575–1642*, p. 157; Arthur M. Clark, *Thomas Heywood: Playwright and Miscellanist*, p. 236; Day, *History of English Literature to 1660*, pp. 344–5; and Van Fossen, Introduction, *A Woman Killed with Kindness*, pp. xxx–xxxi.
59 Levin argues that Frankford's domestic servants 'are an integral part of ... [the] household, and, through their ultimate relationship with him, impart a homely and genre-like quality to the portrayal of his world ...' ('The Elizabethan "Three-Level" Play,' p. 32). Yet the maid's gesture idealizes the loyalty of servants in an age when cynicism towards them was widespread. See Castan, 'Politics and Private Life,' p. 54 and Kussmaul, *Servants in Husbandry in Early Modern England*, pp. 33–5.

60 'An Homily of the State of Matrimony,' *Certain Sermons or Homilies Appointed to be Read in Churches in the Time of Queen Elizabeth*, p. 538.

61 Cicero, *Offices*, pp. 20–1; cited in McNeir, 'Heywood's Sources for the Main Plot of *A Woman Killed with Kindness*,' p. 207. Frankford's charity, adds McNeir, has parallels in Gascoigne and Greene, 'and sanction in the condemnation of wrathful vengeance by ... medieval ... and Renaissance authorities' (p. 207).

62 A few commentators have pointed to Frankford's complicity in Anne's death, but have reached different conclusions about the dramatic significance of his actions. For Ornstein, 'Heywood deliberately creates the ambiguity of Frankford's mildness' but the play raises no 'serious moral questions about Anne's guilt and suffering [or] about ... Frankford's motives' ('Bourgeois Morality and Dramatic Convention in *A Woman Killed with Kindness*,' p. 139). Vanita interprets Anne's punishment and the method of Frankford's forgiveness as morally and dramatically conventional: 'The titillating title [of the play] directs audience expectation to the kill; hence all that leads up to it is relatively unimportant and moves within an uncritically and unimpressively handled conventional formula ... Frankford restores to Anne the name of "wife" only when he is sure she is nearly dead and he will never have to live with her as a wife' ('Men Beware Men: Shakespeare's Warnings for Unfair Husbands,' pp. 205–13). Panek argues that while Frankford's 'kindness' obscures his vengeance, Heywood is deliberately criticizing the punishment: 'the idea that a repentant adulteress ... *ought* to be forgiven' is widely accepted by 'contemporary conduct-book authors,' so that 'the reader or audience [is] less than comfortable with Frankford's methods of punishing adultery' ('Punishing Adultery,' pp. 375 and 377, n. 19).

63 Battus, *The Christian Man's Closet*, sig. T3r–3v. Gutierrez interprets Anne Frankford's fall in relation to seventeenth-century Puritan discourses of resistance: 'The religious ideology identified as puritan takes on local meaning as Heywood carefully configures the triangle of adultery as the relationship between a possessed Christian and her demon: Anne Frankford, violating her own personal as well as community values, is possessed by Wendoll, a devil figure, with whom she commits adultery, and whom she then exorcises by fasting and prayer so as to be returned to God ... [T]he rhetoric of possession and exorcism ... along with Anne's ... retribution of self-starvation, signals the play's participation in ... Puritan resistance to episcopal authority' ('Exorcism by Fasting in *A Woman Killed with Kindness*, pp. 49–50). On Heywood's relation to early modern Puritanism, see also Atkinson, 'An Approach to the Main Plot of Thomas

Heywood's *A Woman Killed with Kindness*,' p. 25, and Ornstein, *The Moral Vision of Jacobean Tragedy*, p. 17. Elsewhere, Gutierrez contends that 'the ethical pattern of sin, repentance, and punishment that is the framework of so many domestic tragedies is absent in *A Woman Killed with Kindness*' ('The Irresolution of Melodrama,' p. 283). Scobie also argues that Anne Frankford's sentence does not conform to the homiletic ending of the morality play in that her punishment is 'more intense in its moral assertion through being self-inflicted ... Choosing her own punishment, she confirms the truth of the moral judgement as she understands it. Acknowledgement points the way to ... the possibility of salvation, through action that affirms without imposing a moral code' (Introduction, *A Woman Killed With Kindness*, pp. xxi–xxii).

64 Van Fossen, ed., *A Woman Killed with Kindness*, p. 96, n. 44.

65 Heywood, *Apology*, F3v (emphasis added).

66 See Contamine, 'Peasant Hearth to Papal Palace,' p. 496.

67 Dollimore, *Radical Tragedy*, p. 14.

68 Wine proposes that '*Arden* is the first extant play of its type,' and suggests that 'two that are not extant, *Murderous Michael* and *The Cruelty of a Step-Mother*, both of the late 1570s, may be forerunners' (Introduction, *The Tragedy of Master Arden of Faversham*, p. lviii, n. 1). Sturgess is more cautious about the play's uniqueness, suggesting that 'if not the first of these plays it was an important early example' (Introduction, *Three Elizabethan Domestic Tragedies*, p. 19). In addition to the texts which I have cited, the play's sources and analogues include Stow's papers, Hasted's history of Kent, Southouse's survey, Jacob's *History of the Town and Port of Faversham*, the *Breviat Chronicle*, and Heywood's *Troia Britannica*.

69 Day, *History of English Literature to 1600*, p. 349; Trainor, '"Guilty Creatures at a Play,"' p. 40.

70 Leggatt, '"Arden of Faversham,"' p. 124.

71 On the play's modifications of its sources and its interest in character, see Wine, Introduction, *The Tragedy of Master Arden of Faversham*, pp. lxvi–lxxiv. Sturgess argues that 'character portrayal is the play's outstanding feature. The characters are presented not as types or moral symbols but as individuals' (Introduction, *Three Elizabethan Domestic Tragedies*, p. 23). A minority opinion is expressed by Walz, in '*Arden of Faversham* as Tragic Satire,' p. 26, for whom 'the characters are clearly recognizable types. And they are the types associated with domestic satires, the farcical and moral interludes that constituted such a large part of sixteenth-century stage fare.'

72 Douglas, 'Deciphering a Meal,' p. 61.

73 Harrison, *Description of England*, p. 144.

74 LeBlanc, 'Dinner With Chichikov,' p. 76.

75 Harrison, *Description of England*, p. 141.

76 Brown, *Fictional Meals and Their Function in the French Novel, 1798–1848*, p. 38.

77 Although the reasons for Alice's crime, argues Kato, 'are not mentioned in the play itself,' the spectator infers that she murders her husband 'because she has her lover and Arden is the object of her bitter hatred and the obstacle to their enjoying illicit love' ('Alice Arden of Feversham and her Company of Evil,' p. 189). For Brodwin, while *Arden* adheres closely to Holinshed's account, it develops the character of Alice in such a way that it explains 'the desperate quality of her love for Mosbie which drives her to murder for its preservation,' (*Elizabethan Love Tragedy 1587–1625*, p. 191).

78 See Attwell, 'Property, Status, and the Subject in a Middle-class Tragedy: *Arden of Faversham*,' p. 339.

79 Orlin convincingly demonstrates that 'Alice Arden represents both the theoretical threat posed by women to patriarchal philosophy and the suspected inadequacy in practice of an elaborate mechanism of domestic prescription' (*Private Matters and Public Culture*, p. 105). I disagree, however, with her contention that *Arden of Feversham* capitulates to a 'thoroughgoing political orthodoxy' which is 'insufficient to one challenge to its intellectual integrity: it is fatally uncertain of how to treat, manage, and contain its disorderly woman' (p. 104).

80 Bruster, '"In a Woman's Key": Women's Speech and Women's Language in Renaissance Drama,' p. 244.

81 Barbaro, 'On Wifely Duties,' p. 206. While 'silence [is] the most outstanding ornament of women' (p. 206), Barbaro charges men with the duty to speak eloquently 'on those matters that they know well' (p. 204).

82 Gainsford, *The Rich Cabinet*, p. 163.

83 Although I concur with Belsey that in many instances *Arden of Feversham* 'presents Alice Arden's challenge to the institution of marriage as an act of heroism' (*The Subject of Tragedy*, p. 134), in my analysis I depart from her claim that 'a definitive meaning for Alice['s] ... crime ... remains elusive' (p. 135).

84 T.E., *The Lawes Resolutions of Womens Rights*, p. 6.

85 Jardine, *Still Harping on Daughters*, pp. 42–3.

86 Underdown, 'The Taming of the Scold,' p. 119. For my analysis of Alice Arden's recalcitrance I am also indebted to Woodbridge's suggestion that 'the charge of sexual immorality' in early modern discourses 'is levelled

at female[s] ... who have attained some measure of freedom of action,' so that 'one of the major charges in the Renaissance misogynist's catalogue, lust, may have been no more than a backlash against feminine freedom and assertiveness in the real world' (*Women and the English Renaissance*, p. 177). See also Newman, *Fashioning Femininity*, p. xviii.

87 Mendelson, 'Stuart Women's Diaries and Occasional Memoirs,' pp. 192, 191.

88 Ezell, *The Patriarch's Wife*, p. 107.

89 Lewalski, *Writing Women in Jacobean England*, pp. 3, 2. The nine women whom Lewalski studies are Queen Anne, Princess Elizabeth, Arabella Stuart, the Countess of Bedford, Anne Clifford, Rachel Speght, Elizabeth Cary, Amelia Lanyer, and Mary Wroth. See also Krontiris, *Oppositional Voices: Women as Writers and Translators of Literature in the English Renaissance*, on the strategies employed by Englishwomen who challenge conservative ideologies of gender, and Otten's carefully documented account of non-literary writings by women from different social groups, in which they describe a wide range of female experience including suffering as a result of domestic abuse, unjust imprisonment, and economic exploitation (*English Women's Voices, 1540–1700*).

90 Jardine, '*The Duchess of Malfi*: A Case Study in the Literary Representation of Women,' p. 116.

91 For a useful analysis of how 'Arden's prosperity and place in the social hierarchy is premised on the dispossession and displacement' of others, see Breen, 'The Carnival Body in *Arden of Faversham*,' p. 16.

92 See Ferry, *The 'Inward' Language*, p. 49.

93 Although insisting that 'in every other case, human justice and theological judgment are in complete agreement' in the play, Adams admits that 'there is no explanation for this miscarriage of justice,' that 'moral justice is far from perfectly executed' (*English Domestic or, Homiletic Tragedy 1575–1642*, p. 107, n. 14). Youngblood, in 'Theme and Imagery in *Arden of Feversham*,' p. 208, argues that like 'every tragedy,' *Arden* 'postulates a world of moral order and moral sanctions which human actions temporarily violate, with tragic human consequences; a moral order which at the close of the play has been, however artificially, restored and reaffirmed.'

94 See Wine, Introduction, *The Tragedy of Master Arden of Faversham*, p. lxxiv; and Orlin, for whom 'the brief closing scenes satisfy our instinct for justice, but not tidily' ('Man's House as His Castle,' p. 81).

95 Trainor, '"Guilty Creatures at a Play,"' p. 43.

96 Dolan, 'Gender, Moral Agency, and Dramatic Form in *A Warning for Fair Women*,' pp. 202, 209.

97 Orlin, 'Familial Transgressions, Societal Transition on the Elizabethan Stage,' p. 46; *Private Matters and Public Culture*, p. 112.

98 For Mehl, 'the playwright's technique becomes rather simple,' as evidenced by the 'alternat[ion]' between 'realistic tragedy' and 'a morally instructive pantomime in which the characters taking part appear to be only the victims of the virtues and vices struggling for mastery of them' (*The Elizabethan Dumb Show*, pp. 94, 92). Dolan suggests that the dumb shows 'veil the playwright's reluctance to speak about such transgressions as a wife's infidelity and her plot against her husband's life. In their visual presentation of the unspeakable, the dumb shows reinforce Anne's role as a silent, passive figure even in this crime, her own tragedy' ('Gender, Moral Agency, and Dramatic Form in *A Warning for Fair Women*,' p. 211).

99 Mehl, *The Elizabethan Dumb Show*, pp. 95–6.

100 Boas, in *An Introduction to Tudor Drama*, suggests that Tragedy employs 'murky rhetoric' in order to set forth 'the meaning of these "Shows"' (p. 108). Whereas Boas views this development as being 'in uneasy contrast with the homely dialogue of the main action' (p. 109), I consider it more in keeping with the play's resistance to the cults of civility and domesticity.

101 Bradbrook, *Themes and Conventions of Elizabethan Tragedy*, p. 18.

102 Bakhtin, *Rabelais and His World*, p. 48.

103 Freud, 'The "Uncanny,"' p. 220.

104 Freud, 'The "Uncanny,"' p. 222.

105 Freud, 'The "Uncanny,"' pp. 220–5.

106 Freud, 'The "Uncanny,"' pp. 224–5.

107 Strachey, trans. and ed., 'The "Uncanny",' by Sigmund Freud, p. 225, n. 1.

108 On the sources of the play, which in addition to Golding's tract include Holinshed's and Stow's accounts of George Sanders's murder, see Cannon, Introduction, *A Warning for Fair Women*, pp. 64–75.

109 Golding, *A Briefe Discourse*, p. 230.

110 Golding, *A Brief Discourse*, pp. 236–8 (emphasis added).

111 Bradford, 'Daily Meditations,' in *Writings of the Rev. John Bradford*, p. 444.

112 Augustine, St, *The Confessions*, p. 377.

113 Gore, *The Way to Prosper*, pp. 137–8.

114 *Edward de Vere Newsletter*, No. 21 (November 1990), p. [1].

115 *A Yorkshire Tragedy*, ed. A.C. Cawley and Barry Gaines. Further references to the play will be to this edition.

116 See above, chap. 3; for further discussion of *The Miseries of Enforced Marriage* see chap. 5, below.

117 Dolan, *Dangerous Familiars*, pp. 13–14.
118 *Two Most Unnatural and Bloodie Murthers (1605)*, in Cawley and Gaines, eds., *A Yorkshire Tragedy*, Appendix A, p. 96. Further references to the pamphlet will be to this edition.
119 Macdonald, *Mystical Bedlam*, pp. 131, 165.
120 Adams, *English Domestic or, Homiletic Tragedy 1575–1642*, p. 128.
121 While I find valuable Leggatt's contention, in *English Drama: Shakespeare to the Restoration 1590–1660*, p. 183, that in *A Yorkshire Tragedy* 'no saving conventions contain or neutralize the central character's drive to ruin,' I disagree with his suggestion that the playwright ascribes no motive to the Husband's behaviour beyond 'his drive to self-destruction' (p. 184): the 'threat ... that destroys the comfortable home to which the domestic play aspires as its ideal' is strictly 'from within ... and destroys it for no discernible reason' (pp. 185–6).
122 Cawley and Gaines, eds., *A Yorkshire Tragedy*, p. 61, n. 74.
123 Foucault, *Madness and Civilization*, p. 37.
124 Tyrrell, Preface to *A Yorkshire Tragedy*, in *The Doubtful Plays of Shakspere*, pp. 82–3.
125 Cawley and Gaines, Introduction, *A Yorkshire Tragedy*, pp. 19–20.
126 'The Wife's thoughts,' write Cawley and Gaines, 'are engrossed by her husband, who seems to get the major share of her sorrow and her love. We must either accept the Wife's behaviour as a miracle of forgiveness or suppose that she concentrates her emotions on her husband in order to suppress an unbearable sorrow for her dead children. But neither the miraculous nor the psychological explanation is really convincing' (p. 20). Dolan similarly remarks that 'despite the loss of two of her children,' the Wife 'forgives' the Husband (*Dangerous Familiars*, p. 159).
127 Yarrington, *Two Lamentable Tragedies*, ed. John S. Farmer. Further references to the play will be to this edition.
128 Adams, *English Domestic or, Homiletic Tragedy 1575–1642*, p. 108. See also Chambers, *The Elizabethan Stage*, vol. 3, p. 518.
129 *Two Lamentable Tragedies* has attracted little scholarly interest since Adams's denunciation of Yarrington's craft as 'characterized by ... naïve psychology' (*English Domestic or, Homiletic Tragedy 1575–1642*, p. 108) and Andrew Clark's complaint that the text 'employs, *ad nauseum*, the customary dramatic device of divine providence and the popular religious beliefs of the sermons' (*Domestic Drama*, vol. 1, p. 155). Recently, Tessitore and Orlin have argued for a more complex dramaturgy. Although not disputing the providentialist reading, Tessitore views the homiletic design as complemented by an Aristotelian mimetic structure whose

ultimate effect is to induce catharsis, or moral purification ('purificazione morale'), in the spectator ('*Two Lamentable Tragedies* [1601],' p. 53). Focusing on the characterization of Rachel in the English plot, Orlin demonstrates that 'order in the macrocosm – civic order' is 'dependent upon the betrayal of degree in the microcosm – household hierarchy' ('Familial Transgressions,' p. 35).

130 Adams, *English Domestic or, Homiletic Tragedy 1575–1642*, p. 110.

131 Harrison, *Description of England*, p. 118; Smith, *De Republica Anglorum*, p. 46.

132 Slack, in *Poverty and Policy in Tudor and Stuart England*, p. 64, notes that 'in the three Kent parishes of Chatham, Gillingham and the Isle of Grain, in 1596, 71 per cent of the population had no corn, and there were more people with than without only in the Isle.' Between 1580 and 1620 'many Essex parishes were complaining that they were "very sore charged with poor," and the clothing villages in the north of the country were overwhelmed by "poor artisans" in the 1590s.' Similar 'pressures were felt to a much greater degree, and from an earlier date, in towns' (p. 67).

133 Slack, *Poverty and Policy in Tudor and Stuart England*, p. 67.

134 See Beier, *The Problem of the Poor in Tudor and Early Stuart England*, p. 13; Amussen, *An Ordered Society*, p. 31; Walter and Wrightson, 'Dearth and the Social Order in Early Modern England,'pp. 22–42; and Slack, *Poverty and Policy in Tudor and Stuart England*, p. 101.

135 Peter Clark, *The English Alehouse*, pp. 5, 123–31.

136 Amussen, *An Ordered Society*, p. 170.

137 See Adams, *English Domestic or, Homiletic Tragedy 1575–1642*, p. 108; and Andrew Clark, for whom 'the excessive crudity of the work manifests itself in all matters of dramaturgy' (*Domestic Drama*, vol. 1, p. 155).

138 Walter and Wrightson observe that 'it is difficult to exaggerate the extent to which people in the late sixteenth and early seventeenth century were conscious of the threat of dearth' ('Dearth and the Social Order in Early Modern England,' p. 22).

139 Stubbs, *The Anatomy of Abuses*, sig. Ry.

140 Gouge, *Gods Three Arrows; Plague, Famine, Sword* (1631), p. 5.

141 Stubbs, *The Anatomy of Abuses*, sig. Ry.

142 Thomas Smith (?), *Discourse of the Common Weal*, p. 154.

143 See Palliser, *The Age of Elizabeth*, p. 154. Palliser points out that 'a measure of the increased understanding of economics during the second half of the century' is 'that the apparent paradox which Smith tried to explain in 1549 no longer seemed a problem in 1593. Fulke Greville could argue in a parliamentary debate in that year that high prices did

not indicate national poverty but the opposite: "our dearth of everything amongst us, sheweth plenty of money"' (p. 155).

144 See Slack, *Poverty and Policy*, pp. 48–52.

145 Starkey, *A Dialogue between Pole and Lupset*, p. 54; Harrison, *Description of England*, pp. 115–16. Palliser notes that in the early 1580s a number of commentators were calling 'for a reduction in unnecessary imports, especially silk, wine and spices ...' (*The Age of Elizabeth*, p. 330).

146 Law, 'Yarrington's "Two Lamentable Tragedies",' p. 171.

4: 'Retrograde and Preposterous'

1 The English Renaissance plays that treat the subject of witchcraft divide into four broad categories: (1) those whose chief interest is in benign forms of magic; (2) those with historical subjects, in which a main character either practises or is influenced by witchcraft; (3) those in which the witch-figure has only a minor role; (4) witch plays. For a useful synopsis of the features of each group, see Thomas Heywood and Richard Brome, *An Edition of The Late Lancashire Witches*, Introduction by Laird H. Barber, p. 20.

2 Clark, *Domestic Drama*, vol. 2, p. 340.

3 Cooper, *The Mystery of Witchcraft*, title page and p. 5.

4 Cooper, *The Mystery of Witchcraft*, p. 206. In 'Philomela Strikes Back,' p. 433, Gutierrez observes that early modern commentators often point 'to woman's desire to end her subjection to men, her desire for power, as a motivating factor in her choice for adultery or witchcraft. In other words, the woman deliberately chooses to ally herself with a power that is an enemy to the patriarchal system in which she is living.'

5 Coudert, 'Witchcraft Studies to Date,' p. 10. See also Jean R. Brink et al., Introduction, *The Politics of Gender in Early Modern Europe*, p. 9. Although witch beliefs and the relation between women and witches are cross-cultural phenomena, it is only in early modern Europe and America that the belief in witchcraft led to a witchcraze resulting in 'the death of between 60,000 and 200,000 people,' most of them women (Coudert, 'The Myth of the Improved Status of Protestant Women,' p. 61). In England and Scotland, intermittent witch hunts and persecutions were most intensive between 1590 and 1650. In 1542, 1563, and 1604 respectively, three successive Acts of Parliament made witchcraft a statutory crime in England. In England, approximately 2,000 persons were tried in English assize courts from 1542–1736 'and some 300 executed'; among the latter,

approximately 85 to 93 per cent were women (Macfarlane, *Witchcraft in Tudor and Stuart England*, p. 62. See also Thomas, *Religion and the Decline of Magic*, p. 520, and Larner, *Enemies of God*, p. 89).

6 Larner, *Enemies of God*, p. 92.

7 Kramer and Sprenger, *Malleus Maleficarum*, pp. 43–4.

8 James I, *Daemonologie*, pp. 43–4.

9 Kors and Peters, Introduction, *Witchcraft in Europe 1100–1700*, p. 12.

10 Wiesner, *Women and Gender in Early Modern Europe*, p. 225.

11 Nelson, 'Why Witches Were Women,' pp. 347, 346.

12 Coudert, 'Witchcraft Studies to Date,' p. 21.

13 See Stuart Clark, 'Inversion, Misrule and the Meaning of Witchcraft,' pp. 98–127.

14 In city comedies such as Lyly's *Mother Bombie* (1594) and Thomas Heywood's *The Wise Woman of Hogsdon* (1604) the titular heroines are not witches but crones whose magic is benign because they do not practise conjuring or devil-worship. Mother Bombie's claim – 'If neuer to doo harme, be to doo good, I dare saie I am not ill' (III.iv.91–2) – is never disputed in the play, and her activities lead to positive reconciliations in the denouement (Lyly, *Mother Bombie*, in vol. 3 of *The Complete Works of John Lyly*, ed. R. Warwick Bond). Similarly, Heywood's Wise Woman practises fortune-telling, palmistry, and midwifery, but in the end all of the couples whom she has matched are joined in marriage, and she attends the celebrations as the guest of honour.

15 Lyly, *Endimion, The Man in the Moon*, in vol. 3 of *The Complete Works of John Lyly*. Further references to the play will be to this edition.

16 See Briggs, *Pale Hecate's Team*, p. 64.

17 Kramer and Sprenger, *Malleus Maleficarum*, p. 44.

18 *Daemonologie*, p. 55. James is here echoing the authors of the *Malleus Maleficarum* (see Kramer and Sprenger, *Malleus Maleficarum*, p. 1).

19 See Coudert, 'The Myth of the Improved Status of Protestant Women,' p. 66.

20 Peter Corbin and Douglas Sedge observe that in Middleton's *The Witch* 'continental and English witchcraft practices are mingled indiscriminately': the gathering of witches 'in a sabbath in which the Devil was worshipped, the sexual assaults on the community by incubus and succubus, the transvection of witches into the air by means of anointing ... belong ... to continental conceptions of witchcraft ... They co-exist in the play alongside more characteristically English ingredients of witch-lore such as the familiar, the use of waxen effigies and the laming of cattle ... ' (Introduction, *Three Jacobean Witchcraft Plays*, p. 15).

21 Knight, 'The Milk of Concord: An Essay on Life-Themes in *Macbeth*,' in *The Imperial Theme*, p. 139. The scenes in *The Witch* involving Hecate were so successful that *Macbeth* was revised so as to include a dance and two songs from *The Witch* as well as the figure of Hecate, who, like her counterpart in Middleton, 'takes advantage of the flying machinery at the Blackfriars theatre' (Corbin and Sedge, Introduction, *Three Jacobean Witchcraft Plays*, p. 3).

22 Middleton, *The Witch*, in *Three Jacobean Witchcraft Plays*, ed. Corbin and Sedge. Further references to the play will be to this edition.

23 Cited in Thomas Bayly Howell, ed., *A Complete Collection of State Trials*, vol. 2 (1603–1627), pp. 799–801.

24 Cooper, *The Mystery of Witchcraft*, p. 206.

25 *Macbeth*, in *The Complete Works of Shakespeare*, ed. David Bevington. Further references to the play will be to this edition.

26 Stallybrass, '*Macbeth* and Witchcraft,' p. 196.

27 On Lady Macbeth's transgression of 'her wifely roles as hostess and helpmate' see Klein, 'Lady Macbeth "Infirm of Purpose,"' pp. 240–55.

28 Coudert, 'The Myth of the Improved Status of Protestant Women,' p. 78.

29 Luther, *Luther's Works*, vol. 1, p. 203.

30 Brauner, 'Martin Luther on Witchcraft: A True Reformer?', p. 37. In *Fearless Wives and Frightened Shrews*, p. 58, Brauner further notes that for Luther 'women are by nature fearful; they practice witchcraft in order to overcome their fears, but this only binds them all the more to their fearful nature. A woman can free herself from fear only if she accepts her weakness and becomes an obedient wife who trusts in God.'

31 Hobbes, *Leviathan, or the Matter, Form, and Power of a Commonwealth, Ecclesiastical and Civil* (1651), chap. 20, para. 15.

32 Janet Adelman, '"Born of Woman": Fantasies of Maternal Power in *Macbeth*,' p. 97. In *Malevolent Nurture*, pp. 212–13, Willis suggests that while *Macbeth* 'associates demonic agency with unruly women and constructs the murder of a father-king as a profoundly unnatural act, it also arouses considerable anxiety about the "godly" social/political order headed by Duncan and then Malcolm. The interplay between the witches and Macbeth highlights a problematic associated not so much with women as with fathers and kings; a tragic mechanism inheres in godly patriarchal rule, seemingly dooming it to produce traitors out of loyal subjects.'

33 Adelman, '"Born of Woman": Fantasies of Maternal Power in *Macbeth*,' p. 98. The passage also alludes to menstruation. Fox has demonstrated that 'visitings of Nature' was 'a common euphemism for menstruation' ('Obstetrics and Gynecology in *Macbeth*,' p. 129). 'In the play's context of

unnatural births,' writes Adelman, 'the thickening of the blood and the stopping up of access and passage to remorse begin to sound like attempts to undo reproductive functioning and perhaps to stop the menstrual blood that is the sign of its potential' (p. 97).

34 Brain, 'An Anthropological Perspective on the Witchcraze,' p. 18.

35 Marston, *The Wonder of Women*, in *Three Jacobean Witchcraft Plays*, ed. Corbin and Sedge. Further references to the play will be to this edition.

36 For the plot involving Erichto, Marston borrows heavily from Book VI of Lucan's *Pharsalia*. On the sexual and scatological underpinning of Erichto's necrophilic and necrophagous rites, Chauchaix observes: 'La magicienne manifeste, en effet, un intérêt particulier pour ce qui concerne les fonctions sexuelles et excrémentielles. Elle est nécrophile et nécrophage: elle s'acharne avec avidité ... sur des cadavres ... ' ('Visages de Femmes dans La *Sophonisbe* de J. Marston,' pp. 46–7).

37 Kramer and Sprenger, *Malleus Maleficarum*, p. 47.

38 Heywood and Brome, *An Edition of The Late Lancashire Witches by Thomas Heywood and Richard Brome*, ed. Barber. Further references to the play will be to this edition.

39 Berry, 'The Globe Bewitched and *El Hombre Fiel*,' p. 218.

40 Brain, 'An Anthropoligical Perspective on the Witchcraze,' p. 15.

41 Dekker, *The Witch of Edmonton*, in vol. 3 of *The Dramatic Works of Thomas Dekker*. Further references to the play will be to this edition.

42 Monter, 'The Pedestal and the Stake: Courtly Love and Witchcraft,' p. 134.

43 Monter, 'The Pedestal and the Stake,' p. 134.

44 Dollimore, *Radical Tragedy*, p. 40. 'The Witch of Edmonton,' writes Dollimore, 'is remarkable for the way it depicts how habit, socially coerced, becomes another – or rather "anti" – nature' (p. 176). Dawson has suggested that 'Mother Sawyer's turn to witchcraft' is portrayed as 'a direct response to her particular social circumstances'; her 'malignity ... is unequivocally motivated by the scapegoat role she has been forced to play' ('Witchcraft/Bigamy,' p. 80).

45 Klaits, *Servants of Satan*, p. 51.

46 Thomas, *Religion and the Decline of Magic*, p. 562.

47 Onat, Introduction, *The Witch of Edmonton: A Critical Edition*, p. 94; Hattaway, 'Women and Witchcraft,' p. 53. Atkinson observes that 'the play does not make it entirely clear whether or not the witch really is responsible for the death of Anne Ratcliff,' and suggests that 'the episode was probably imperfectly assimilated from the source' ('Moral Knowledge and the Double Action in *The Witch of Edmonton*,' p. 431, n. 8).

48 Wier, *De Praestigiis Daemonum*, vol. 1, p. 300. The debate about demonol-

ogy is well documented in Walker, *Spiritual and Demonic Magic from Ficino to Campanella*; Trevor-Roper, *The European Witch-Craze of the Sixteenth and Seventeenth Centuries*; and Anglo, 'Melancholia and Witchcraft,' pp. 209–28.

49 Trevor-Roper, *The European Witch-Craze of the Sixteenth and Seventeeth Centuries*, pp. 132–4. Thomas, in *Religion and the Decline of Magic*, p. 579, claims that it was easier for Neoplatonists 'to advance a "natural" explanation for the witches' *maleficium* than it was for those who had been educated in the tradition of scholastic Aristotelianism' which frequently supported diabolical explanations.

50 Stuart Clark notes that before coming to England, James I had dealt cautiously and even sceptically with accusations of witchcraft; however, he later 'became a witch-hunter and demonologist' apparently 'to satisfy political and religious pretensions at a time when they could be expressed in few other ways,' finding 'in the theory and practice of witch persecution a perfect vehicle for his nascent ideals of kingship.' Foremost among these ideals was the duty of the king to be 'the people's teacher and patriarch' ('King James's *Daemonologie*: Witchcraft and Kingship,' pp. 164–5). Elsewhere, Clark suggests that James's 'attempt in 1590–1 to write into the confessions of the North Berwick witches a special antipathy between demonic magic and godly magistracy had been a way of authenticating his own, as yet rather tentative initiatives as ruler of Scotland' ('Inversion, Misrule and the Meaning of Witchcraft,' p. 117).

51 Scot, *The Discoverie of Witchcraft*, Book 1, chap. 1, para. 1.

52 Scot, *The Discoverie of Witchcraft*, Book 1, chap. 1, para. 1.

53 Scot, *The Discoverie of Witchcraft*, Book 1, chap. 3, paras. 1 and 2.

54 See George Gifford, *A Dialogue concerning Witches and Witchcraft*.

55 See Notestein, *A History of Witchcraft in England from 1558–1718*, p. 143.

56 Rao, *The Domestic Drama*, p. 187; Herndl, *The High Design*, p. 272.

57 Kramer and Sprenger, *Malleus Maleficarum*, pp. 44–7.

58 Adams, *English Domestic or, Homiletic Tragedy 1575–1642*, p. 136.

59 Herndl, *The High Design*, p. 272. My reading of the denouement of *The Witch of Edmonton* takes issue with Herndl's claim that 'religious piety provid[es] again [as in *A Woman Killed with Kindness*] some reconciliation to the otherwise intolerable suffering of a man we cannot blame' (p. 272).

60 Brodwin, 'The Domestic Tragedy of Frank Thorney in *The Witch of Edmonton*,' p. 322. Elsewhere, Brodwin contends that Frank's 'final desire is that death may extinguish the despair which [his] ultimate self-recognition has brought' (*Elizabethan Love Tragedy*, p. 174). Onat, conceding that Frank's repentance is 'not the mere stock convention of homiletic drama,'

observes that it is 'dramatically credible' because 'Frank has been characterized as a man of some conscience and feeling' (Introduction, *The Witch of Edmonton*, p. 86).

61 The 'Church courts,' observes Stone, 'declared a marriage in church to be adulterous and of no validity if there could be proved a prior oral contract *per verba de praesenti* by one of the pair with another person' (*The Family, Sex and Marriage in England 1500–1800*, p. 32). In *Church Courts, Sex and Marriage in England, 1570–1640*, p. 190, Ingram points out that 'marriage in church was undoubtedly normal practice in the late sixteenth and the seventeenth centuries. But an unsolemnised or unwitnessed union, though irregular, might nonetheless be fully binding.'

5: Developments in Comedy

1 Harbage, *Shakespeare and the Rival Traditions*, p. 235.
2 See Grivelet, *Thomas Heywood et le Drame Domestique Elizabéthain*, pp. 166–74, and Clark, *Domestic Drama*, vol. 2, p. 249, n. 36.
3 On the thematic importance of the testing motif in domestic comedy, see Manheim, 'The Thematic Structure of Dekker's 2 *Honest Whore*,' p. 365; Clark, *Domestic Drama*, vol. 2, chaps. 6 and 7; Quinn, Introduction, *The Faire Maide of Bristow*, p. 27; and Rao, *The Domestic Drama*, pp. 13 and 89–92.
4 Clark, *Domestic Drama*, vol. 2, p. 267.
5 *The Faire Maide of Bristow*, ed. Arthur H. Quinn. Further references to the play will be to this edition.
6 *The London Prodigal*, in *The Shakespeare Apocrypha*, ed. C.F. Tucker Brooke. Further references to the play will be to this edition.
7 I am indebted to Leggatt's observation that *The London Prodigal* leaves 'room for sombre reflection ... on the abuse of marriage and on the rights of parents and children' (*English Drama*, p. 183).
8 Champion, in 'From Melodrama to Comedy: A Study of the Dramatic Perspective in Dekker's *The Honest Whore*, Parts I and II,' p. 194, demonstrates that in content and in the amount of stage time it receives, the Candido plot is equivalent to the two other plots: the Candido scenes total 859 lines, compared with 669 lines for the Bellafront plot and 605 for the romance plot.
9 Feldman, *The Morality-Patterned Comedy of the Renaissance*, p. 98; Keyishian, 'Dekker's *Whore* and Marston's *Courtesan*,' p. 264.
10 Haselkorn, in *Prostitution in Elizabethan and Jacobean Comedy*, p. 125, argues that 'Bellafront is not naive; she knows men,' and her 'conversion in Part I

runs less than a straight course. She teeter-totters between Hippolito and Matheo, going from one to the other, until she finally settles on Matheo, the man she can get ... set[ting] up a situation which will be fraught with unhappiness.'

11 'Candido's humour,' writes Ure, 'makes him seem ridiculous and touchingly *good* at one and the same time; we look up to him with one auspicious and one dropping eye' ('Patient Madman and Honest Whore: The Middleton-Dekker Oxymoron,' p. 26).

12 *The Honest Whore, Part I*, in vol. 2 of *The Dramatic Works of Thomas Dekker*. Further references to the play will be to this edition.

13 Comensoli, 'Merchants and Madcaps: Dekker's *Honest Whore* Plays and the *Commedia dell'Arte*,' pp. 125–39.

14 It is generally agreed that 2 *Honest Whore* is primarily Dekker's, and that 'Middleton's contribution may have consisted principally in touches given to individual passages throughout the play' (Hoy, *Introductions, Notes, and Commentaries*, vol. 2, p. 6).

15 In *The Restoration Rake-Hero*, p. 137, Weber observes that 'men not only refuse to believe in her [Bellafront's] ability to change, but actively discourage it. Her reform frustrates both their lust and their easy assumptions of male superiority and female weakness. Male definitions of a woman's nature simply do not allow for the possibility of reform.'

16 *The Honest Whore, Part II*, in vol. 2 of *The Dramatic Works of Thomas Dekker*. Further references to the play will be to this edition.

17 Frye, *Anatomy of Criticism*, p. 48.

18 Wotton, *Elements of Architecture*, p. 82. See above, chap. 3.

19 On the proliferation of the concept of hospitality in the sixteenth and seventeenth centuries, see Heal, 'The Idea of Hospitality in Early Modern England,' p. 75, and *Hospitality in Early Modern England*.

20 The enormous importance placed on hospitality in the early modern period is evidenced by the practice of inscribing householders' neighbourliness and beneficence on their tombstones. Among the tombstones in Oxford county, for example, the epitaph to Christopher Kempster, a London freeman and mason who assisted in the building of St Paul's Cathedral, is typical: the engraved eulogy emphasizes that in addition to having 'liv'd in perfect Love and Amity with his dear Wife,' Kempster 'left behind him the Character of ... a loving Father, a Hospitable Neighbour and a Compasionate Benefactor to the poor' (St John Baptist Church, Burford, England).

21 Heal, 'The Idea of Hospitality,' p. 67.

22 Taylor, 'The Pennyless Pilgrimage, p. 127.

23 *Xenophon's Treatise of Hovseholde*, p. 6.

24 Ellis, *The Gentile Sinner*, p. 179.

25 Wotton, *Elements of Architecture*, p. 82.

26 Gore, 'The Way to Prosper,' in *Register of Sermons Preached at Paul's Cross 1534–1642*, p. 137.

27 Wotton, *Elements of Architecture*, p. 4.

28 Tilney, *Flower of Friendship*, pp. 135–6, 137.

29 Pearson, *Elizabethans at Home*, p. 556.

30 Markham, *The English Hus-Wife*, p. 4.

31 See Burton, *The Early Tudors at Home: 1485–1558*, p. 138, and Mennell, *All Manners of Food*, p. 45.

32 Andrew Clark, *Domestic Drama*, vol. 2, p. 247.

33 Porter, *The Two Angry Women of Abington*, ed. Jardine and Simons (emphasis added). Further references to the play will be to this edition.

34 Ure, 'Patient Madman and Honest Whore,' p. 27; Palumbo, 'Trade and Custom in *1 Honest Whore*,' p. 34.

35 Palmer, *Hospitable Performances*, p. 28.

36 Ball, in *Merchants and Merchandise*, p. 156, writes that 'the last years for which the enrolled customs accounts are available suggest some buoyancy in the trade: 104,000 shortcloths exported by London in 1601, 118,000 in 1602, 92,000 in 1603, and 112,000 in 1604 ... the dying away of complaints of the over-expansion of cloth manufacture, together with positive contemporary comments on the prosperity of the trade, make it reasonable to believe that the peak of 127,000 shortcloths exported by English merchants from London in 1614 was not an isolated phenomenon, but the culmination of a decade of expansion.'

37 Aymard writes that 'friendship bound families more than individuals, or, rather, it bound individuals through their families ... Friendship was ubiquitous, commonplace, and necessary. It took many forms and was a part of the fabric of social relations, which it helped to shape. It kept the social machinery running smoothly' ('Friends and Neighbors,' p. 453).

38 For a survey of the pictorial and poetic representations, see Goodman-Soellner, 'Poetic Interpretations of the "Lady at her Toilette" Theme in Sixteenth-Century Painting,' pp. 426–42.

39 Ranum, 'The Refuges of Intimacy,' p. 228.

40 della Casa, *Galateo Ovvero de' Costumi*, p. 385.

41 Serlio, *Tutte l'opere d'architettura*, pp. 45–7; translation mine.

42 My analysis of the Bedlam scene takes issue with Price's claim that 'Setting the denouement in Bedlam permits Dekker to entertain his audience with a show of madmen, which has but little relation to his drama' (*Thomas Dekker*, p. 63).

43 Some commentators have been uneasy with the shift in perspective in the play's final scene. For Haselkorn, although the Bridewell episode is not gratuitous because it is 'connected with Bellafront's personal Bridewell,' it is nevertheless an extension of 'Dekker's Puritan morality [which] implies that one can achieve purification and atonement for sins only by submitting to ... harsh measures' (*Prostitution in Elizabethan and Jacobean Comedy*, p. 133). Others have offered qualified praise: for Conover, 'the "whores" are vital, lively, and interesting,' their presence 'help[ing] to end the play in a strong, theatrical manner, appropriate in mood, if not in terms of action, to the play which has preceded that ending' (*Thomas Dekker*, 1969, p. 110). Sherbo suggests that the procession of the obstreperous prostitutes 'serves to counteract and weaken the sentimental effect of the fifth act with its reformations and reconciliations' (*English Sentimental Drama*, p. 108); and Hunt, although complaining of the 'appeal to the gallery,' observes the ending's tragic elements: 'The closing scenes ... to the present-day reader ... are terrible rather than comic; and perhaps they were to Dekker, too' (*Thomas Dekker*, pp. 100–1).

44 Frye, *Anatomy of Criticism*, p. 44.

45 In my reading of the Bridewell episode I depart from the contention, put forth separately by Shaw and Salgādo, that Dekker merely draws on the popular, idealistic conception of the workhouse as reformatory. Shaw suggests that while the episode is informed by 'topographical and vocational realism ... the penology is somewhat idealized' and Bridewell is portrayed as 'a work house for correction rather than a prison for punishment' ('The Position of Thomas Dekker in Jacobean Prison Literature,' pp. 369, 370). For Salgādo, Dekker's treatment of confinement 'gives an idealized picture of Bridewell both as a house of correction and as a recruiting centre' (*The Elizabethan Underworld*, p. 189).

46 Stow, *A Survey of London*, vol 2, p. 145.

47 Stow, *A Survey of London*, vol. 2, p. 145.

48 'By being forced to work within the institution, the prisoners would form industrious habits and would receive a vocational training at the same time. When released, it was hoped, they would voluntarily swell the labor market' (Rusche and Kirchheimer, *Punishment and Social Structure*, p. 42). Cf. Sharpe, *Crime in Early Modern England 1550–1750*, p. 179: 'To the established notions of punishment as deterrence and retribution was added the

idea that it might be possible to cure criminal instincts through a healthy dose of labour discipline.'

49 Foucault, *Madness and Civilization*, p. 59.

50 According to McConville, 'the penal side of Bridewell was ... emphasized by the preliminary flogging of certain categories of new prisoners – chiefly prostitutes and vagrants. This punishment was inflicted in public – either at a cart's tail or in Bridewell's whipping room. Only after this induction did these prisoners pass on to the industrial parts of the prison. Retributive and reformative ends were thus jointly served' (*A History of English Prison Administration*, p. 33).

51 The belief in the educational value of imprisonment was commonplace, but after the publication of 2 *Honest Whore* it was increasingly ridiculed by Dekker's contemporaries. The reformatory notion of prison became 'a standing joke. ... The lessons ironically supposed to be taught at such universities were villainy, blasphemy, drunkenness – and law' (Pendry, *Elizabethan Prisons and Prison Scenes*, vol. 2, pp. 270–2).

Epilogue

1 'A tragic-comic vogue,' writes Andrew Clark, 'established by Beaumont and Fletcher also meant that domestic drama was now frequently limited to a portion of the dramatic action. Authors, for the sake of variety or fashion, introduce material extraneous to the genre' *Domestic Drama*, vol. 2, p. 325. See also Adams, who notes that plays such as *Fortune by Land and Sea*, *Women Beware Women*, *The English Traveller*, *The Vow Breaker*, and *'Tis Pity She's a Whore* 'illustrate the debility of the genre and ... its imminent disappearance from the stage' (*English Domestic or, Homiletic Tragedy 1575–1642*, p. 160).

2 Collier, *A Defence of the Short View of the Profaneness and Immorality of the English Stage* (1698), ed. Arthur Freeman, p. 139.

3 Diderot, 'Entretiens sur Le fils naturel,' in *Le Drame Bourgeois*, p. 116.

4 Diderot, 'Entretiens sur Le fils naturel,' passim.

5 Diderot, 'De la poésie dramatique,' in *Le Drame Bourgeois*, p. 368; translation mine.

6 Diderot, 'De la poésie dramatique,' p. 368; translation mine.

7 Grivelet, *Thomas Heywood et le Drame Domestique Elizabéthain*, p. 346.

8 Grivelet, *Thomas Heywood et le Drame Domestique Elizabéthain*, p. 345.

9 Diderot, 'Entretiens sur Le fils naturel,' p. 150.

10 Ibsen, *A Doll's House*, trans. Sharp, Marx-Aveling, and Hannas, Act III, p. 66. Further references to the play will be to this edition.

11 Miller, 'Tragedy and the Common Man,' pp. 4, 6.
12 Miller, 'The Family in Modern Drama,' p. 74.
13 O'Neill, *Long Day's Journey Into Night*, s.d., Act I, p. 11. Further references
   to the play will be to this edition.

Works Cited

Abbreviations

EETS, e.s.   Early English Text Society, extra series or supplementary
 or s.s.   series
STC   A Short-Title Catalogue of Books Printed in England, Scotland, and
               Ireland, 1477–1640, ed. A.W. Pollard and G.R. Redgrave
Wing   A Short-Title Catalogue of Books Printed in England, Scotland, Wales,
               and British America, 1641–1700, ed. Donald Wing

Primary Sources

Plays

Adam: A Twelfth-Century Play. Trans. Lynette R. Muir. Leeds: Leeds Philo-
     sophical and Literary Society, 1970.
The Chester Mystery Cycle. Ed. R.M. Lumiansky and David Mills. 2 vols. EETS,
     s.s. 3 and 9. London, New York, Toronto: Oxford University Press,
     1974–86.
Dekker, Thomas. *The Dramatic Works of Thomas Dekker*. Ed. Fredson Bowers.
     4 vols. Cambridge: Cambridge University Press, 1953–61.
The Faire Maide of Bristow. Ed. Arthur H. Quinn. Vol. 8, no. 1 of *Publications of
     the University of Pennsylvania*. Series in Philology and Literature. Phila-
     delphia: University of Pennsylvania, 1902.
Garter, Thomas. *The Most Virtuous & Godly Susanna*. 1578. Ed. W.W. Greg.
     Malone Society Reprints. Oxford: Oxford University Press, 1936
     (1937).

Heywood, John. *Johan Johan*. In *The Plays of John Heywood*. Ed. Richard Axton and Peter Happé. Cambridge: D.S. Brewer, 1991.

Heywood, Thomas. *The Captives*. Prepared by Arthur Brown. Malone Society Reprints. Oxford: Oxford University Press, 1953.

– *How a Man May Choose a Good Wife from a Bad*. In *A Select Collection of Old English Plays*. 1744. Ed. Robert Dodsley. Vol. 4, Part 2. 4th edn. Ed. W. Carew Hazlitt. 1874–6. Rpt. New York and London: Blom, 1964. 1–96.

– *The Rape of Lucrece*. In *The Dramatic Works of Thomas Heywood*. Ed. R.H. Shepherd. Vol. 5. London: John Pearson, 1874.

– *A Woman Killed with Kindness*. Ed. R.W. Van Fossen. The Revels Plays. London: Methuen, 1961.

– and Richard Brome. *An Edition of The Late Lancashire Witches by Thomas Heywood and Richard Brome*. Ed. Laird H. Barber. New York and London: Garland, 1979.

Ibsen, Henrik. *A Doll's House*. Trans. Farquharson Sharp, E. Marx-Aveling, and L. Hannas. London and New York: Dent and Dutton, 1958.

Ingelend, Thomas. *The Disobedient Child*. In *A Select Collection of Old English Plays*. 1744. Ed. Robert Dodsley. Vol. 1, Part 2. 4th edn. Ed. W. Carew Hazlitt. 1874–6. Rpt. New York and London: Blom, 1964. 265–320.

The London Prodigal. In *The Shakespeare Apocrypha*. Ed. C.F. Tucker Brooke. Oxford: Clarendon Press, 1908.

Lyly, John. *The Complete Works of John Lyly*. Ed. R. Warwick Bond. 8 vols. 1902. Rpt. Oxford: Clarendon Press, 1967.

Marston, John. *The Wonder of Women or the Tragedy of Sophonisba*. In *Three Jacobean Witchcraft Plays: The Tragedy of Sophonisba, The Witch, The Witch of Edmonton*. Ed. Peter Corbin and Douglas Sedge. Manchester: Manchester University Press, 1986.

Middleton, Thomas. *The Witch*. In *Three Jacobean Witchcraft Plays*. Ed. Peter Corbin and Douglas Hedge. Manchester: Manchester University Press, 1986.

Non-cycle Plays and Fragments. Ed. Norman Davis. EETS, S.S. 1. London, New York, Toronto: Oxford University Press, 1970.

The N-Town Play: Cotton MS Vespasian D.8. Ed. Stephen Spector. 2 vols. EETS, s.s. 11–12. Oxford, New York, Toronto: Oxford University Press, 1991.

O'Neill, Eugene. *Long Day's Journey Into Night*. New Haven: Yale University Press, 1956.

Phillip, John. *The Play of Patient Grissell*. Prepared by R.B. McKerrow and W.W. Greg. Malone Society Reprints. London: Oxford University Press, 1909.

Porter, Henry. *The Two Angry Women of Abington*. Ed. Michael Jardine and John Simons. Nottingham: Nottingham Drama Texts, 1987.

Shakespeare, William. *The Complete Works of Shakespeare*. Ed. David Beving-
ton. 3rd edn. London: Scott, Foresman, 1980.
The Towneley Plays. Ed. Martin Stevens and A.C. Cawley. 2 vols. EETS.
Oxford, New York, Toronto: Oxford University Press, 1994.
The Tragedy of Master Arden of Faversham. Ed. M.L. Wine. The Revels Plays.
London: Methuen, 1973.
Two Coventry Corpus Christi Plays. Ed. Hardin Craig. 2nd edn. EETS, e.s. 87.
1902. Rpt. London, New York, Toronto: Oxford University Press, 1957.
A Warning for Fair Women. Ed. Charles Dale Cannon. The Hague and Paris:
Mouton, 1975.
Wilkins, George. *The Miseries of Enforced Marriage*. In *A Select Collection of Old
English Plays*. 1744. Ed. Robert Dodsley. Vol. 4, Part 2. 4th edn. Ed. W.
Carew Hazlitt. 1874–6. Rpt. New York and London: Blom, 1964. 465–576.
Yarrington, Robert. *Two Lamentable Tragedies* (1601). Ed. John S. Farmer.
Tudor Facsimile Texts. 1913. Rpt. New York: AMS Press, 1970.
The York Plays. Ed. Richard Beadle. York Medieval Texts. Second Series. Lon-
don: Edward Arnold, 1982.
A Yorkshire Tragedy. Ed. A.C. Cawley and Barry Gaines. The Revels Plays.
Manchester: Manchester University Press, 1986.

Nondramatic Works

Augustine, St. *The Confessions of the Incomparable Doctour S. Avgvstine*. Trans.
Toby Matthew. London, 1620.
– *Saint Augustine: Confessions*. Trans. Vernon J. Bourke. New York: Fathers of
the Church, 1953.
Baldwin, William. *A Mirroure for Magistrates* (1599). In *The Mirror for Magis-
trates*, ed. Lily B. Campbell. Cambridge: Cambridge University Press, 1938.
Barbaro, Francesco. 'On Wifely Duties.' In *The Earthly Republic*. Ed. B. Kohl
and R. Witt. Philadelphia: University of Pennsylvania Press, 1978. 189–228.
Battus, Bartholomeus. *The Christian Man's Closet*. Trans. William Lowth. Lon-
don, 1581; *STC* 1591.
Becon, Thomas. *The Golden Boke of Christen Matrimony* (1542). Vol. 2 of *The
Worckes of Thomas Becon*. London: John Day, 1564. *STC* 1723.
Boccaccio, Giovanni. *The Decameron*. Trans. and ed. Mark Musa and Peter E.
Bondanella. New York: Norton, 1977.
Bodin, Jean. *The Six Bookes of a Commonweale*. Trans. Richard Knolles. London,
1606. Rpt. Ed. Kenneth D. McRae. Cambridge, MA: Harvard University
Press, 1962.
Bond, Ronald B., ed. *Certain Sermons or Homilies (1547) AND A Homily against*

Disobedience and Wilful Rebellion (1570): A Critical Edition. Toronto, Buffalo, London: University of Toronto Press, 1987.

Bradford, John. *Writings of the Rev. John Bradford, Prebendary of St. Paul's and Martyr, A.D. 1555.* London: The Religious Tract Society, n.d.

Bruni, Leonardo. *De Studiis et Literis* (1409). Trans. William Harrison Woodward. In *Vittorino da Feltre and Other Humanist Educators.* Rpt. Ed. Eugene F. Rice, Jr. 1897. Rpt. New York: Teachers College, Columbia University Press, 1963.

Bryan, W.F., and Germaine Dempster, eds. *Sources and Analogues of Chaucer's Canterbury Tales.* New York: Humanities Press, 1958.

Casa, Giovanni della. *Galateo Ovvero de' Costumi* (1558). In *Opere di Baldassare Castiglione, Giovanni della Casa, Benvenuto Cellini.* Ed. Carlo Cordié. Milan and Naples: Riccardo Ricciardi, 1960. 365–440.

Certain Sermons or Homilies Appointed to be Read in Churches in the Time of Queen Elizabeth. London: Society for Promoting Christian Knowledge, 1908.

Certayne Sermons Appointed by the Queen's Majesty. London, 1569.

Chaucer, Geoffrey. *The Works of Geoffrey Chaucer.* Ed. F.N. Robinson. 2nd edn. Boston: Houghton Mifflin, 1961.

Cicero. *Offices.* London: Bohn Classical Library, 1853.

Cleaver, Robert. *A Codly [Godly] Form of Householde Governement: For the Ordering of Private Families.* London, 1598. STC 5382.

Collier, Jeremy. *A Defence of the Short View of the Profaneness and Immorality of the English Stage* (1698). Ed. Arthur Freeman. New York: Garland, 1972.

Cooper, Thomas. *The Mystery of Witchcraft.* London, 1617. STC 5701.

Dekker, Thomas. *Foure Birds of Noahs Arke.* Ed. F.P. Wilson. Oxford: Basil Blackwell, 1924.

Deloney, Thomas. *The Garland of Good Will.* Ed. J.H. Dixon. London: Percy Society, 1852.

D'Ewes, Sir Simonds. *The Diary of Sir Simonds D'Ewes (1622–1624).* Ed. Elisabeth Bourcier. Paris: Didier, 1974.

Diderot, Denis. *Le Drame Bourgeois.* Vol. 10 of *Diderot: Oeuvres Complètes.* Ed. Jacques Chouillet and Anne-Marie Chouillet. Paris: Hermann, 1980.

Ellis, Clement. *The Gentile Sinner.* Oxford, 1660. Wing 556.

Erasmus, Desiderius. *A ryght frutefull epystle ... in laude and prayse of matrymony.* Trans. Richard Taverner. n.p. 1536? STC 10492.

– *Literary and Educational Writings 3: De Conscribendis Epistolis Formula / De Civilitate.* Vol. 25 of *Collected Works of Erasmus.* Ed. J.K. Sowards. Toronto: University of Toronto Press, 1985.

Gainsford, Thomas. *The Rich Cabinet Furnished with varietie of Excellent discriptions, exquisite Characters.* London, 1616. STC 11522.

Golding, Arthur. *A Briefe Discourse of the Late Murther of Master George Saunders a Worshipfull Citizen of London* (1573). In vol. 2 of *The School of Shakspere*. Ed. Richard Simpson. London: Chatto and Windus, 1878. 220–39.

Goodcole, Henry. *The Wonderfull Discouerie of Elizabeth Savvyer, a Witch*. London, 1621. STC 12014.

The Good Hous-wives Treasurie. Being a . . . booke instructing to the dressing of meates. London: Edward Allde, 1588. STC 13854.

The Good Hows-holder. London, 1607. STC 13851.

The Good Huswives Handmayde; contayning many principall poyntes of Cookery. London, 1591.

Gore, John. *The Way to Prosper. A Sermon Preached at St. Pauls Crosse on Sunday the 27 day of May, being Trinity Sunday, 1632*. STC 12083. In *Register of Sermons Preached at Paul's Cross 1534–1642* by Millar MacLure. Rev. by Jackson Campbell Boswell and Peter Pauls. Ottawa: Dovehouse Editions, 1989, pp. 137–8.

Gosynhyll, Edward. *The Scole House of Women* (c. 1541). STC 1204.5.

– *The Vertuous Scholehous of Vngracious Women* (c. 1550). STC 12104.

Gouge, William. *Gods Three Arrows; Plague, Famine, Sword*. London, 1631. STC 12116.

– *Of Domesticall Duties: Eight Treatises*. 3rd edn. 1622; London: Bladen/Haviland, 1634. STC 12121.

[Greene, John?]. *A Refutation of the Apology for Actors* (1615) by I.G. New York: Scholars' Facsimiles & Reprints, 1941.

Griffith, Matthew. *Bethel: or a Forme for Families*. London, 1633. STC 12368.

Guazzo, M. Steeven. *The Civile Conversation of M. Steeven Guazzo*. Trans. George Pettie and Bartholomew Young (1581, 1586). Ed. Edward Sullivan. 2 vols. New York: AMS Press, 1967.

Harrison, William. *The Description of England* (1577, 1587). Ed. Georges Edelen. Ithaca: Cornell University Press, 1968.

Heywood, Thomas. *An Apology for Actors* (1612). New York: Scholars' Facsimiles & Reprints, 1941.

– *A Curtaine Lecture*. London, 1637. STC 13312.

– *Gunaikeion; or nine bokes of various history concerninge women; inscribed by ye names of ye nine muses*. London, 1624. STC 13326.

Hobbes, Thomas. *Leviathan, or the Matter, Form, and Power of a Commonwealth, Ecclesiastical and Civill*. London, 1651. Wing 2246.

– *Philosophical Rudiments Concerning Government and Society*. Vol. 2 of *The English Works of Thomas Hobbes of Malmesbury*. Ed. Sir William Molesworth. 1839. Rpt. London: Scientia Aalen, 1962.

Hooker, Richard. *The Works*. Ed. John Keble. 7th edn. 3 vols. 1888. Rpt. New York: Burt Franklin, 1970.

Howell, Thomas Bayly, ed. *A Complete Collection of State Trials*. Vol. 2 (1603–1627). London: Longman, 1811.

James I. *Daemonologie, in Forme of a Dialogue*. London, 1597.

Kramer, Heinrich, and Jacob Sprenger. *Malleus Maleficarum*. Trans. Montague Summers. London: Pushkin Press, 1928.

Luther, Martin. *Luther's Works*. Gen. ed. J. Pelikan. 30 vols. St. Louis: Concordia, 1955–.

MacLure, Millar. *Register of Sermons Preached at Paul's Cross 1534–1642*. Rev. by Jackson Campbell Boswell and Peter Pauls. Ottawa: Dovehouse Editions, 1989.

Markham, Gervase. *The English Hus-wife*. London, 1615. STC 17342.

McIlwain, Charles H., ed. *The Political Works of King James I*. Cambridge, MA: Harvard University Press, 1918.

The Mirror for Magistrates. Ed. Lily B. Campbell. Cambridge: Cambridge University Press, 1938.

Montaigne, Michel de. *The Essayes of Montaigne*. Trans. John Florio. New York: Modern Library [1933?].

More, Henry. *An Account of Virtue: Or, Dr. Henry Moore's Abridgment of Morals, Put into English*. London, 1690. Wing 2637.

Nichols, Josias. *An Order of Household Instruction*. London, 1596. STC 18540.

Perkins, William. *Christian Oeconomie or, A Short Survey of the Right Manner of Erecting and Ordering a Family, according to the Scriptures*. 1609. London, 1618. STC 19677.

Puttenham, George. 'The Maner of Reioysings at Mariages and Weddings.' In *Edmund Spenser: Epithalamion*. Ed. Robert Beum. Columbus, OH: Merrill, 1968. 53–5.

Roper, William. *The Lyfe of Sir Thomas Moore, Knyghte*. Ed. James Cline. New York: Swallow Press, 1950.

Scot, Reginald. *The Discoverie of Witchcraft* (1584). London, 1930. Rpt. New York: Dover, 1972.

Serlio, Sebastiano. *Tutte l'opere d'architettura*. Venice, 1519.

Smith, Thomas. *De Republica Anglorum: A Discourse on the Commonwealth of England* (1583). Ed. L. Alston. 1906. Rpt. Shannon, Ireland: Irish University Press, 1972.

Somi, Leone di. *Dialogues and Stage Affairs*. Trans. Allardyce Nicoll. In Allardyce Nicoll, *The Development of the Theatre*. 5th edn. 1946. Rpt. New York: Harcourt, Brace, Jovanovich, 1966. 252–78.

Spenser, Edmund. *Amoretti*. In *Spenser: Poetical Works*. Ed. J.C. Smith and E. De Selincourt. London: Oxford University Press, 1970.

Starkey, Thomas. *A Dialogue between Pole and Lupset* (c. 1529–32). Ed. T.F. Mayer. Camden (Society), 4th series. Vol. 37. London: Royal Historical Society, 1989.

Stow, John. *A Survey of London* (1603). Ed. Charles Lethbridge Kingsford. 2 vols. 1908. Rpt. Oxford: Clarendon Press, 1971.

Stubbs, Philip. *The Anatomy of Abuses*. London, 1583. *STC* 23376. Rpt. New York and London: Johnson Reprint Corporation, 1972.

T.E. *The Lawes Resolutions of Womens Rights*. London, 1632. Early Printed Books Published in Facsimile, no. 922. Amsterdam and Norwood, NJ: Walter J. Johnson and Theatrum Orbis Terrarum, 1979.

Taylor, Jeremy. *A Course of Sermons for All the Sundays of the Year* (1653); Sermons XVII and XVIII: 'The Marriage Ring,' Parts I and II. In vol. 4 of *Jeremy Taylor: The Whole Works*. Ed. Reginald Heber and Charles P. Eden. 10 vols. 1850. Rpt. Hildeshein and New York: Verlag, 1970.

Taylor, John. '"The Pennyless Pilgrimage," or the Moneylesse Perambulation of John Taylor, Alias, the King's Majesties Water-Poet' (1618). In *Early Travellers in Scotland*. Ed. P. Hume Brown. 1891. Rpt. New York: Burt Franklin, 1970. 107–31.

Tilney, Edmund. *A briefe and pleasant discourse of duties in Mariage, called the Flower of Friendshippe* (1573). In *The Flower of Friendship: A Renaissance Dialogue Contesting Marriage By Edmund Tilney*. Ed. Valerie Wayne. Ithaca and London: Cornell University Press, 1992.

Two Most Unnatural and Bloodie Murthers (1605). In A.C. Cawley and Barry Gaines, eds. *A Yorkshire Tragedy*. The Revels Plays. Manchester: Manchester University Press, 1986. 94–110.

Tyrrell, Henry, ed. *The Doubtful Plays of Shakspere*. London and New York, 1851.

Vives, Juan Luis. *The Instruction of a Christen Woman*. Trans. R. Hyrd. n.p. 1529. *STC* 24856.5.

– *The Office and Duties of an Husband*. Trans. Thomas Paynell. n.p. 1555? *STC* 24855.

Whately, William. *A Bride-Bush Or, A Wedding Sermon*. London, 1617. *STC* 25296. Early Printed Books Published in Facsimile, no. 769. Amsterdam and Norwood, NJ: Walter J. Johnson and Theatrum Orbis Terrarum, 1975.

Wier, Johann. *De Praestigiis Daemonum* (1563). In vol. 1 of *Histoires Disputes et Discours des Illusions et Impostures des Diables*. Ed. J. Bourneville. Paris, 1885.

Wotton, Henry. *The Elements of Architecture By Sir Henry Wotton: A Facsimile*

Reprint of the First Edition (London, 1624). Charlottesville: University Press of Virginia, 1968.

Xenophon's Treatise of Hovseholde. Trans. Gentian Hervet. London, 1532. *STC* 26069.

Secondary Sources

Adams, Henry H. *English Domestic or, Homiletic Tragedy 1575–1642.* New York: Columbia University Press, 1943.

Adelman, Janet. '"Born of Woman": Fantasies of Maternal Power in *Macbeth.'* In *Cannibals, Witches, and Divorce: Estranging the Renaissance.* Ed. Marjorie Garber. Baltimore and London: Johns Hopkins University Press, 1987. 90–121.

Aers, David, et al., eds. *Literature, Language and Society in England 1580–1680.* Dublin and Totowa: Gill and Macmillan; Barnes and Noble, 1981.

Althusser, Louis. *Lenin and Philosophy and Other Essays.* Trans. Ben Brewster. New York and London: Monthly Review Press, 1971.

Amussen, Susan Dwyer. *An Ordered Society: Gender and Class in Early Modern England.* Oxford and New York: Basil Blackwell, 1988.

– 'Gender, Family and the Social Order, 1560–1725.' In *Order and Disorder in Early Modern England.* Ed. Anthony Fletcher and John Stevenson. Cambridge: Cambridge University Press, 1985. 196–217.

Anglo, Sydney, ed. *The Damned Art: Essays in the Literature of Witchcraft.* London, Henley, and Boston: Routledge & Kegan Paul, 1977.

– 'Melancholia and Witchcraft: The Debate between Wier, Bodin, and Scot.' In *Folie et deraison à la Renaissance.* International Federation for the Study of the Renaissance. Brussels: University of Brussels, 1976. 209–28.

Ariès, Philippe. *Centuries of Childhood: A Social History of Family Life.* Trans. Robert Baldick. New York: Knopf, 1962.

– and Georges Duby, eds. *A History of Private Life.* 4 vols. Cambridge, MA and London: Harvard University Press, 1987–91.

Atkinson, David. 'An Approach to the Main Plot of Thomas Heywood's *A Woman Killed with Kindness.' English Studies* 70 (February 1989): 15–27.

– 'Moral Knowledge and the Double Action in *The Witch of Edmonton.' Studies in English Literature* 25 (Spring 1985): 419–37.

Attwell, David. 'Property, Status, and the Subject in a Middle-class Tragedy: *Arden of Faversham.' English Literary Renaissance* 21 (Autumn 1991): 328–48.

Aymard, Maurice. 'Friends and Neighbors.' In *Passions of the Renaissance.* Ed. Roger Chartier. Trans. Arthur Goldhammer. Vol. 3 of *A History of Private*

Life. Ed. Philippe Ariès and Georges Duby. Cambridge, MA and London: Harvard University Press, 1989. 447–91.

Babcock, Barbara. *The Reversible World: Symbolic Inversion in Art and Society.* Ithaca: Cornell University Press, 1978.

Bakhtin, Mikhail. *The Dialogic Imagination: Four Essays.* Trans. Caryl Emerson and Michael Holquist. Ed. Michael Holquist. Austin and London: University of Texas Press, 1988.

– *Problems of Dostoevsky's Poetics.* Trans. C. Emerson. Manchester: Manchester University Press, 1984.

– *Rabelais and His World.* Trans. Hélène Iswolsky. 1965. Rpt. Bloomington: Indiana University Press, 1984.

Baldwin, Anna. 'From the *Clerk's Tale* to *The Winter's Tale*.' In *Chaucer Traditions: Studies in Honour of Derek Brewer.* Ed. Ruth Morse and Barry Windeatt. Cambridge and New York: Cambridge University Press, 1990. 199–212.

Ball, J.N. *Merchants and Merchandise: The Expansion of Trade in Europe 1500–1630.* New York: St. Martin's Press, 1977.

Barthélemy, Dominique. 'Civilizing the Fortress: Eleventh to Thirteenth Century.' In *Revelations of the Medieval World.* Ed. Georges Duby. Vol. 2 of *A History of Private Life.* Ed. Philippe Ariès and Georges Duby. Cambridge, MA and London: Harvard University Press, 1988. 397–423.

Beadle, Richard. 'The York Cycle.' In *The Cambridge Companion to Medieval English Theatre.* Ed. Richard Beadle. Cambridge: Cambridge University Press, 1994. 85–108.

– ed. *The Cambridge Companion to Medieval English Theatre.* Cambridge: Cambridge University Press, 1994.

Beier, A.L. *Masterless Men: The Vagrancy Problem in England 1560–1640.* London: Methuen, 1985.

– *The Problem of the Poor in Tudor and Early Stuart England.* London and New York: Methuen, 1983.

Belsey, Catherine. *The Subject of Tragedy: Identity and Difference in Renaissance Drama.* London: Methuen, 1985.

– 'Alice Arden's Crime.' *Renaissance Drama* n.s. 13 (1982): 83–102.

Berry, Herbert. 'The Globe Bewitched and *El Hombre Fiel*.' *Medieval and Renaissance Drama in England* 1 (1984): 211–30.

Bescou, Yves. 'Thomas Heywood et le problème de l'adultère dans *Une femme tuée par la bonté*.' *Revue Anglo-Américaine* 9 (1931): 127–40.

Bettridge, William Edwin, and Francis Lee Utley. 'New Light on the Origin of the Griselda Story.' *Texas Studies in Literature and Language* 13 (Spring 1971): 153–208.

Bevington, David. *Medieval Drama.* Boston: Houghton Mifflin, 1975.

– *From Mankind to Marlowe: Growth and Structure of the Popular Drama of Tudor England.* Cambridge, MA: Harvard University Press, 1962.

Blayney, Glenn H. 'Enforcement of Marriage in English Drama (1600–1650).' *Philological Quarterly* 38 (1959): 459–72.

Bliss, Lee. 'The Renaissance Griselda: A Woman for all Seasons.' *Viator: Medieval and Renaissance Studies* 23 (1992): 301–43.

Bloch, Marc. *Feudal Society.* Trans. L.A. Manyon. 2 vols. Chicago: University of Chicago Press, 1961.

Boas, F.S. *An Introduction to Tudor Drama.* Oxford: Clarendon Press, 1933.

Bowers, Rick. '*A Woman Killed With Kindness*: Plausibility on a Smaller Scale.' *Studies in English Literature* 24 (Spring 1984): 293–306.

Bradbrook, Muriel. *Themes and Conventions of Elizabethan Tragedy.* Cambridge: Cambridge University Press, 1960.

Bradley, Andrew Cecil. *Shakespearean Tragedy: Lectures on Hamlet, Othello, King Lear, Macbeth.* 2nd edn. 1905. Rpt. London: Macmillan, 1963.

Bradner, Leicester. 'The Rise of Secular Drama in the Renaissance.' *Studies in the Renaissance* 3 (1956): 7–22.

Brain, James L. 'An Anthropological Perspective on the Witchcraze.' In *The Politics of Gender in Early Modern Europe.* Ed. Jean R. Brink et al. 15–27.

Brauner, Sigrid. *Fearless Wives and Frightened Shrews: The Construction of the Witch in Early Modern Germany.* Ed. Robert H. Brown. Amherst: University of Massachusetts Press, 1995.

– 'Martin Luther on Witchcraft: A True Reformer?' In *The Politics of Gender in Early Modern Europe.* Ed. Jean R. Brink et al. 29–42.

Breen, J.M. 'The Carnival Body in *Arden of Faversham.*' *Cahiers Elisabéthains: Late Medieval and Renaissance English Studies* 45 (April 1994): 13–20.

Briggs, K.M. *Pale Hecate's Team: An Examination of the Beliefs on Witchcraft and Magic among Shakespeare's Contemporaries and His Immediate Successors.* London: Routledge & Kegan Paul, 1962.

Brink, Jean R., Allison P. Coudert, and Maryanne C. Horowitz, eds. *The Politics of Gender in Early Modern Europe.* Sixteenth Century Essays and Studies. Vol. 12. Kirksville, MO: Sixteenth Century Journal Publishers, 1989.

Brockett, Oscar G. *History of the Theatre.* 3rd edn. Boston and London: Allyn and Bacon, 1977.

– *Elizabethan Love Tragedy, 1587–1625.* New York and London: New York and London University Presses, 1971.

Brodwin, Leonora Leet. 'The Domestic Tragedy of Frank Thorney in *The Witch of Edmonton.*' *Studies in English Literature* 7 (1967): 311–28.

Bromley, Laura G. 'Domestic Conduct in *A Woman Killed with Kindness.*' *Studies in English Literature* 26 (Spring 1986): 259–76.

Bronfman, Judith. 'Griselda, Renaissance Woman.' In *The Renaissance English-woman in Print: Counterbalancing the Canon*. Ed. Anne M. Haselkorn and Betty Travitsky. 211–23.

Brooke, Christopher N.L. *The Medieval Idea of Marriage*. Oxford, New York, Toronto: Oxford University Press, 1989.

Brown, Arthur. 'Citizen Comedy and Domestic Drama.' In *The Jacobean Theatre*. Ed. J.R. Brown and Barnard Harris. New York: Capricorn Books, 1967. 63–83.

Brown, James W. *Fictional Meals and their Function in the French Novel, 1798–1848*. Toronto: University of Toronto Press, 1984.

Bruster, Douglas. '"In a Woman's Key": Women's Speech and Women's Language in Renaissance Drama.' *Exemplaria* 4 (Fall 1992): 235–66.

Butler, Martin. *Theatre and Crisis 1632–1642*. Cambridge: Cambridge University Press, 1984.

Burton, Elizabeth. *The Early Tudors at Home 1485–1558*. London: Allen Lane and Penguin, 1976.

– *The Elizabethans at Home*. London: Secker & Warburg, 1958.

Canuteson, John. 'The Theme of Forgiveness in the Plot and Subplot of *A Woman Killed with Kindness*.' *Renaissance Drama* n.s. 2 (1969): 123–41.

Carson, Ada Lou, and Herbert L. Carson. *Domestic Tragedy in English: Brief Survey*. 2 vols. Salzburg: Universität Salzburg, 1982.

Castan, Yves. 'Politics and Private Life.' In *Passions of the Renaissance*. Ed. Roger Chartier. Vol 3 of *A History of Private Life*. Ed. Philippe Ariès and Georges Duby. 21–67.

Cawley, A.C. '*A Yorkshire Tragedy* Considered in Relation to Biblical and Moral Plays.' In *Everyman & Company: Essays on the Theme and Structure of the European Moral Play*. Ed. Donald Gilman. New York: AMS Press, 1989. 155–68.

Cerasano, Susan P. 'Alleyn's Fortune: The Biography of a Playhouse.' PhD diss., University of Michigan, 1981.

Chambers, E.K. *The Elizabethan Stage*. Vol. 3. Oxford: Clarendon Press, 1923.

Champion, Larry. *Thomas Dekker and the Traditions of English Drama*. New York: Peter Lang, 1985.

– 'From Melodrama to Comedy: A Study of the Dramatic Perspective in Dekker's *The Honest Whore*, Parts I and II.' *Studies in Philology* 69 (1972): 192–209.

Chartier, Roger, ed. *Passions of the Renaissance*. Trans. Arthur Goldhammer. Vol. 3 of *A History of Private Life*. Ed. Philippe Ariès and Georges Duby.

Chauchaix, Jacqueline. 'Visages de Femmes Dans La *Sophonisbe* de J. Marston.' In *Visages de féminité*. Ed. A.-J. Bullier and J.-M. Racault. St. Denis: Université de Réunion, 1984. 41–56.

Clark, Alice. *Working Life of Women in the Seventeenth Century*. London: Routledge & Kegan Paul, 1982.

Clark, Andrew. *Domestic Drama: A Survey of the Origins, Antecedents and Nature of the Domestic Play in England, 1500–1640*. 2 vols. Salzburg: Universität Salzburg, 1975.

Clark, Arthur M. *Thomas Heywood: Playwright and Miscellanist*. Oxford: Basil Blackwell, 1931.

Clark, Peter. *The English Alehouse: A Social History 1200–1830*. London and New York: Longman, 1983.

Clark, Stuart. 'Inversion, Misrule and the Meaning of Witchcraft.' *Past and Present* 87 (May 1980): 98–127.

– 'King James's *Daemonologie*: Witchcraft and Kingship.' In *The Damned Art: Essays in the Literature of Witchcraft*. Ed. Sydney Anglo. London, Henley, and Boston: Routledge & Kegan Paul 1977. 156–81.

Cohen, Walter. *Drama of a Nation: Public Theater in Renaissance England and Spain*. Ithaca and London: Cornell University Press, 1985.

Cole, Douglas. *Suffering and Evil in the Plays of Christopher Marlowe*. 1962. Rpt. New York: Gordian, 1972.

Colie, Rosalie Littell. *The Resources of Kind: Genre-Theory in the Renaissance*. Ed. Barbara Kiefer Lewalski. Berkeley: University of California Press, 1973.

Collier, J.P. *The History of English Dramatic Poetry to the Time of Shakespeare: and Annals of the Stage to the Restoration*. 3 vols. London: John Murray, 1831.

Comensoli, Viviana. 'Merchants and Madcaps: Dekker's *Honest Whore* Plays and the *Commedia dell'Arte*.' In *Shakespeare's Italy: Functions of Italian Locations in Renaissance Drama*. Ed. Michele Marrapodi et al. Manchester and New York: Manchester University Press, 1993. 125–39.

Conover, James H. *Thomas Dekker: An Analysis of Dramatic Structure*. Studies in English Literature 38. The Hague: Mouton, 1969.

Contamine, Philippe. 'Peasant Hearth to Papal Palace: The Fourteenth and Fifteenth Centuries.' In *Revelations of the Medieval World*. Ed. Georges Duby. Vol. 2 of *A History of Private Life*. Ed. Philippe Ariès and Georges Duby. 425–505.

Cook, Albert Spaulding. *The Dark Voyage and the Golden Mean: A Philosophy of Comedy*. Cambridge, MA.: Harvard University Press, 1949.

Cook, Ann Jennalie. *The Privileged Playgoers of Shakespeare's London, 1576–1642*. Princeton: Princeton University Press, 1981.

Cook, David. '*A Woman Killed with Kindness*: An Unshakespearian Tragedy.' *English Studies* 45 (1964): 353–72.

Coudert, Allison P. 'The Myth of the Improved Status of Protestant Women: The Case of the Witchcraze.' In *The Politics of Gender in Early Modern Europe*. Ed. Jean R. Brink et al. 61–90.

– 'Witchcraft Studies to Date' (unpublished MS).

Cromwell, Otelia. *Thomas Heywood: A Study in the Elizabethan Drama of Everyday Life*. New Haven: Yale University Press, 1928.

Davidson, Clifford, et al., eds. *The Drama of the Middle Ages: Comparative and Critical Essays*. New York: AMS Press, 1982.

Davis, Natalie Zemon. *Society and Culture in Early Modern France*. Stanford: Stanford University Press, 1975.

Dawson, Anthony B. 'Witchcraft/Bigamy: Cultural Conflict in *The Witch of Edmonton*.' *Renaissance Drama* 20 (1989): 77–98.

Day, Martin S. *History of English Literature to 1600*. Garden City, NY: Doubleday, 1963.

Denley, Marie. 'Strictures on Interludes and Plays to Religious and Lay People in the Earlier Sixteenth Century.' *Notes and Queries* 35 (December 1988): 444–5.

Dinshaw, Carolyn. *Chaucer's Sexual Poetics*. Madison, WI and London: University of Wisconsin Press, 1989.

Dolan, Frances E. *Dangerous Familiars: Representations of Domestic Crime in England, 1550–1700*. Ithaca and London: Cornell University Press, 1994.

– 'Gender, Moral Agency, and Dramatic Form in *A Warning for Fair Women*.' *Studies in English Literature* 29 (Spring 1989): 201–18.

Dollimore, Jonathan. *Radical Tragedy: Religion, Ideology and Power in the Drama of Shakespeare and his Contemporaries*. Chicago and Brighton: University of Chicago Press and Harvester Press, 1984.

Donahue, Charles, Jr. 'The Canon Law in the Formation of Marriage and Social Practice in the Later Middle Ages.' *Journal of Family History* 8 (1983): 144–58.

Doran, Madeleine. *Endeavors of Art*. Madison: University of Wisconsin Press, 1954.

Douglas, Mary. 'Deciphering a Meal.' *Daedalus* 10 (Winter 1972): 61–81.

Dubrow, Heather. *A Happier Eden: The Politics of Marriage in the Stuart Epithalamium*. Ithaca and London: Cornell University Press, 1990.

Duby, Georges, ed. *Revelations of the Medieval World*. Trans. Arthur Goldhammer. Vol 2 of *A History of Private Life*. Ed. Philippe Ariès and Georges Duby.

Edward de Vere Newsletter, No. 21 (November 1990).

Elias, Norbert. *The Civilizing Process: The History of Manners*. Trans. Edmund Jephcott. 2 vols. 1939. Rpt. New York: Urizen, 1978.

Ellis, Deborah S. 'Domestic Treachery in the *Clerk's Tale*.' In *Ambiguous Realities: Women in the Middle Ages and Renaissance*. Ed. Carole Levin and Jeanie Watson. Detroit: Wayne State University Press, 1987. 99–113.

Emmison, F.G. *Morals and the Church Courts*. Vol. 2 of *Elizabethan Life*. Chelmsford: Essex Record Office, 1973.

Ezell, Margaret J.M. *The Patriarch's Wife: Literary Evidence and the History of the Family*. Chapel Hill and London: University of North Carolina Press, 1987.

Farley-Hills, David. *Shakespeare and the Rival Playwrights 1600–1606*. London and New York: Routledge, 1990.

Febvre, Lucien. *The Problem of Unbelief in the Sixteenth Century: The Religion of Rabelais*. Trans. Beatrice Gottlieb. Cambridge, MA and London: Harvard University Press, 1982.

Feldman, Sylvia D. *The Morality-Patterned Comedy of the Renaissance*. The Hague and Paris: Mouton, 1970.

Ferry, Anne. *The 'Inward' Language: Sonnets of Wyatt, Sidney, Shakespeare, Donne*. Chicago and London: University of Chicago Press, 1983.

Fisher, Frederick J. 'The Development of London as a Centre of Conspicuous Consumption in the Sixteenth and Seventeenth Centuries.' In vol. 2 of *Essays in Economic History*. Ed. E.M. Carus-Wilson. London: Edward Arnold, 1954. 199–220.

Fletcher, Anthony, and John Stevenson, eds. *Order and Disorder in Early Modern England*. Cambridge: Cambridge University Press, 1985.

Foucault, Michel. *Madness and Civilization: A History of Insanity in the Age of Reason*. Trans. Richard Howard. 1965. Rpt. New York: Vintage, 1973.

Fowler, Alastair. *Kinds of Literature: An Introduction to the Theory of Genres and Modes*. Cambridge, MA: Harvard University Press, 1982.

Fox, Alice. 'Obstetrics and Gynecology in *Macbeth*.' *Shakespeare Studies* 12 (1979): 127–41.

Freud, Sigmund. 'The "Uncanny."' In vol. 17 of *The Standard Edition of the Complete Psychological Works of Sigmund Freud*. Trans. and ed. James Strachey. London: Hogarth Press, 1968. 218–56.

Frye, Northrop. *Anatomy of Criticism*. Princeton: Princeton University Press, 1957.

Gash, Anthony. 'Carnival against Lent: The Ambivalence of Medieval Drama.' In *Medieval Literature: Criticism, Ideology & History*. Ed. David Aers. New York: St. Martin's Press, 1986. 74–98.

Goodman-Soellner, Elise. 'Poetic Interpretations of the "Lady at her Toilette" Theme in Sixteenth-Century Painting.' *The Sixteenth Century Journal* 14, 4 (1983): 426–42.

Goody, Jack. *The Development of the Family and Marriage in Europe*. Cambridge and New York: Cambridge University Press, 1983.

- *Cooking, Cuisine, and Class: A Study in Comparative Sociology*. Cambridge, Cambridge University Press, 1982.

Greene, Thomas M. *The Light in Troy: Imitation and Discovery in Renaissance Poetry*. New Haven and London: Yale University Press, 1982.

Griffith, D.D. *The Origin of the Griselda Story*. Seattle: University of Washington Press, 1931.

Grivelet, Michel. *Thomas Heywood et le Drame Domestique Elizabéthain*. Paris: Didier, 1957.

Guillēn, Claudio. *Literature as System: Essays Toward the Theory of Literary History*. Princeton: Princeton University Press, 1971.

Gurr, Andrew. *Playgoing in Shakespeare's London*. Cambridge: Cambridge University Press, 1987.

- *The Shakespearean Stage 1574–1642*. 2nd edn. Cambridge: Cambridge University Press, 1980.

Gutierrez, Nancy A. 'Exorcism by Fasting in *A Woman Killed with Kindness*: A Paradigm of Puritan Resistance?' *Research Opportunities in Renaissance Drama* 23 (1994): 43–62.

- 'The Irresolution of Melodrama: The Meaning of Adultery in *A Woman Killed with Kindness*.' *Exemplaria* 1 (Fall 1989): 265–91.

- 'Philomela Strikes Back: Adultery and Mutilation as Female Self-assertion.' *Women's Studies* 16 (1989): 429–43.

Hanawalt, Barbara A. *The Ties that Bound: Peasant Families in Medieval England*. New York: Oxford University Press, 1986.

Hanley, Sarah. 'Engendering the State: Family Formation and State Building in Early Modern France.' *French Historical Studies* 16 (Spring 1989): 4–27.

Hansen, Elaine Tuttle. 'The Powers of Silence: The Case of the Clerk's Griselda.' In *Women and Power in the Middle Ages*. Ed. Mary Erler and Maryanne Kowaleski. Athens, GA and London: University of Georgia Press, 1988. 230–49.

Harbage, Alfred. *Shakespeare and the Rival Traditions*. New York: Macmillan, 1952.

Hardison, O.B. 'Three Types of Renaissance Catharsis.' *Renaissance Drama* n.s. 2 (1969): 3–22.

Haselkorn, Anne M. *Prostitution in Elizabethan and Jacobean Comedy*. New York: Whitson, 1983.

- and Betty S. Travitsky, eds. *The Renaissance Englishwoman in Print: Counterbalancing the Canon*. Amherst, MA: University of Massachusetts Press, 1990.

Hattaway, Michael. 'Women and Witchcraft.' *Trivium* 20 (May 1985): 49–68.

– *Elizabethan Popular Theatre: Plays in Performance*. London: Routledge & Kegan Paul, 1982.

Hawkins, Harriet. 'The Victim's Side: Chaucer's *Clerk's Tale* and Webster's *Duchess of Malfi*.' *Signs* (Winter 1975): 339–61.

Heal, Felicity. *Hospitality in Early Modern England*. Oxford: Clarendon Press, 1990.

– 'The Idea of Hospitality in Early Modern England.' *Past & Present* 102 (February 1984): 66–93.

– and Rosemary O'Day, eds. *Church and Society in England: Henry VIII to James I*. Hamden, CT: Archon Books, 1977.

Henderson, Diana E. 'Many Mansions: Reconstructing *A Woman Killed with Kindness*.' *Studies in English Literature* 26 (Spring 1986): 277–94.

Herlihy, David. *Medieval Households*. Cambridge, MA: Harvard University Press, 1985.

Herndl, George. *The High Design: English Renaissance Tragedy and the Natural Law*. Lexington: University Press of Kentucky, 1970.

Herrup, Cynthia B. 'Law and Morality in Seventeenth-Century England.' *Past & Present* 106 (February 1985): 102–23.

Hodge, Bob. 'Marlowe, Marx and Machiavelli: Reading into the Past.' In *Literature, Language and Society in England 1580–1680*. Ed. David Aers et al. 1–22.

Hoffman, Dean. '"Both bodily deth and werdly shame": "Little Musgrave and Lady Barnard" as Source for *A Woman Killed with Kindness*.' *Comparative Drama* 23 (Summer 1989): 166–78.

Holbrook, Peter. *Literature and Degree in Renaissance England: Nashe, Bourgeois Tragedy, Shakespeare*. Newark: University of Delaware Press; London and Toronto: Associated University Presses, 1994.

Hoskins, W.G. *Provincial England: Essays in Social and Economic History*. London: Macmillan, 1963.

Houlbrooke, Ralph. *The English Family 1450–1700*. London: Longman, 1984.

– *Church Courts and the People During the English Reformation 1520–1570*. Oxford: Oxford University Press, 1979.

Howard, Jean E. *The Stage and Social Struggle in Early Modern England*. London and New York: Routledge, 1994.

Howell, Martha C. *Women, Production, and Patriarchy in Late Medieval Cities*. Ed. Catharine Stimpson. Chicago and London: University of Chicago Press, 1986.

Hoy, Cyrus. *Introductions, Notes, and Commentaries to Texts in 'The Dramatic Works of Thomas Dekker' Ed. by Fredson Bowers*. 4 vols. Cambridge: Cambridge University Press, 1980.

Hull, Suzanne W. *Chaste, Silent & Obedient: English Books for Women 1475–1640*. San Marino: Huntington Library, 1982.

Hulse, Clark. *Metamorphic Verse: The Elizabethan Minor Epic*. Princeton: Princeton University Press, 1981.

Hunt, Mary Leland. *Thomas Dekker: A Study*. New York: Columbia University Press, 1911.

Ingram, Martin. *Church Courts, Sex and Marriage in England, 1570-1640*. Cambridge: Cambridge University Press, 1987.

James, Mervyn. *Family, Lineage and Civil Society: A Study of Society, Politics and Mentality in the Durham Region, 1500-1640*. Oxford: Clarendon Press, 1974.

Jameson, Frederic. *The Political Unconscious: Narrative as a Socially Symbolic Act*. Ithaca: Cornell University Press, 1981.

– *Marxism and Form*. Princeton: Princeton University Press, 1971.

Jardine, Lisa. *Still Harping on Daughters: Women and Drama in the Age of Shakespeare*. 2nd edn. New York: Columbia University Press, 1989.

– 'The Duchess of Malfi: A Case Study in the Literary Representation of Women.' In *John Webster's 'The Duchess of Malfi.'* Ed. Harold Bloom. New York: Chelsea House, 1987. 115–27.

Jeanneret, Michel. *A Feast of Words: Banquets and Table Talk in the Renaissance*. Trans. Jeremy Whiteley and Emma Hughes. Chicago and Cambridge: University of Chicago Press and Polity Press, 1991.

Jenkins, Harold. *The Life and Work of Henry Chettle*. London: Sidgewick & Jackson, 1934.

Johnston, Alexandra F. 'The Inherited Tradition: The Legacy of Provincial Drama.' In *The Elizabethan Theatre* 13. Ed. A.L. Magnusson and C.E. McGee. Toronto: P.D. Meany, 1994. 1–25.

– 'Cycle Drama in the Sixteenth Century: Texts and Contexts.' In *Early Drama to 1600*. Ed. Albert H. Tricomi. Binghamton: State University of New York, 1987. 1–15.

Jordan, Constance. *Renaissance Feminism: Literary Texts and Political Models*. Ithaca and London: Cornell University Press, 1990.

Jourdain, M[argaret]. *English Decoration and Furniture of the Early Renaissance (1500–1650): An Account of Its Development and Characteristic Forms*. London: B.T. Batsford, 1924.

Kahn, Victoria. *Rhetoric, Prudence, and Skepticism in the Renaissance*. Ithaca and London: Cornell University Press, 1985.

Kastan, David Scott, and Peter Stallybrass, eds. *Staging the Renaissance: Reinterpretations of Elizabethan and Jacobean Drama*. New York and London: Routledge, 1991.

Kato, Sadahide. 'Alice Arden of Feversham and her Company of Evil.' In

Poetry and Drama in the Age of Shakespeare. Ed. Peter Milward and Tetsuo Anzai. Tokyo: Sophia University, 1982. 184–98.

Keiser, George R. 'The Middle English *Planctus Mariae* and the Rhetoric of Pathos.' In *The Popular Literature of Medieval England*. Ed. Thomas J. Heffernan. Tennessee Studies in Literature 28. Knoxville: University of Tennessee Press, 1985. 167–94.

Keyishian, Harry. 'Griselda on the Elizabethan Stage: The *Patient Grissil* of Dekker, Chettle, and Haughton.' *Studies in English Literature* 16 (1976): 253–61.

– 'Dekker's *Whore* and Marston's *Courtesan*.' *English Language Notes* 4 (1967): 261–6.

Kiefer, Frederick. 'Heywood as Moralist in *A Woman Killed with Kindness*.' *Medieval & Renaissance Drama in England* 3 (1986): 83–98.

King, T.J. *Shakespeare and Staging 1599–1642*. Cambridge, MA: Harvard University Press, 1971.

Klaits, Joseph. *Servants of Satan: The Age of the Witch Hunts*. Bloomington: Indiana University Press, 1985.

Klapisch-Zuber, Christiane. *Women, Family, and Ritual in Renaissance Italy*. Trans. Lydia G. Cochrane. Chicago: University of Chicago Press, 1985.

Klein, Joan Larsen. ed. *Daughters, Wives, and Widows: Writings by Men about Women and Marriage in England, 1500–1640*. Urbana and Chicago: University of Illinois Press, 1992.

– 'Lady Macbeth "Infirm of Purpose."' In *The Woman's Part: Feminist Criticism of Shakespeare*. Ed. Carolyn Ruth Swift Lenz et al. Urbana, Chicago, and London: University of Illinois Press, 1980. 240–55.

Knight, G. Wilson. *The Imperial Theme: Further Interpretations of Shakespeare's Tragedies Including the Roman Plays*. 3rd edn. London: Methuen, 1951.

Kohl, Benjamin G., and Ronald G. Witt, eds. *The Earthly Republic: Italian Humanists on Government and Society*. Philadelphia: University of Pennsylvania Press, 1978.

Kors, Alan C., and Edward Peters, eds. *Witchcraft in Europe 1100–1700: A Documentary History*. Philadelphia: University of Pennsylvania Press, 1972.

Krontiris, Tina. *Oppositional Voices: Women as Writers and Translators of Literature in the English Renaissance*. London and New York: Routledge, 1992.

Kussmaul, Ann. *Servants in Husbandry in Early Modern England*. Cambridge and New York: Cambridge University Press, 1981.

Larner, Christina. *Enemies of God: The Witch-hunt in Scotland*. Baltimore: Johns Hopkins University Press, 1981.

Law, R.A. 'Yarrington's "Two Lamentable Tragedies."' *Modern Language Review* 5 (1910): 167–77.

LeBlanc, Ronald. 'Dinner with Chichikov: The Fictional Meal as Narrative Device in Gogol's *Dead Souls.' Modern Language Studies* 18 (Fall 1988): 68–80.

Leggatt, Alexander. *English Drama: Shakespeare to the Restoration 1590–1660*. London and New York: Longman, 1988.

– '"Arden of Faversham."' *Shakespeare Survey* 36 (1983): 121–33.

– *Citizen Comedy in the Age of Shakespeare*. Toronto: University of Toronto Press, 1973.

Levin, Harry. 'Notes toward a Definition of City Comedy.' In *Renaissance Genres: Essays on Theory, History, and Interpretation*. Ed. Barbara Kiefer Lewalski.

Levin, Richard. *The Multiple Plot in English Renaissance Drama*. Chicago: University of Chicago Press, 1971.

– 'The Elizabethan "Three-Level" Play.' *Renaissance Drama* n.s. 2 (1969): 23–37.

Lewalski, Barbara Kiefer. *Writing Women in Jacobean England*. Cambridge, MA and London: Harvard University Press, 1993.

–, ed. *Renaissance Genres: Essays on Theory, History, and Interpretation*. Cambridge, MA: Harvard University Press, 1986.

Lieblein, Leanore. 'The Context of Murder in English Domestic Plays, 1590–1610.' *Studies in English Literature* 23 (Spring 1983): 181–96.

Lucas, R. Valerie. 'Puritan Preaching and the Politics of the Family.' In *The Renaissance Englishwoman in Print: Counterbalancing the Canon*. Ed. Anne M. Haselkorn and Betty S. Travitsky. 224–40.

Lumiansky, R.M. 'Comedy and Theme in the Chester *Harrowing of Hell.' Tulane Studies in English* 10 (1960): 5–12.

Luxton, Imogen. 'The Reformation and Popular Culture.' In *Church and Society in England: Henry VIII to James I*. Ed. Felicity Heal and Rosemary O'Day. 57–77.

Macdonald, Michael. *Mystical Bedlam: Madness, Anxiety and Healing in Seventeenth-Century England*. Cambridge: Cambridge University Press, 1981.

Macfarlane, Alan. *Marriage and Love in England: Modes of Reproduction 1300–1840*. Oxford and New York: Basil Blackwell, 1986.

– *Witchcraft in Tudor and Stuart England: A Regional and Comparative Study*. New York and Evanston: Harper & Row, 1970.

Maclean, Ian. *The Renaissance Notion of Woman: A Study in the Fortunes of Scholasticism and Medical Science in European Intellectual Life*. Cambridge: Cambridge University Press, 1980.

Manheim, Michael. 'The Thematic Structure of Dekker's 2 *Honest Whore.' Studies in English Literature* 5 (1965): 363–81.

Marshall, Sherrin. *The Dutch Gentry: 1500–1650*. New York, Westport, CT, and London: Greenwood Press, 1987.

McConville, Sean. *A History of English Prison Administration*. London, Boston, and Henley: Routledge & Kegan Paul, 1981.

McKeon, Michael. *The Origins of the English Novel 1600–1740*. Baltimore: Johns Hopkins University Press, 1987.

McLuskie, Kathleen E. *Dekker and Heywood: Professional Dramatists*. New York: St. Martin's Press; London: Macmillan, 1994.

– *Renaissance Dramatists*. New York, London, and Toronto: Harvester Wheatsheaf, 1989.

– '"Tis But A Woman's Jar": Family and Kinship in Elizabethan Domestic Drama.' *Literature and History* 9 (1983): 228–39.

McNeir, Waldo. 'Heywood's Sources for the Main Plot of *A Woman Killed with Kindness*.' In *Studies in the English Renaissance Drama*. Ed. Josephine W. Bennett et al. New York: New York University Press, 1959. 189–211.

– 'Corpus Christi Passion Plays as Dramatic Art.' *Studies in Philology* 48 (January 1951): 601–28.

Medvedev, P.N., and M.M. Bakhtin. *The Formal Method in Literary Scholarship: A Critical Introduction to Sociological Poetics*. Trans. Albert J. Wehrle. Baltimore and London: Johns Hopkins University Press, 1978.

Mehl, Dieter. *The Elizabethan Dumb Show: The History of a Dramatic Convention*. Cambridge, MA: Harvard University Press, 1966.

Mendelson, Sara Heller. 'Stuart Women's Diaries and Occasional Memoirs.' In *Women in English Society 1500–1800*. Ed. Mary Prior. London and New York: Methuen, 1985. 187–210.

Mennell, Stephen. *All Manners of Food: Eating and Taste in England and France from the Middle Ages to the Present*. Oxford: Basil Blackwell, 1985.

Meredith, Peter. Introduction. *The Passion Play from the N. Town Manuscript*. Ed. Peter Meredith. London and New York: Longman, 1990.

Miller, Arthur. 'The Family in Modern Drama.' In *The Theater Essays of Arthur Miller*. Ed. Robert A. Martin. New York: Viking Penguin, 1978. 69–82.

– 'Tragedy and the Common Man.' In *The Theater Essays of Arthur Miller*. Ed. Robert A. Martin. 1–12.

Mills, David. 'The Chester Cycle.' In *The Cambridge Companion to the Medieval Theatre*. Ed. Richard Beadle. 109–33.

Miner, Earl. 'Some Issues of Literary "Species, or Distinct Kind".' In *Renaissance Genres: Essays on Theory, History, and Interpretation*. Ed. Barbara Kiefer Lewalski. 15–44.

Monter, E. William. 'The Pedestal and the Stake: Courtly Love and Witchcraft.' In *Becoming Visible: Women in European History*. Ed. R. Bridenthal and C. Koonz. Boston: Houghton Mifflin, 1977. 119–36.

Munson, William F. 'Audience and Meaning in Two Medieval Dramatic Realisms.' In *The Drama of the Middle Ages*. Ed. Clifford Davidson, C.J. Giankaris and John H. Stroupe. New York: AMS Press, 1982. 183–206.

Neale, J.E. *Elizabeth I and Her Parliaments 1584–1601*. London: Jonathan Cape, 1957.

Neely, Carol Thomas. 'Remembering Shakespeare Always but Remembering him Differently.' *Bulletin of the Shakespeare Association of America* 13 (January 1990): 1.

Nelson, Mary. 'Why Witches Were Women.' In *Women: A Feminist Perspective*. Ed. Jo Freeman. Palo Alto, CA: Mayfield, 1975. 335–50.

Newman, Karen. *Fashioning Femininity and English Renaissance Drama*. Chicago and London: University of Chicago Press, 1991.

Nicholas, David. *The Domestic Life of a Medieval City: Women, Children, and the Family in Fourteenth-Century Ghent*. Lincoln, NB and London: University of Nebraska Press, 1985.

Nicoll, Allardyce. *The Development of the Theatre: A Study of Theatrical Art from the Beginnings to the Present Day*. 5th edn. 1946. Rpt. New York: Harcourt, Brace, Jovanovich, 1966.

Norland, Howard B. 'Formalizing English Farce: *Johan Johan* and Its French Connection.' *Comparative Drama* 17 (Summer 1983): 141–52.

Notestein, Wallace. *A History of Witchcraft in England from 1558–1718*. 1909. Rpt. New York: Crowell, 1968.

Nuttall, A.D. *A New Mimesis: Shakespeare and the Representation of Reality*. London and New York: Methuen, 1983.

Onat, Etta Soiref. Introduction. *The Witch of Edmonton: A Critical Edition*. Ed. Etta Soiref Onat. New York: Garland, 1980.

Orlin, Lena Cowen. '"The Causes and Reasons of all Artificial Things" in the Elizabethan Domestic Environment.' *Medieval and Renaissance Drama in England* 7 (1995): 19–75.

– *Private Matters and Public Culture in Post-Reformation England*. Ithaca and London: Cornell University Press, 1994.

– 'Familial Transgressions, Social Transition on the Elizabethan Stage.' In *Sexuality and Politics in Renaissance Drama*. Ed. Carole Levin and Karen Robertson. Studies in Renaissance Literature 10. Lewiston, Queenston, and Lampeter: Edwin Mellen Press, 1991. 27–55.

– 'Man's House as his Castle in *Arden of Feversham*.' *Medieval and Renaissance Drama in England* 2 (1985): 57–89.

- 'Man's House as His Castle in Elizabethan Domestic Tragedy.' PhD diss., University of North Carolina, 1985.

Ornstein, Robert. 'Bourgeois Morality and Dramatic Convention in *A Woman Killed with Kindness.*' In *English Renaissance Drama.* Ed. Standish Henning et al. Carbondale and Edwardsville: Southern Illinois University Press, 1976. 128–41.

- *The Moral Vision of Jacobean Tragedy.* Madison: University of Wisconsin Press, 1960.

Otten, Charlotte F. *English Women's Voices, 1540–1700.* Miami: Florida International University Press, 1992.

Owst, G.R. *Literature and Pulpit in Medieval England.* Oxford: Basil Blackwell, 1966.

Palliser, D.M. *The Age of Elizabeth: England under the Later Tudors 1547–1603.* 2nd edn. 1983. Rpt. London and New York: Longman, 1992.

Palmer, Daryl W. *Hospitable Performances: Dramatic Genre and Cultural Practices in Early Modern England.* West Lafayette, IN: Purdue University Press, 1992.

Palumbo, R.J. 'Trade and Custom in 1 *Honest Whore.*' *American Notes and Queries* 15, no. 3 (1976): 34–5.

Panek, Jennifer. 'Punishing Adultery in *A Woman Killed with Kindness.*' *Studies in English Literature* 34 (Spring 1994): 357–78.

Parente, James A., Jr. *Religious Drama and the Humanist Tradition: Christian Theater in Germany and in the Netherlands 1500–1680.* Leiden and New York: E.J. Brill, 1987.

Partridge, Eric. *Shakespeare's Bawdy.* 3rd edn. 1947. Rpt. London and New York: Routledge, 1968.

Pearson, Lu Emily. *Elizabethans at Home.* Stanford: Stanford University Press, 1957.

Pechter, Edward. '*Patient Grissil* and the Trials of Marriage.' *The Elizabethan Theatre* 14. Ed. A.L. Magnusson and C.E. McGee. Toronto: P.D. Meany, 1995. 1–25.

Pendry, E.D. *Elizabethan Prisons and Prison Scenes.* 2 vols. Salzburg: Universität Salzburg, 1974.

Phythian-Adams, Charles. *Desolation of a City: Coventry and the Urban Crisis of the Late Middle Ages.* Cambridge: Cambridge University Press, 1979.

Powell, Chilton L. *English Domestic Relations: 1487–1653.* New York: Columbia University Press, 1917.

Price, George. *Thomas Dekker.* New York: Twayne, 1969.

Ranum, Orest. 'The Refuges of Intimacy.' In *Passions of the Renaissance.* Ed. Roger Chartier. Trans. Arthur Goldhammer. Vol. 3 of *A History of Private Life.* Ed. Philippe Ariès and Georges Duby. 207–63.

Rao, G. Nageswara. *The Domestic Drama*. Tirupati: Sri Venkateswara University Press, [1978?].

Rauchbaur, Otto. 'Visual and Rhetorical Imagery in Th. Heywood's *A Woman Killed with Kindness.' English Studies* 57 (1976): 200–10.

Revel, Jacques. 'The Uses of Civility.' In *Passions of the Renaissance*. Ed. Roger Chartier. Vol. 3 of *The History of Private Life*. Ed. Philippe Ariès and Georges Duby. 167–205.

Reynolds, George F. *The Staging of Elizabethan Plays at the Red Bull Theater: 1605–1625*. 1940. Rpt. New York: Kraus, 1966.

Roberts, Charles Walter. 'An Edition of John Phillip's Commodye of Pacient and Meeke Grissill.' PhD diss., University of Illinois, 1938.

Robinson, J.W. 'The Art of the York Realist.' In *Medieval English Drama: Essays Critical and Contextual*. Ed. Jerome Taylor and Alan H. Nelson. Chicago and London: University of Chicago Press, 1972. 230–44.

Rose, Mary Beth. *The Expense of Spirit: Love and Sexuality in English Renaissance Drama*. Ithaca and London: Cornell University Press, 1988.

Rusche, Georg, and Otto Kirchheimer. *Punishment and Social Structure*. 1939. Rpt. New York: Russell & Russell, 1967.

Salgādo, Gāmini. *The Elizabethan Underworld*. London and Totowa, NJ: Dent, Rowman & Littlefield, 1977.

Schaeffer, Jean-Marie. 'Literary Genres and Textual Genericity.' In *The Future of Literary Theory*. Ed. Ralph Cohen. New York and London: Routledge, 1989. 167–87.

Schell, Edgar. 'The Distinctions of the Towneley Abraham.' *Modern Language Quarterly* 41 (December 1980): 315–27.

Schochet, Gordon J. *Patriarchalism in Political Thought*. Oxford: Basil Blackwell, 1975.

Scobie, Brian. Introduction. *A Woman Killed with Kindness*. Ed. Brian Scobie. New Mermaids. London: A & C Black; New York: Norton, 1985.

Shaffer, Brian W. '"To Manage Private and Domestic Quarrels": Shakespeare's *Othello* and the Genre of Elizabethan Domestic Tragedy.' *Iowa State Journal of Research* 62 (February 1988): 453–7.

Shahar, Shulamith. *Childhood in the Middle Ages*. London and New York: Routledge, 1990.

Sharpe, J.A. *Crime in Early Modern England 1550–1750*. London and New York: Longman, 1984.

Shaw, Phillip. 'The Position of Thomas Dekker in Jacobean Prison Literature.' *Publications of the Modern Language Association* 62 (1947): 366–91.

Sherbo, Arthur. *English Sentimental Drama*. East Lansing: Michigan State University Press, 1957.

Siegel, Paul N. 'English Humanism and the New Tudor Aristocracy.' *Journal of the History of Ideas* 13 (1952): 450–68.

Simon, Joan. *Education and Society in Tudor England*. Cambridge: Cambridge University Press, 1967.

Slack, Paul. *Poverty and Policy in Tudor and Stuart England*. London and New York: Longman, 1988.

Southern, Richard. *The Medieval Theatre in the Round: A Study of the Staging of 'The Castle of Perseverance' and Related Matters*. London: Faber and Faber, 1957.

Spacks, Patricia Meyer. 'Honor and Perception in *A Woman Killed with Kindness*.' *Modern Language Quarterly* 20 (1959): 321–32.

Spivack, Bernard. *Shakespeare and the Allegory of Evil: The History of a Metaphor in Relation to his Major Villains*. New York and London: Columbia University Press, 1958.

Stallybrass, Peter. 'Patriarchal Territories: The Body Enclosed.' In *Rewriting the Renaissance*. Ed. Margaret W. Ferguson et al. Chicago and London: University of Chicago Press, 1986. 123–42.

– '*Macbeth* and Witchcraft.' In *Focus on Macbeth*. Ed. John Russell Brown. London, Boston, and Henley: Routledge, 1982. 192–201.

Sticca, Sandro. *The Planctus Mariae in the Dramatic Tradition of the Middle Ages*. Trans. Joseph R. Berrigan. Athens, GA, and London: University of Georgia Press, 1988.

Stone, Lawrence. *The Family, Sex and Marriage in England 1500–1800*. London: Weidenfeld and Nicolson; New York: Harper & Row, 1977.

– *The Crisis of the Aristocracy 1558–1641*. Oxford: Oxford University Press, 1965.

Sturgess, Keith. Introduction. *Three Elizabethan Domestic Tragedies*. Ed. Keith Sturgess. Harmondsworth and Baltimore: Penguin, 1969.

Sutherland, Sarah. '"Not or I see more neede": The Wife of Noah in the Chester, York, and Towneley Cycles.' In *Shakespeare and Dramatic Tradition: Essays in Honor of S.F. Johnson*. Ed. W.R. Elton and William B. Long. Newark: University of Delaware Press; London and Toronto: Associated University Presses, 1989. 181–93.

Taylor, Jerome, and Alan H. Nelson, eds. *Medieval English Drama: Essays Critical and Contextual*. Chicago and London: University of Chicago Press, 1972.

Telle, Emile Villemeur. *Erasme de Rotterdam et le Septième Sacrement*. Geneva: Droz, 1954.

Tessitore, Maria Vittoria. '*Two Lamentable Tragedies* (1601).' In vol. 1 of *Le Forme del Teatro: Contributi del Gruppo di ricerca sulla communicazione teatrale in Inghilterra.* Ed. Giorgio Melchiori. Rome: University of Rome, 1979. 53–80.

Thomas, Keith. *Religion and the Decline of Magic.* New York: Scribner's, 1971.

– 'The Social Origins of Hobbes's Political Thought.' In *Hobbes Sudies.* Ed. K.C. Brown. Oxford: Basil Blackwell, 1965. 185–236.

– 'Women and the Civil War Sects.' In *Crisis in Europe 1560–1660.* Ed. Trevor Aston. London: Routledge & Kegan Paul, 1965. 317–40.

Todd, Margo. *Christian Humanism and the Puritan Social Order.* Cambridge and New York: Cambridge University Press, 1987.

Todorov, Tzvetan. *Genres in Discourse.* Trans. Catherine Porter. Cambridge: Cambridge University Press, 1990.

Townsend, Freda. 'The Artistry of Thomas Heywood's Double Plots.' *Philological Quarterly* 25 (1946): 97–119.

Trainor, Stephen L. '"Guilty Creatures at a Play": Rhetoric and Repentance in Renaissance Domestic Tragedy.' *Ball State University Forum* 24, No. 2 (1983): 40–6.

Trevor-Roper, H.R. *The European Witch-Craze of the Sixteenth and Seventeenth Centuries.* New York and Evanston: Harper, 1967.

Tricomi, Albert H., ed. *Early Drama to 1600. ACTA* XIII. Binghamton: State University of New York, 1987.

Twycross, Meg. 'The Theatricality of Medieval English Plays.' In *The Companion to Medieval English Theatre.* Ed. Richard Beadle. 37–84.

Tydeman, William. *The Theatre in the Middle Ages: Western European Stage Conditions, c. 800–1576.* Cambridge: Cambridge University Press, 1978.

Tyrrell, Henry, ed. *The Doubtful Plays of Shakspere.* London and New York, 1851.

Underdown, D.E. 'The Taming of the Scold: the Enforcement of Patriarchal Authority in Early Modern England.' In *Order and Disorder in Early Modern England.* Ed. Anthony Fletcher and John Stevenson. 116–36.

Ure, Peter. 'Marriage and the Domestic Drama in *A Woman Killed with Kindness.*' In *Shakespeare's Contemporaries: Modern Studies in English Renaissance Drama.* Ed. Max Bluestone and Norman Rabkin. 2nd edn. Englewood Cliffs, NJ: Prentice-Hall, 1970. 194–203.

– 'Patient Madman and Honest Whore: The Middleton-Dekker Oxymoron.' *Essays and Studies* n.s. 19 (1966): 18–40.

– 'Marriage and the Domestic Drama in Heywood and Ford.' *English Studies* 32 (1951): 200–16.

Vanita, Ruth. 'Men Beware Men: Shakespeare's Warnings for Unfair Husbands.' *Comparative Drama* 28 (Summer 1994): 201–20.

Velte, Mowbray. *The Bourgeois Elements in the Dramas of Thomas Heywood.* 1924. Rpt. New York: Haskell House, 1966.

Walker, D.P. *Spiritual and Demonic Magic from Ficino to Campanella*. London: Warburg Institute, University of London, 1958.

Walter, John, and Keith Wrightson. 'Dearth and the Social Order in Early Modern England.' *Past and Present* 71 (1976): 22–42.

Walz, Eugene P. '*Arden of Faversham* as Tragic Satire.' *Massachusetts Studies in English* 4, no. 11 (1973): 23–41.

Ward, A.W. Preface. *A Woman Killed with Kindness*. Ed. A.W. Ward. London: Dent, 1897.

Wayne, Valerie. Introduction. *The Flower of Friendship: A Renaissance Dialogue Contesting Marriage By Edmund Tilney*. Ed. Valerie Wayne. Ithaca and London: Cornell University Press, 1992.

Weber, Harold. *The Restoration Rake-Hero: Transformations in Sexual Understanding in Seventeenth-Century England*. Madison: University of Wisconsin Press, 1986.

Weimann, Robert. *Shakespeare and the Popular Tradition in the Theater: Studies in the Social Dimension of Dramatic Form and Function*. Baltimore and London: Johns Hopkins University Press, 1978.

Wentworth, Michael. 'Thomas Heywood's *A Woman Killed with Kindness* as Domestic Morality.' In *Traditions and Innovations: Essays on British Literature of the Middle Ages and the Renaissance*. Ed. David G. Allen and Robert A. White. Newark: University of Delaware Press; London and Toronto: Associated University Presses, 1990. 150–62.

White, Paul Whitfield. *Theatre and Reformation: Protestantism, Patronage, and Playing in Tudor England*. Cambridge: Cambridge University Press, 1993.

Wiesner, Merry E. *Women and Gender in Early Modern Europe*. Cambridge: Cambridge University Press, 1993.

Williams, Raymond. *The Long Revolution*. London: Chatto & Windus, 1961.

Willis, Deborah. *Malevolent Nurture: Witch-hunting and Maternal Power in Early Modern England*. Ithaca and London: Cornell University Press, 1995.

Wilson, F.P. *The English Drama 1485–1585*. Ed. G.K. Hunter. Oxford: Clarendon Press, 1969.

Woodbridge, Linda. *Women and the English Renaissance: Literature and the Nature of Womankind, 1540–1620*. Urbana and Chicago: University of Illinois Press, 1984.

Wright, Louis B. *Middle-Class Culture in Elizabethan England*. 1935. Rpt. Ithaca: Cornell University Press, 1958.

Wrightson, Keith. 'The Social Order of Early Modern England: Three Approaches.' In *The World We Have Gained: Histories of Population and Social Structure*. Ed. Lloyd Bonfield, Richard M. Smith, and Keith Wrightson. Oxford and New York: Basil Blackwell, 1986. 177–202.

Youngblood, Sarah. 'Theme and Imagery in *Arden of Feversham.*' *Studies in English Literature* 3 (Spring 1963): 207–18.

Zagorin, Perez. *Ways of Lying: Dissimulation, Persecution, and Conformity in Early Modern Europe.* Cambridge, MA and London: Harvard University Press, 1990.

Index

Abraham and Isaac plays, 31–4, 47, 165nn20–2, 166n26. *See also* cycle plays

Adam: A Twelfth-Century Play, 36, 166n33

Adams, Henry H., 4, 5, 6, 16, 103, 160n62; *English Domestic or, Homiletic Tragedy*, 154nn10–11, 164n2, 178n58, 182n93, 184n120 and nn128–9, 185n130 and n137, 190n58, 195n1

Adelman, Janet, 117, 118, 188n32, 188–9n33

adultery, 5, 19, 20, 43, 65, 79, 81, 82, 88, 92, 93, 132, 135, 161n78, 172n1, 176n51, 177n53, 178n58, 179nn62–3, 186n4

alienation, 25, 99–100, 124

Althusser, Louis, 14, 23, 158n51, 162n96

Amussen, Susan Dwyer, 156n30 and n33, 161n78, 162n82, 172n26 and n1, 185n134 and n136

Anglicanism, 4, 18, 161n70

Anglo, Sydney, 190n48

architecture, 70–2, 74–5

Arden of Feversham. See *Tragedy of Master Arden of Feversham, The*

Ariès, Philippe, 164n7

Aristotle, 111, 160n66, 190n49

Atkinson, David, 179–80n63, 189n47

Attwell, David, 160n62, 181n78

audiences, 14, 30, 37, 40, 41, 45, 62, 81–2, 88, 91, 95, 129, 145, 148, 169n3, 194n42; and class, 5, 6, 11, 154n13 and n16

Augustine, St, 27, 97; *Confessions*, 38, 166n40, 183n112

Axton, Richard, 167n54 and n56

Aymard, Maurice, 193n37

Babcock, Barbara, 163n105

Bakhtin, Mikhail, 14, 67, 95, 158n50 and nn52–4, 173n10, 183n102

Baldwin, Anna, 169n1

Baldwin, William: *A Mirroure for Magistrates*, 8, 156n23

Ball, J.N., 193n36

Barbaro, Francesco, 88, 181n81

Barber, Laird H., 186n1, 189n38

Barthélemy, Dominique, 164n5